The World that is the Book
Paul Auster's Fiction

Aliki Varvogli

LIVERPOOL UNIVERSITY PRESS

First published in 2001 by
LIVERPOOL UNIVERSITY PRESS
4 Cambridge Street, Liverpool L69 7ZU

British Library Cataloguing-in-Publication Data
A British Library CIP record is available.

ISBN 0-85323-687-9 *hardback*
ISBN 0-85323-697-6 *paperback*

Typeset in Sabon with Gill Sans by
Northern Phototypesetting Co. Ltd, Bolton, Lancs.
Printed and bound in the European Union by
Bell & Bain Ltd, Glasgow

Contents

Acknowledgments

I would like to thank Allan Lloyd-Smith, who supervised the thesis on which this book is based. He read my work perceptively, and his comments were always helpful, insightful and encouraging.

David Seed encouraged me to approach Liverpool University Press, and I am grateful for his friendship, trust and support. Emory Elliott and Brian Harding did more than anyone else to convince me of the merit of my work. Their faith in this project has made all the difference, and it is a great pleasure to be able to thank them.

Paul Auster kindly allowed me to quote from an as yet unpublished interview he gave to Christopher Bigsby of the University of East Anglia, and I thank him for that and for the interest he has shown in my work.

Many friends and colleagues provided moral support and intellectual stimulation. My thanks to Lia Yoka, Boris Wastiau, Simon Waters, Gloria Cronin, Alan Rice and Josh Cohen.

My parents I can never thank enough. They made it all possible by offering emotional, intellectual and practical support, and they still insist on finding my gratitude excessive, which only goes to show how lucky I am to have them. This book is dedicated to them as a small token of gratitude, and love.

Author's Note

All translations from French and Spanish sources are my own.

List of abbreviations

Unless otherwise indicated, the editions of Auster's works cited parenthetically in the text are abbreviated as follows:

AH   *The Art of Hunger: Essays, Prefaces, Interviews* (Harmondsworth: Penguin, 1993)

CLT *In the Country of Last Things* (London: Faber, 1987)

GW   *Ground Work: Selected Poems and Essays 1970–1979* (London: Faber, 1990)

HM   *Hand to Mouth: A Chronicle of Early Failure* (London: Faber, 1997)

IoS   *The Invention of Solitude* (London: Faber, 1982)

Lev   *Leviathan* (London: Faber, 1992)

MC   *The Music of Chance* (London: Faber, 1990)

MP   *Moon Palace* (London: Faber, 1989)

MV   *Mr Vertigo* (London: Faber, 1994)

NYT *The New York Trilogy* (London: Faber, 1988)
       CG   *City of Glass*
       Gh   *Ghosts*
       LR   *The Locked Room*

Tm   *Timbuktu* (London: Faber, 1999).

Introduction

Between 1982 and 1984 Paul Auster sent his manuscript for *City of Glass* to seventeen publishers; they all turned it down. Twelve years later, he sold his manuscripts to the Berg Collection in the New York Public Library, where they now lie in the company of those of Charles Dickens, Mark Twain and Vladimir Nabokov. Since 1984, Auster has published nine novels as well as books of non-fiction, while some of his early plays, along with a pseudonymous detective novel originally published in 1982, have been published in the form of appendices to new work. Meanwhile, his career in film has progressed from a cameo appearance in Philip Haas's adaptation of *The Music of Chance* to writing and co-directing *Smoke* and *Blue in the Face* with Wayne Wang, to a film written and directed by himself, *Lulu on the Bridge*.[1] In the 1970s, Auster felt that everything he touched 'turned to failure' (*HM* 3); by the early 1990s, he could support himself through writing, and now the story has it that his books are kept behind the counter in many bookshops because he is a favourite among shoplifters.[2] The critical attention he has received is no less impressive than his reversal of fortune; in a book published in 1995 Dennis Barone predicted an 'exponential growth' in Auster criticism in the late 1990s, and in 1996 alone four books on *Moon Palace* appeared in France.[3]

---

1. For a list of Auster's works, see the Bibliography.
2. Suzie Mackenzie confirms this rumour in her profile of Paul Auster, 'The Searcher', *The Guardian Weekend*, 29 May 1999, p. 8.
3. Dennis Barone, ed., *Beyond the Red Notebook: Essays on Paul Auster* (Philadelphia: University of Pennsylvania Press, 1995), p. 1. The books on *Moon Palace* are: François Fallix, ed., *Lectures d'une œuvre: Moon palace de Paul Auster* (Paris: Editions du Temps, 1996); Catherine Pesso-Miquel, ed., *Toiles Trouées et déserts lunaires dans Moon palace de Paul Auster* (Paris: Presses de la Sorbonne Nouvelle, 1996); Yves-Charles Granjeat, ed., *Moon Palace, collectif* (Paris: Ellipses, 1996); Marc Chénetier, *Paul Auster as the Wizard of Odds: Moon Palace* (Paris: Didier Erudition–CNED, 1996).

Despite this success, Sven Birkerts has a point when he describes Auster as 'the ghost at the banquet of contemporary American letters',[4] while Auster himself feels that what he is doing is 'so contrary to what most novelists are trying to accomplish that I often have trouble thinking of myself as a novelist at all' (*AH* 305). There are, as we shall see, various factors that may help to explain the peculiar position that Auster occupies in American letters. His fiction is hard to classify, as it borrows from different traditions and participates in, without belonging to, various 'schools' of writing. His work combines metafictive elements with a clearly articulated interest in, and engagement with, the contemporary world. Overt references to the act and the nature of writing and self-conscious subversions of traditional notions of story-telling are never divorced from questions pertaining to urban living, Western history, capitalism, the tyranny of money, and the role of the author in society. Especially in the novels that follow *The New York Trilogy*, a delicate balance is maintained between what can be broadly termed 'realism' and 'experimentation', between an enquiry into the world and an exploration of the nature of the self as it appears in language.

Auster's autobiographical piece *Hand to Mouth* provides some insight into his interest in the relationship between the world and the word. Recalling his years at Columbia (1965–69), the author remembers them as being chiefly about two things, books and the war in Vietnam. By 1967, when he went to Paris with Columbia's Junior Year Abroad Program, he had spent two years 'living in a delirium of books'; 'whole new worlds had been poured into my head, life-altering transfusions had reconstituted my blood. Nearly everything that is still important to me in the way of literature and philosophy I first encountered during those two years' (*HM* 29). In Paris, he found that he had to take language lessons instead of the courses he had been dreaming of ('Roland Barthes at the Collège de France, for example'), and his disappointment was such that he decided to quit university altogether. He knew that meant he would be drafted into the army, but he had made up his mind to refuse and go to jail: 'That was a categorical decision – an absolute, unbudgeable stance' (*HM* 31). Much like his fictional character Benjamin Sachs in *Leviathan*, Auster's interest in books is what prompts him to take a political stance, so that the public and private spheres are seen to exist in a new, unexpected relationship.

---

4. Sven Birkerts, *American Energies: Essays on Fiction* (New York: William Morrow, 1992), p. 338.

Back at Columbia, where he was talked out of his decision and re-admitted so that he wouldn't have to go to Vietnam, Auster recalls a time of turmoil: 'The campus became a war zone of demonstrations, sit-ins, and moratoriums. There were riots, police raids, slugfests, and factional splits. Rhetorical excesses abounded, ideological lines were drawn, passions flowed from all sides' (*HM* 33). Although Auster helped occupy a campus building and was sufficiently involved to get arrested and spend a night in jail, on the whole he felt that he was too much of a 'loner' to join in group action. 'I could never quite bring myself to climb aboard the great ship *Solidarity*. For better or worse,' he writes, 'I went on paddling my little canoe' (*HM* 34). Paul Auster has been paddling his little canoe ever since. His books, products of solitude, not solidarity, deal with questions pertaining to the notion of the self, the nature of language, the power of story-telling. The recurring image is that of a man alone in his room, but illumination is found when that solitude enables the individual to arrive at a better understanding of connectedness, and of the individual's complex, infinite relations with the world at large. Mark Ford makes a similar point when he observes that Auster is 'obsessively concerned with the powers of solitude to convert *socially* induced anxieties of self-division into the creative forces of self-awareness' (added emphasis).[5]

In the context of contemporary American writing, Auster's work occupies an unusual position. He is reluctant to discuss other writers, and even when pressed he will only mention his friendship with Don DeLillo and Salman Rushdie, while his own critical essays mainly focus on earlier European writers. Although throughout his fiction he willingly enters into dialogue with other texts, these are usually the writings of the American Renaissance, or the works of European writers such as Kafka, Beckett or Hamsun. The formative years he spent in France from 1971 to 1974, his translations of French poetry, and his editorial work on the *Random House Book of Twentieth-Century French Poetry* go some way towards explaining the common perception of his body of work as one that displays a European, or more specifically French, sensibility, but just as the course of French literature was significantly altered by Baudelaire's active interest in Edgar Allan Poe's work, so Auster's own supposedly French qualities may be attributed to his abiding interest in nineteenth-century American writing. His work may deal with abstract notions, and the emphasis may appear to be on form and style, but many of his chosen

5. Mark Ford, 'Inventions of Solitude: Thoreau and Auster', *Journal of American Studies*, 33.2 (1999), p. 204.

themes and tropes are borrowed from the American tradition. He writes about baseball, the Statue of Liberty, the Depression; about the American West and the anonymity of the great city. However, his references to American culture are often subordinated to a larger project of a more philosophical quality. Auster bemoans the loss of a 'philosophical dimension' from recent American writing; he sees it in Melville, Hawthorne, Poe and Thoreau, but finds that it has all but disappeared from contemporary fiction in his country:

> The fact is... that the American novel changed. The novels of Melville and Hawthorne, the stories of Poe and the writings of Thoreau for example, all of whom I am passionately interested in, were not about sociology, which is what the novel has come to concern itself [with] in the United States. It's something else. They had a metaphysical dimension, a philosophical dimension to them which I think has been forgotten and ignored.[6]

The New York Trilogy is a good example of how Auster reconciles 'realism' with 'experiment', and 'sociology' with writing that has a metaphysical dimension. The book has been described as a postmodern detective story; like Umberto Eco, Thomas Pynchon or Borges before him, Auster borrows some elements from detective fiction and uses his own writing to explore the nature and expose the limitations of the genre, and to ask questions of a more philosophical nature concerning perception, interpretation, and the availability of truth, or meaning. Michael Holquist has claimed that this practice may be identified as a major trend in postmodern fiction: 'what the structural and philosophical presuppositions of myth... were to modernism... the detective story is to postmodernism'.[7] *The New York Trilogy* also belongs to the tradition of metafictional writing by virtue of its self-conscious nature. Auster not only violates traditional conventions of time, place, causality and unity of action, he also crosses ontological boundaries by creating a character named Paul Auster in *City of Glass*,[8] and by an authorial intrusion in *The Locked Room*, where the reader is addressed by the author who explains

6. From an unpublished interview with Professor Christopher Bigsby, University of East Anglia, quoted with Paul Auster's kind permission. Subsequent references will be to 'Interview by Christopher Bigsby'.
7. Michael Holquist, 'Whodunit and Other Questions: Metaphysical Detective Stories in Postwar Fiction', *New Literary History*, 3.1 (1971), pp. 135–56; repr. in *The Poetics of Murder*, ed. Glenn Most and William Stowe (San Diego: Harcourt, 1983), p. 149.
8. In the graphic novel version of *City of Glass*, this character is drawn to look like Paul Auster as well. Paul Karasik and David Mazzucchelli, *Paul Auster's City of Glass: A Graphic Mystery* (New York: Avon Books, 1994).

that the three stories 'are finally the same story, but each one represents a different stage in my awareness of what it is about' (*LR* 294).

Daniel Quinn, the main character in *City of Glass*, is a poet who writes detective novels for a living; this is how his work is described: 'Like most people, Quinn knew almost nothing about crime... Whatever he knew about these things, he had learned from books, films, and newspapers. He did not, however, consider this to be a handicap. What interested him about the stories he wrote was not their relation to the world but their relation to other stories' (*CG* 7). Throughout *The New York Trilogy*, Paul Auster himself stresses the relation of his stories to other stories: Quinn writes his detective novels using the pseudonym William Wilson, while the character Paul Auster has an elaborate theory concerning the authorship of *Don Quixote*, which he explains to Quinn in a passage that both reflects and serves to add another twist to the ontological complexities of *City of Glass*, while also evoking the work of Borges, whose 'Pierre Menard, author of the Quixote' also deals with *Don Quixote* and questions of authorship. *Ghosts* is, by the author's admission, a rewrite of Henry David Thoreau's *Walden*: 'Walden Pond in the heart of the city' (*AH* 271), and when the two main characters, Blue and Black, meet, the latter tells the former the plot of Hawthorne's story 'Wakefield'. Being the story of the inexplicable disappearance of a man, 'Wakefield' clearly foreshadows the plot of *The Locked Room*, whose absent protagonist is named Fanshawe in homage to Hawthorne's character in his first novel of the same name. *The New York Trilogy* as a whole has been described as 'Kafka gone gumshoe', and, as I shall argue later, the affinity between the two writers goes much deeper than the trope of ordinary man caught in nightmarish situation, which is what the term 'Kafkaesque' so often implies. Auster has also said that the influence Samuel Beckett had on him was so great that for a long time he could not see his way beyond it (*AH* 265). Although there are no overt references to Beckett in *The New York Trilogy*, its structural and thematic similarities with Beckett's *Trilogy* are taken for granted by Steven Connor, who talks of 'Paul Auster's rewriting of Beckett's *Trilogy* of novels in his *New York Trilogy*' in the same breath as he speaks of Robert Coover's 'extrapolation of the Pinocchio story in *Pinocchio in Venice*'.[9]

All these references to other writers and books are not simply a display of erudition, and Auster has never underplayed their importance. He

9. Steven Connor, *The English Novel in History 1950–1995* (London and New York: Routledge, 1996), p. 166.

talks about his passion for nineteenth-century American literature, and considers Beckett and Kafka to have had an unquestionable impact on him. Yet when asked if he identifies with Quinn's interest in the relation of his books to other books he says, 'Not at all. I do the exact opposite. My stories come out of the world and not out of books.'[10] And whereas *City of Glass* may be described as a metaphysical thriller, Auster prefers to think of it as 'an homage to Siri [his wife, novelist Siri Hustvedt], as a love letter in the form of a novel. I tried to imagine what would have happened to me if I hadn't met her, and what I came up with was Quinn. Perhaps my life would have been something like his' (*AH* 306). *The New York Trilogy*, as its title suggests, is also about the experience of living in the city. Quinn's wanderings around New York are described in detail, and his route could be traced on a map (indeed, many readers have tried to do this in the hope that his steps, like Stillman's, would contain a message, but they don't). *Ghosts* records the solitary existences of city dwellers, people who feel so lonely among the crowds that they hire a private eye to watch them so that someone will bear witness, and thus give meaning, to their existence. New York is a city in which 'the brokenness is everywhere, the disarray is universal' (*CG* 78). *The Locked Room* charts the love affair between the narrator and his vanished friend's wife, and it contains a moving evocation of childhood friendship.

Auster insists that 'in the strictest sense of the word', he considers himself a realist (*AH* 277). Yet to claim that one's books come out of 'the world' and not out of other books is a very problematic statement, as it presupposes a clear distinction between lived experience and books, between the world and the word. The evidence from Auster's fiction seems to contradict rather than support his statement. It is true that many of the characters he creates, and some incidents in his books, come from 'real life', and the effect in later novels especially is one of deceptive realism. At the same time, however, Auster's fictions are, if anything, overdetermined, full of allusions and references to other books and writers. Even if that were not the case, it would still be problematic to say that his books come out of the real world. Books are written, and received, with reference to other books, while 'lived experience' itself is not available in any pure, unmediated form. *The New York Trilogy* is the most allusive of Auster's works; it reads like a catalogue of the writers Auster admires, the ones who helped to form his own sensibilities. But if later novels become

---

10. Santiago del Rey, 'Paul Auster: Al compas de un ritmo pendular', *Quimera: Revista de Literatura*, 109 (May 1992), p. 25.

progressively less allusive, the presence of other writers and other books still haunts them. Anna Blume, named after a character in a poem by Kurt Schwitters, is also Scheherazade, and she owes her existence to Kafka's and Hamsun's hunger artists as much as to her own creator. Auster explains that there was very little he had to make up in his depiction of the country of last things, but can any book that presents a vision of a dystopia ever be said to come out of the real world uncontaminated by all the dystopian novels that came before it?

In *The Music of Chance*, a character named Pozzi is condemned to live in a field and build a wall that serves no purpose; the allusion here is not only to Beckett and Kafka, but also to a play written by Auster himself, *Laurel and Hardy Go to Heaven*,[11] a metaphysical burlesque in which two characters build a wall on the stage but fail to discover the meaning of their appointed task. *Moon Palace*'s Marco Stanley Fogg is made up of characters real and imaginary, and his initials, MS, are the clearest clue to his identity. He likens himself to an orphan in a nineteenth-century novel, and he narrates a story which charts the discovery of his artistic identity, thus placing the narrative in the tradition of the *Bildungsroman*. The centre of the novel is taken up by his grandfather's narrative of his adventures in the Wild West, but he is the first to acknowledge that this mythical West can only be seen through the lens of its mythologisers. The unavailability of unadulterated experience is further underscored by the fact that this story is itself embedded in the narrator's story.

Auster has often told the story of how he came to write *The New York Trilogy*, of how it all started with a wrong number. In his memoir *Hand to Mouth: A Chronicle of Early Failure*, the genesis of other works can be traced. Auster writes of his early adulthood, his forays into the literary world, and his attempts to support himself financially in order to devote himself to writing. Among other jobs connected with writing and the literary world, Auster once agreed to work for Jerzy Kosinski; his task was to go through *Cockpit* in order to make sure that the English was correct, and to make minor alterations where necessary. Kosinski would not let him take the manuscript away, so Auster had to work in the writer's home. He recounts how Kosinski interrupted him every twenty minutes and told him stories and anecdotes: 'What made these interruptions

---

11. This play is now reprinted in Paul Auster's *Hand to Mouth: A Chronicle of Early Failure* (London: Faber, 1997). It is interesting to note that the book came out in French translation a year before it appeared in the original. *Le Diable par la queue*, trans. Christine Le Bœuf (Paris: Actes Sud, 1996).

doubly odd and intriguing was that nearly every story he told me also appeared in the book he had written – the very novel spread out before me when he came into the room to talk' (*HM* 95). Auster was puzzled by his employer's story-telling:

> The book was supposedly a work of fiction, but when Kosinski told me these stories, he presented them as facts, real events from his life. Did he know the difference? I can't be sure, can't even begin to guess, but if I had to give an answer, I would say that he did… Perhaps. And then again, perhaps not. The only thing I know for certain is that Kosinski was a man of labyrinthine complexity. (*HM* 95)

Reading Auster's memoir, one is compelled to ask whether this is a warning to his own readers. This is the same narrative that tells the story of Auster's acquaintance with H.L. Humes, a man who inherited fifteen thousand dollars from his father and decided to use the inheritance to deal a blow to capitalism: he took all the money out of the bank, converted it into fifty-dollar bills, and distributed it to strangers in the street, much as Effing does with the stolen money in *Moon Palace*. Another acquaintance from Auster's days at Columbia University was Ted Gold, a man who later blew himself to 'a thousand pieces' when the bomb he was making exploded in his hands; Benjamin Sachs in *Leviathan* meets the same end. Perhaps Auster offers these stories in order to support his earlier claim: 'What I'm after, I suppose, is to write fiction as strange as the world I live in' (*AH* 278). The practice of constantly blurring the line that ought to separate fact from fiction is nowhere more pronounced than in those novels in which Auster deals with history and politics, and tackles some of his country's most cherished myths. Therefore, it is not only other writers and books that need to be considered in relation to his work, but also wider cultural phenomena and historical events as they appear in his fiction.

In *City of Glass*, the writer-detective Daniel Quinn follows Professor Stillman as he wanders around the streets of New York. When he sketches the old man's itinerary on a sheet, he thinks he sees a different letter of the alphabet spelled every day, making up the phrase 'The Tower of Babel'. If, as I shall argue in the first chapter, 'Legacies', we take Stillman to be a version of Ralph Waldo Emerson, then Quinn's thoughts and actions are a fitting analogue for what the author himself is doing in appropriating the work of his predecessors. Similarly, they offer an image of the reader. Whether Stillman actually spells 'The Tower of Babel' in the streets is something we cannot know; more importantly, it is irrelevant.

Quinn needs to impose a pattern and give meaning to the other man's behaviour. It is not what Stillman does but how Quinn receives it that is of interest. Quinn writes *on top* of Stillman's writings, superimposes his own ideas, projects his own desires, but in so doing he does not erase Stillman's writing. Instead, he brings it to the foreground, in the only form in which one can know it: mediated, seen in its relation to other ideas, other writings.

In *Moon Palace*, the narrative spans three generations, covering most of the twentieth century. The narrator, born like his creator in 1947, is implicated in the historical and cultural events of his time. As his initials, MS, suggest, he is a page on which history is written, and his story is the story of his times. In *Leviathan*, an author gives up writing and decides to 'step into the real world and do something'. His desire for political engagement leads him to become a terrorist. But whether it is history or politics, Auster grounds the debate in the fictional. He does this by exposing the mechanisms of fiction-making (be that fiction a novel or history), by keeping writing always in the foreground. The story of Sachs's career as a terrorist comes to the reader through Peter Aaron, who writes a book about his friend and exposes his own limitations as observer. But, as I shall be arguing, to admit that there can be no immediacy of perception, no unadulterated experience, is not to admit defeat or deny the possibility of recovery from the edge of absence. To evoke other authors, and implicate them in one's own writing, does not efface the author.

An early example of how Auster fuses intense personal experience with the relative detachment of the self-consciously literary can be found in *The Invention of Solitude*. The book is divided into two parts; the first, 'Portrait of an Invisible Man' (1979), offers a first-person account of how the author came to terms with the death of his father, a man who even before his death 'had been absent'. The second part, 'The Book of Memory' (1980–81), is also largely autobiographical, but this time the author tries to imagine himself as other and writes in the third person, identifying the protagonist only as A. As its title suggests, 'Portrait of an Invisible Man' chronicles an attempt to capture absence, but it is not only the physical absence of a man who has died. Auster describes his father as a cold, distant man, of whom nothing could be known, a man who was absent from his family's life even while he was still alive: 'For as long as he lived, he was somewhere between here and there. But never really here. And never really there' (*IoS* 19). The father's absence becomes not only the cause of the narrator's distress, but also an emblem of the unavailability of truth, in writing as in life. 'One could not believe there was such a man – who lacked feeling, who wanted so little of others. And if there was not such a man, that means there was another man, a man hidden inside the man who was not there, and the trick of it, then, is to find him. On the condition that he is there to be found. To recognize, right from the start, that the essence of this project is failure' (*IoS* 20). Already in these personal words, born of grief and frustration, we recognise the questions that Auster will go on asking throughout his work. As 'Portrait of an Invisible Man' unfolds, it becomes increasingly clear that Auster is not only writing about his father, he is also writing about the act of writing, but his self-consciousness does not lessen the emotional impact of the text. The above quotation contains, in all its brevity, a problem that is central in Auster's fiction. He cannot decide whether there was, indeed, another man inside the one who was not there. In the same way, his books often take the form of a quest, but it is never resolved whether meaning is there to be found; instead, the focus shifts to the attempt not so much to recover even some of that meaning, as to fill the gap that its apparent absence leaves. The initial statement that the project is doomed to failure is later modified, when Auster realises that, no matter how inadequate his words are, they are the only means of filling the void. The imaginative act of representation is redemptive not because it restores meaning, but because it creates the only signification that can become available:

> In spite of the excuses I have made for myself, I understand what is happening. The closer I come to the end of what I am able to say, the more reluctant I am to say anything. I want to postpone the moment of ending, and in this way delude myself into thinking that I have only just begun, that the better part of my story still lies ahead. No matter how useless these words might seem to be, they have nevertheless stood between me and a silence that continues to terrify me. When I step into this silence, it will mean that my father has vanished forever. (*IoS* 65)

Words become a deferral, or a displacement, of absence and of silence, and the presence of Samuel Beckett is already felt in these lines. Later, in the novel *In the Country of Last Things*, the words in a woman's journal will become the means of holding together a world that is falling apart. The father is equated with the logos, and a recovery of him in words is a recovery of signification.

The quest for the absent father appears in different guises in much of Auster's fiction. It is, as 'Portrait of an Invisible Man' makes clear, a re-enactment of the author's quest for his own father, and also a metaphor for the author's relation to language and narrative. But a desire to establish one's genealogy is also a desire for legitimacy, a need to be placed inside a recognised tradition. Throughout Auster's *oeuvre* there is this interaction, this transaction: on the one hand he appropriates 'the father' (history, his literary ancestors, writing), and on the other he gives himself back to this family history by a deliberate act of will. These twin impulses become more pronounced in the second part of *The Invention of Solitude*, 'The Book of Memory'.

In 'The Book of Memory' the meditation on fatherhood continues, but this time the son has himself become a father. As the narrative switches from the first person to the third, we witness the passage from the personal to the public, a move underscored by the author's frequent allusions to, and quotations from, literary texts. Auster explains that he had felt no need to write this second part until he finished the first one. In the beginning, he thought that he could go on writing in the first person, but he soon found that he was not happy with it:

> It gave me a great deal of trouble, especially in terms of organization... This part was even more personal than the first, but the more deeply I descended into the material, the more distanced I became from it. In order to write about myself, I had to treat myself as though I were someone else. It was only when I started all over again in the third person that I began to see my way out of the impasse. (*AH* 267)

With 'The Book of Memory', then, Auster moves away from biographical meditation towards a *novelistic* kind of writing, a way of writing about the self as other; subjectivity is not yet thematised, which is why the work cannot be read as novel, but in it the reader may witness the genesis of a novel. As Auster writes about himself as 'other', he also feels the freedom to define this self through other books as well as through his own 'biographical' identity: 'I think in that second part of *The Invention of Solitude*, "The Book of Memory", the reason I quote so liberally from other writers is because I wanted it to be a collective work. This is the hoard of voices which inhabits my skull. These are the voices that I live with and I wanted them to come out and share the work with me.'[12]

As I shall be arguing, this kind of 'sharing' has been going on ever since, even when the voices cannot be heard as clearly as they can in this piece. As pointed out earlier, 'The Book of Memory' can be read as an image of a novel in the process of being born; subsequent novels have

12. Interview by Christopher Bigsby.

come out of this piece, which contains the seeds of both the themes and the techniques that Auster will later use. This is something that the author himself is well aware of: 'In retrospect I can see that everything I have done has come out of that book. The problems and questions and experiences that are examined there have been the meat of the things I have done since.'[13]

Elsewhere, Auster has claimed that all his books are really the same book, so a study of his own *œuvre* needs to take into account how the author gives a different treatment each time to a limited set of questions or themes. My discussion of 'The Book of Memory' will not be exhaustive, but it will concentrate on some major themes that recur in Auster's novels. The title itself, 'The Book of Memory', is an echo of Edmond Jabès's *The Book of Questions*. Auster remarks of the latter:

> *The Book of Questions* is... a mosaic of fragments, aphorisms, dialogues, songs, and commentaries that endlessly move around the central question of the book: how to speak what cannot be spoken... What happens in *The Book of Questions*, then, is the writing of *The Book of Questions* – or rather, the attempt to write it, a process that the reader is allowed to witness in all its gropings and hesitations. Like the narrator in Beckett's *The Unnamable*, who is cursed by 'the inability to speak [and] the inability to be silent', Jabès's narrative goes nowhere but around and around itself. (*AH* 107, 111)

The same words could be used to describe Auster's own 'Book of Memory', but there are more specific thematic connections to be made between the two works, which I shall discuss in 'Austerities'. 'The Book of Memory' takes its epigraph from Carlo Collodi's *Pinocchio*, which the narrator, A., is reading to his son. Auster's interest in the fairy-tale will also be addressed in 'Austerities', but there are aspects of this particular story which recur under different guises in many of his novels. The comical aspects of *Pinocchio* will only surface much later, in *Mr Vertigo*, where an unruly urchin needs to undergo a series of rituals in order to acquire discipline and find, albeit in an unorthodox manner, his place in the world. The images that the writer singles out from *Pinocchio* in 'The Book of Memory' relate to the father–son relationship in the tale, and the image of Gepetto in the belly of the shark. In *City of Glass*, the father–son relationship of *Pinocchio* has been reversed: Stillman Jr has been abused by his father, and when Quinn encounters him he seems more like a puppet than a real person. In a book that is largely about the

---

13. Interview by Christopher Bigsby.

loss of innocence (be it personal, linguistic, or narrative innocence), this reversal of Pinocchio's rescue of his father becomes poignant. In *Moon Palace*, Fogg pushes his father into a freshly dug grave, but he saves him before he dies, and is therefore allowed to reach the maturity denied Peter Stillman.

The image of Gepetto in the belly of the shark loses its comforting fairy-tale associations as it transmutes into the more disturbing images of Jonah devoured by the fish, Hölderlin living out his grief and mental anguish in a tower built for him by the carpenter Zimmer (the name meaning 'room' which is also given to a character in *Moon Palace*), Anne Frank writing her secret diary in a room in Amsterdam, and the Jews storing memories in words, as the writer puts it (*IoS* 165), in the Warsaw ghetto. The image of the solitary artist is a recurring one in Auster's fiction and, as I argue further on, rooms and other enclosures play an important part throughout, although they carry different, and at times conflicting, associations.

In 'The Book of Memory' Auster also meditates on the nature of chance. Among other tales, he tells the story of A. and his wife finding two pianos with the same key missing in the space of only a few months: 'It was at that moment, perhaps, that A. realized the world would go on eluding him forever' (*IoS* 146). He then goes on to consider how what is random and meaningless in life is invested with meaning the moment it is used in literature: 'In a work of fiction, one assumes there is a conscious mind behind the words on the page. In the presence of happenings in the so-called real world, one assumes nothing. The made-up story consists entirely of meanings, whereas the story of fact is devoid of any signifi-cance beyond itself' (*IoS* 146). It is this paradox, and the twin impulses of looking for meaning and accepting the meaningless (or at least unknowability) of the world, that Auster explores in his fiction. His books are both an investigation into these matters and a reflection of them. The coincidences that appear in Auster's fiction are 'meaningful' in that they are selected by the author, and are therefore not as random as the ones occurring in 'real life'; they also produce signification because they often form the basis of the plot.

To summarise my position so far, there are three factors that I take into account in my study of Auster's fiction: the writers and literary texts which appear in the books, the cultural texts of myth and history, and the relations among Auster's books themselves. To talk of an author's inter-textual practices as I just have implies an acceptance of the writer as orig-inator and sole creator of his work, but this is a thesis to which I do not subscribe. The 'intertext' exists independently of the author's will, and it shapes both the production and the reception of any given cultural arte-fact. Therefore, before I begin my discussion of Auster's fiction, I shall consider the theoretical arguments which have determined my approach.

In the previous section, I suggested that Auster was 'influenced' (although I carefully avoided using the term) by the writers of the American Renais-sance, by French Symbolism, and by modernist writers such as Beckett and Kafka. Given the amount of textual evidence there is to justify the claim, this may seem an obvious point to make; however, it can also be highly problematic. To use the term 'influence' in the sense that Bloom employs it in *The Anxiety of Influence* is to accept the author as sole orig-inator and agent of his or her own creation. Bloom's insistence on the subject presupposes the existence of the poetic genius and relies on notions of originality and authenticity that have now been discredited. As a result of his privileging of the subject, Bloom's model of influence is also restrictive in that it leaves no room for interpretation by the reader. It is, therefore, appropriate at this point to turn to theories of inter-textuality, a term that does not privilege the author to the same extent as does Bloom's theory of influence.

'Intertextuality' is a term first used by Julia Kristeva in writings which introduced Bakhtin to French theorists.[14] Whereas Bloom was concerned with static structures and one-to-one relationships, Kristeva proposed that the text was a dynamic site, an 'intersection of textual surfaces' acquiring meaning only in its relation to other texts; in other words, sig-nification was not an inherent quality in texts, but was produced in the interaction between texts. The term 'text' was itself enlarged to include not only literary texts, but also the sign systems that make up history and society. In *Desire in Language*, Kristeva writes that intertextuality 'situ-ates the text within history and society, which are then seen as texts read by the writer, and into which he inserts himself by rewriting them'.[15] Although Kristeva does not privilege the subject in the same way as Bloom does, in that she recognises selfhood itself, or identity, to be the product of socio-linguistic interactions, hers is also an author-centred theory in that she defines intertextuality as a function of writing rather

14. 'Word, Dialogue and Novel' (1966); repr. in Julia Kristeva, *Desire in Language: A Semiotic Approach to Literature and Art*, trans. Thomas Gora, Alice Jardine and Leon S. Roudiez, ed. Leon S. Roudiez (New York: Columbia University Press, 1980).
15. Kristeva, *Desire in Language*, p. 65.

than of reading; as the above quotation suggests, she only makes room for reading as a function performed by the author, who then goes on to assimilate and reproduce his readings.

Two years after Kristeva introduced the concept of intertextuality, Roland Barthes proclaimed the death of the author. In the essay of that title he, like Kristeva, recognised the multiplicity of semantic codes inherent in the text, but he shifted the emphasis away from the author as controlling agent and identified the reader as the site in which signification is produced: 'a text is made of multiple writings, drawn from many cultures and entering into mutual relations of dialogue, parody, contestation, but there is one place where this multiplicity is focused and that place is the reader, not, as was hitherto said, the author'.[16] But Barthes's theory becomes problematic when he goes on to add that 'the reader is without history, biography, psychology', since such a reader can only be trapped in a sealed circle of endless substitution or, to use Umberto Eco's term, unlimited semiosis. Eco, following Barthes, opposes the humanist model which insists on the centrality of the author. In 'Overinterpreting Texts', he distinguishes between the intention of the reader (*intentio lectoris*), and the intention of the text (*intentio operis*), and he writes:

> The text's intention is not displayed by the textual surface... it is possible to speak of the text's intention only as the result of a conjecture on the part of the reader. The initiative of the reader basically consists in making a conjecture about the text's intention. A text is a device conceived in order to produce its model reader. I repeat that this reader is not the one who makes the 'only right' conjecture... Since the intention of the text is basically to produce a model reader able to make conjectures about it, the initiative of the model reader consists in figuring out a model author that is not the empirical one and that, in the end, coincides with the intention of the text.[17]

If Eco's text produces a model reader, then this reader must, like Barthes's, be one without history, biography, psychology, since these particulars would be as irrelevant as the intentions of the empirical author. However, Eco also recognises that this view could authorise the production of endless decodings and encodings, some of which would not be acceptable. Therefore, just as he does not reject the notion of the

16. Roland Barthes, 'The Death of the Author', in *Image–Music–Text*, trans. Stephen Heath (London: Fontana, 1977), p. 147.
17. Umberto Eco with Richard Rorty, Jonathan Culler and Christine Brooke-Rose, *Interpretation and Overinterpretation*, ed. Stefan Collini (Cambridge and New York: Cambridge University Press, 1992), p. 64.

intention of the empirical author, but merely finds it ancillary to the intention of the text, he proposes that a line be drawn beyond which interpretation is no longer acceptable, because it is not productive:

> In spite of the obvious differences in degrees of certainty and uncertainty, every picture of the world (be it a scientific law or a novel) is a book in its own right, open to further interpretation. But certain interpretations can be recognized as unsuccessful because they are like a mule, that is, they are unable to produce new interpretations or cannot be confronted with the traditions of the previous interpretations.[18]

That Eco strikes a delicate balance between humanism and deconstruction can be seen from the responses he receives, in the same volume, from Richard Rorty and Jonathan Culler. For Rorty, Eco's theory is lacking in humanism (although Rorty's use of the term excludes the essentialist nature of humanism), whereas to Culler it seems too humanist in that it does not defend overinterpretation on principle. I find Eco's theory useful precisely because it incorporates the teachings of structuralist and poststructuralist theory while avoiding many of its excesses. In this, of course, he is not alone.

In *Desire in Language*, Kristeva wrote: 'any text is constructed as a mosaic of quotations; any text is the absorption and transformation of another'.[19] We cannot know if the choice of the noun 'absorption' in favour of an active verb is deliberate, but we find the full expression of such a view in Barthes's *The Pleasure of the Text*:

> *Text* means *Tissue*; but whereas hitherto we have always taken this tissue as a product, a ready-made veil, behind which lies, more or less hidden, meaning (truth), we are now emphasizing, in the tissue, the generative idea that the text is made, is worked out in a perpetual interweaving; lost in this tissue – this texture – the subject unmakes himself, like a spider dissolving in the constructive secretions of its web. Were we fond of neologisms, we might define the theory of the text as an *hyphology* (*hyphos* is the tissue and the spider's web).[20]

This passage summarises both the strengths and the drawbacks of Barthes's theory. The realisation that any text is worked out in perpetual interweaving has far-reaching implications: it not only de-centres the

18. Eco et al., *Interpretation*, p. 150.
19. Kristeva, *Desire in Language*, p. 66.
20. Roland Barthes, *The Pleasure of the Text* (1973), trans. Richard Miller (Oxford: Basil Blackwell, 1990), p. 64.

author and rejects notions of the availability of meaning and truth, it also questions our acceptance of all kinds of grand narratives which shape the society we live in. However, feminist and 'minority' theorists have argued successfully that the effacement of the author has political implications as well. To choose the web over the spider is to imply 'the confident posture of mastery that a post-Cartesian subject enjoys in relation to the texts of his culture'.[21] Since women and minorities do not have equal access to these texts, 'to postulate an intending agent as the epicenter of an eclectic, allusive motion is to raise the issues of opportunities and constraints with which the women or minority writers worked but without returning to the expressionist assumptions of a narrower influence theory'.[22]

This is precisely what Nancy Miller proposes in 'Arachnologies': an acknowledgment of the agency of the author which does not, however, operate at the expense of the text, or the reader. Miller uses the story of Arachne, as recounted in Ovid's *Metamorphoses*, as the archetypal image of the woman and her place in cultural production. She concludes:

> To remember Arachne only as the spider, or through the dangers of her web alone, is to retain the archetype and dismember, once again, with Athena, the subject of its history: to underread. The goal of overreading, of reading for the signature, is to put one's finger – figuratively – on the place of production that marks the spinner's attachment to her web. This is also, of course, to come closer to the spider's art itself: in the end, the material of arachnologies may allow us to refuse and refigure the very opposition of subject and text, spider and web.[23]

Miller welcomes the death of the author because she takes it to signal the end of a patriarchal canon based around the notion of the originating powers of authorship, but she insists that a history of female authorship still needs to be established. A distinction needs to be made between Miller's ideological position and her methodology, and it is the latter I am concerned with here. The power relations may be different, but the study of 'the place of production' that marks the author's attachment to the text may be used as a way of approaching any text. Moreover, there is no reason why one could not also study the place of production that marks the *reader's* attachment to the web along with the spinner's. To

21. Nancy Miller, 'Arachnologies', in *Subject to Change: Reading Feminist Writing* (New York: Columbia University Press, 1988), p. 83.
22. Jay Clayton and Eric Rothstein, eds., *Influence and Intertextuality in Literary History* (Wisconsin: University of Wisconsin Press, 1991), p. 11.
23. Miller, 'Arachnologies', p. 97.

read, in this case, Paul Auster in relation to the authors he writes into his own texts is not to return to a strict author-centred model, but precisely to vex the relationship between the author and the text (his own as well as the texts of the past), and between the world and the word.

When Paul Auster refers to Thoreau's *Walden*, he does not send his readers back to the book *Walden* written by Henry David Thoreau, but to the book Auster has read and then inscribed into his own text (and which is in turn decoded by the reader), and also to the mythic status the book has acquired even for those who, like Auster's character Blue, did not have the patience to read it. *Walden* in *Ghosts* is not the same as *Walden* by Thoreau, a book we can find in the library or bookshop. So we return to the *thematisation* of the intertext, which can be seen more clearly in Auster's later novels, where the emphasis moves away from individual authors and works to take into account the larger intertext of politics, history, and myth-making as systems of signification.

It follows from this that an actively intertextual author like Auster does not seek to assert his own authority, but rather to undermine that very concept. This is achieved not only in the thematisation of intertextuality, but also in the choice of individual texts, or the dialogue between texts. Writing – somehow surprisingly – of William Blake, Rajan notes: 'Recognizing that the cultural scene is overdetermined, composed by competing discourses, someone like Blake constructs his work intertextually not to transcend his historical situation, but rather to write himself into it. He clears a space for his own position precisely by inscribing it in a text whose construction makes writing and reading a mirror of their own cultural production.' If the writer signals an awareness of his position within the site of cultural production, he denounces authority and notions of originality precisely because he allows himself to be seen 'insert[ing] himself into an anterior (social) text by rewriting it'.[24]

If writers like Poe, Hawthorne, Beckett and Kafka are brought together on the page, who speaks in a Paul Auster novel? Whereas in Bloom's formulation the author would be trying to assert his own authority by struggling to shake off the influence of his predecessors, Auster's intertextual strategies, as I have argued, undermine traditional notions of authorship and authority. Again in Bloomian terms, Auster's practice could be seen as an assertion of the author's omnipotence, but another shortcoming in Bloom's theory is his insistence that the subject matter of the poem is irrelevant. In the case of Auster's writing, although

24. Clayton and Rothstein, eds., *Influence and Intertextuality*, pp. 73–74.

of course not uniquely, a study of the thematic preoccupations of his novels is crucial in understanding his relationship with literary as well as cultural texts, while a concurrent examination of the literary genres Auster works within, or subverts, also illuminates the author's practices.

This is the organising principle that has shaped the main body of this book. As my theoretical position makes clear, I am not interested in chasing every allusion, identifying every quotation, and considering their relation to Auster's *œuvre*. Instead, I have tried to explore different aspects of the intertext, and to consider how they shape, and are shaped by, Auster's fiction. The first chapter, 'Legacies', offers a close reading of *The New York Trilogy* in the light of the nineteenth-century writers who haunt the text. Since I take the intertext to be a dynamic site rather than a rigid structure, this practice works both ways. As I will argue, we do not only read Auster after Hawthorne, for example, but also Hawthorne after Auster. The specific philosophical stance and the narrative strategies that Auster employs in his exploration of urban living, the nature of language and representation, or the perils of interpretation, all place his writing within a tradition that can be traced to nineteenth-century American writing.

The second chapter, 'Austerities', moves away from the author-based model of 'Legacies' to consider in broader terms Auster's relation to certain modes of writing, especially aspects of literary modernism. I use the term mainly in the interests of taxonomy, since I am not concerned with defining Auster's writing through the use of a modernism/postmodernism dichotomy. I am simply arguing that certain themes and techniques which can be found in *The New York Trilogy*, *In the Country of Last Things* and *The Music of Chance* have previously been the concern of writers such as Samuel Beckett, Franz Kafka and Knut Hamsun, with whose work Auster's has a close affinity. The title of this chapter reflects the spartan, elliptical quality of these narratives, and indeed my discussion of *In the Country of Last Things* and *The Music of Chance* takes into consideration Auster's chosen modes of story-telling, and particular thematic tropes that reflect that practice.

With 'Realities', the final chapter of this book, the field opens up even more widely to allow a consideration of how Auster deals with questions pertaining to history, politics and myth-making. As the title of this chapter implies, in novels like *Moon Palace* and *Leviathan* no easy distinction can be made between the 'real' and the 'fictive'. Both novels deal with characters who are self-mythologisers, while at the same time they are seen to be the products of their own historical time. The emphasis is on the weaving of plots, on writing and representation, and the strategies that Auster employs serve to blur the line between the extra- and the intra-textual. In *Ghosts*, the character Blue feels

> like a man who has been condemned to sit in a room and go on reading a book for the rest of his life. This is strange enough – to be only half alive at best, seeing the world only through words, living through the lives of others... he no longer wants any part of it. But how to get out? How to get out of the room that is the book that will go on being written for as long as he stays in the room? (*Gh* 169–70)

What Blue doesn't know is what Auster's fiction so powerfully demonstrates: the book, or the room, that Blue is trapped in is also the world. We see the world through words, and we live through the lives of others.

I

Legacies

'Legacies' offers an analysis which takes the form of a juxtaposition between Auster's *New York Trilogy* and texts by his American forefathers. As I have already stated, my aim is not to trace influences or chase allusions, if only because Auster makes such a task superfluous by drawing attention to them in a very explicit manner. Nor does my method involve a study of the historical progression of American literature from the nineteenth century to the present, and this is not only due to the fact that any such history may be ideologically suspect, and often necessarily simplistic, but also because it has for a long time been recognised that literature is also read backwards from the present. In 'Tradition and the Individual Talent' (1917), T.S. Eliot called attention to this effect when he wrote: 'What happens when a new work of art is created is something that happens simultaneously to all works of art which preceded it... The past [is] altered by the present as much as the present is directed by the past.'[1] Borges gave a more specific example, emphasising the contribution of individual authors to the way we read earlier texts. In his essay on Nathaniel Hawthorne, he drew parallels between 'Wakefield' and Kafka's stories, and he concluded:

> The circumstance, the strange circumstance, of perceiving in a story written by Hawthorne at the beginning of the nineteenth century the same quality that distinguishes the stories Kafka wrote at the beginning of the twentieth must not cause us to forget that Hawthorne's particular quality has been created, or determined, by Kafka. 'Wakefield' prefigures Franz Kafka, but Kafka modifies and refines the reading of 'Wakefield'. The debt

---

1. T.S. Eliot, 'Tradition and the Individual Talent', in *Selected Essays* (London: Faber, 1961), p. 15.

is mutual; a great writer creates his precursors. He creates and somehow justifies them.[2]

In his book *Reverse Tradition: Postmodern Fictions and the Nineteenth Century Novel*, Robert Kiely expands on this proposition, and offers readings of nineteenth-century texts through contemporary ones. The importance of his contribution lies in the fact that, like Borges, he considers individual texts, looking at how later ones 'modify' the earlier ones, while at the same time, like Eliot, he sees this as a phenomenon that exists independently of individual authors' intentions. In his introduction, he explains that he chose texts from both periods 'without any thought of suggesting indirectly a hidden but "real" historical influence... An almost infinite variety of other combinations is possible, since, of course, none of these writers "belongs" with any other.'[3] My approach differs from Kiely's to the extent that my choices are often guided by textual allusions and references, as well as Auster's own critical writings. But, like Kiely, I recognise that nineteenth-century fiction can now be read through the postmodern lens, and this applies both to Auster's reading of this fiction and to my own interpretation of that reading as it manifests itself in the text.

Paul Auster, who admits that he is 'passionately interested' and 'absolutely immersed' in nineteenth-century American literature, displays his familiarity with the works of that period throughout his *œuvre*. *The New York Trilogy* alone contains references to texts that range from the well known, such as Thoreau's *Walden*, to the nearly obscure, such as Melville's 'Jimmy Rose', while the author character Benjamin Sachs in *Leviathan* writes a novel whose characters include Emerson, Hawthorne's daughter Rose, and Walt Whitman. Auster shares many preoccupations with his American forefathers, ranging from the investigation into language and its relation to reality to questions of identity, solitude and artistic creativity, and the contrasting views of America that emerge from its cityscapes and the large expanses of nature. It need hardly be said that Auster comes to very different conclusions, but what needs to be stressed is that, by bringing these writers into his own work,

---

2. Jorge Luis Borges, 'Nathaniel Hawthorne', in *Other Inquisitions: 1937–1952*, trans. Ruth L.C. Simms (Austin: University of Texas Press, 1964); repr. in *Nathaniel Hawthorne's Tales: Authoritative Texts, Backgrounds, Criticism*, ed. James McIntosh (New York and London: W.W. Norton, 1987), p. 410.
3. Robert Kiely, *Reverse Tradition: Postmodern Fictions and the Nineteenth Century Novel* (Cambridge, MA and London: Harvard University Press, 1993), p. 7.

he shifts the emphasis away from an author-based model, away from certainty, towards an investigation which is rooted in the fictive, the textual. This is not to deny the existence of an extra-textual world, and therefore to be caught in a circle of self-referentiality, but rather to recognise mediation as a necessary condition for the act of perception and interpretation. In this sense, the presence of Ralph Waldo Emerson in *City of Glass*, which I examine in detail in the first part of this chapter, is largely ironic. Emerson was the major advocate of literary and intellectual independence for his country. 'Our days of dependence, our long apprenticeship to the learning of other lands, draws to a close', he proclaimed in 'The American Scholar'. 'The millions that around us are rushing into life, cannot always be fed on the sere remains of foreign harvests.'[4] This call stemmed from Emerson's desire to see the emergence of writers who would create a new idiom for a newly independent country, and also from his belief in the authenticity and originality of the Romantic genius: 'Insist on yourself; never imitate', he urged in 'Self-Reliance' (199). Auster's disagreement with this doctrine is clearly registered in *The New York Trilogy*, where Emerson metamorphoses into an inspired madman who inhabits a text which owes its particular nature as much to cultural events and literary texts, ranging from the writings of Kafka and Beckett to film noir and baseball, as to Auster's 'original' authorship.

But this 'backwards' reading of Transcendentalism does not use as its departure point only the texts of the twentieth century, but also contemporary ones. Writers such as Melville and Hawthorne were already registering their disagreement with the Transcendentalist doctrine, and Auster explores this tension, which has provided the organising principle for 'Legacies'. The first part, 'Yea-Saying', comprises a reading of *The New York Trilogy* in relation to Emerson and Thoreau, whom I identify as the main figures in *City of Glass* and *Ghosts* respectively. 'Nay-Saying' begins with *The Locked Room*, which, as the author points out, is related to Hawthorne's writing, and I also look at the intertextual ghosts of Melville and Poe, who haunt the entire *Trilogy*.

Another factor that needs to be considered in relation to Auster's treatment of American Romantic texts is the fact that *The New York Trilogy* takes the form of a postmodernist rewrite of the detective novel. Daniel Quinn, the protagonist of *City of Glass*, writes detective novels using the pseudonym William Wilson and, as is usual in Auster's writing, the

---

4. Ralph Waldo Emerson, *Selected Essays*, ed. Larzer Ziff (Harmondsworth: Penguin, 1982), p. 83. Subsequent references are to this edition.

choice of name is not accidental. Apart from serving to announce early
in the book the theme of the double that runs throughout the *Trilogy*, this
reference may also be read as an indication of Auster's allegiance to a particular 'school' of detective fiction which begins with Poe and culminates
with the great noir hard-boiled stories of Dashiell Hammett and Raymond Chandler. To the extent that any writer can ever be said to create
a new genre, Edgar Allan Poe is credited with the invention of the detective story with the publication of 'The Murders in the Rue Morgue' in
1841. However, Stefano Tani successfully argues that Poe's detective
stories are not canonical, or conventional, in the sense that they display
fundamental differences from the detective fiction of writers such as
Agatha Christie or Arthur Conan Doyle. For instance, Tani claims that in
'The Murders in the Rue Morgue' there is no culprit in the traditional
sense of the word, since the murderer's creativity is morally neutral. In
order to support his argument concerning the problematic nature of
Poe's detective stories, Tani also refers to non-detective stories which still
involve an element of mystery, such as 'Ligeia', where the reader is presented with a 'false' solution, and 'William Wilson', where the solution
destroys the solver.[5] The famous debate about Poe's 'The Purloined
Letter', initiated by Lacan's 'seminar', is further proof that the detective
genre was not, in its birth, a representation of a simple world in which
good and evil, reason and unreason, truth and lies were clearly defined.[6]
The moral and narrative ambiguity of Poe's stories suggests that, paradoxically, Poe violated the very principles he created, and although these
anomalies were ironed out in traditional mystery novels, they survive in
the hard-boiled tradition to which Auster's writing is closer.

In 'The Typology of Detective Fiction', Tzvetan Todorov begins with
the proposition that the whodunit contains two stories: the story of the
crime, and the story of the subsequent investigation. He goes on to illustrate how, in the hard-boiled novel, the two stories unfold simultaneously: 'the narrative coincides with the action... there is no point reached

---

5. Stefano Tani, *The Doomed Detective: The Contribution of the Detective Novel to
   Postmodern American and Italian Fiction* (Carbondale and Edwardsville: Southern
   Illinois University Press, 1984).
6. Jacques Lacan, 'Seminar on "The Purloined Letter"', *Yale French Studies*, 48 (1956),
   pp. 339–72. In response to Lacan's 'Seminar', Jacques Derrida wrote 'The Purveyor
   of Truth', *Yale French Studies*, 52 (1975), pp. 31–113. Barbara Johnson kept the
   debate going with her essay 'The Frame of Reference: Poe, Lacan, Derrida', in *The
   Critical Difference* (Baltimore and London: Johns Hopkins University Press, 1980),
   pp. 110–76.

where the narrator comprehends all past events'.[7] The private eye therefore moves in a world of shifting, elusive signifiers, and there is no guarantee that he will discover meaning, even if he arrives at a solution. This
is certainly true of the detective figures in *The New York Trilogy*, but
there is one further twist: the private eye has been romanticised in our
collective imagination; through the many representations in film and literature, the iconography of this figure no longer carries associations of a
world of peril and uncertainty. It is evoked in our culture – a term which
I use to include the production and the reception of *The New York Trilogy* – with a certain nostalgia for the 'Golden Age' of the private investigator, and nostalgia implies not only a hankering after the past, but also
the acceptance that a return to this past is no longer possible. The point
is not that Quinn is a hard-boiled detective; it is, rather, that things would
be a lot easier if only he were. This nostalgia is also evident in Auster's
attitude towards Transcendentalism. As with his use of detective fiction
elements, his inclusion of texts such as Emerson's *Nature* or Thoreau's
Walden does not imply an intention to ridicule them, nor an unques-
tioning acceptance of them. Their recontextualisation draws attention to
their inapplicability in the 'age of suspicion', while it also demonstrates
Auster's deep involvement with the texts of the past.

What the detective story shares with Emerson's essays and addresses,
or Thoreau's introspective diaries and meditations, is the quest for truth
and meaning, even though it is conducted in differing contexts and for
different purposes. In a sense, the detective's investigation is a secular
version of the Transcendentalist search for signification. The signifying
field is no longer nature, which Emerson and Thoreau saw as a large
hieroglyph, but the city, which is man-made, composed of conflicting elements, a collection of contradictory signs which cloud the investigator's
vision and expose him to dangers. As I shall argue, Auster explores these
two opposing sites through the juxtaposition of the recurring images of
the Garden of Eden and the Tower of Babel. But it is the detective genre
in general that Auster uses to great effect in his trilogy. As he told Joseph
Mallia, 'In the same way that Cervantes used chivalric romances as a
starting point for *Don Quixote*, or the way that Beckett used the standard
vaudeville routine as the framework for *Waiting for Godot*, I tried to use
certain genre conventions to get to another place, another place altogether' (*AH* 269). Unlike Cervantes, though, Auster's intention is not to

---

7. Tzvetan Todorov, 'The Typology of Detective Fiction', in *The Poetics of Prose*, trans.
   Richard Howard (Oxford: Blackwell, 1977), p. 47.

mock the original genre – in this case that of the detective novel – but, through a process of defamiliarisation, to startle his readers out of the certainties and assumptions which are formed by the closely defined rules of the genre. The precise methods he employs will be discussed in the pages that follow, but it would be useful at this point to consider Auster's fiction in the light of genre in general.

Auster began his literary career as a poet, but he gave up during the late 1970s; he never denounced his own efforts, or poetry in general, but he felt he needed more scope in his writing:

> My poems were a quest for what I would call a uni-vocal expression. They expressed what I felt at any given moment, as if I'd never felt anything before and would never feel anything again. They were concerned with essences, with bedrock beliefs, and their aim was always to achieve a purity and consistency of language. Prose, on the other hand, gives me a chance to articulate my conflicts and contradictions. Like everyone else, I am a multiple being, and I embody a whole range of attitudes and responses to the world... Writing prose allows me to include all of these responses. I no longer have to choose among them. (*AH* 297)

To the interviewer's suggestion that this sounds like Bakhtin's notion of 'the dialogic imagination', Auster replies, 'Exactly. Of all the theories of the novel, Bakhtin's strikes me as the most brilliant, the one that comes closest to understanding the complexity and magic of the form' (*AH* 297). In *The Dialogic Imagination*, Bakhtin writes: 'the novel parodies other genres (precisely in their roles as genres); it exposes the conventionality of their forms and their language; it squeezes out some genres and incorporates others into its own peculiar structure, reformulating and re-accentuating them'.[8] Bakhtin is comparing the novel to genres that predate it, such as the epic, but his comments may also be used in the study of how a novel incorporates elements from various other novelistic genres. Elements of the detective novel, science fiction, the picaresque, the *Bildungsroman*, all find their way into Auster's fiction, but they are reformulated and reaccentuated. *The New York Trilogy*, for instance, charts not so much a search for truth as a questioning of its existence in the first place. Daniel Quinn tries to adopt the language of the hard-boiled private eye, but he is after all a poet, and the detective he thinks he is impersonating turns out to be a writer himself. In other words, the detective fiction elements are never allowed to take over the

8. M.M. Bakhtin, *The Dialogic Imagination*, trans. Caryl Emerson and Michael Holquist, ed. Michael Holquist (Austin: University of Texas Press, 1981), p. 5.

story. *In the Country of Last Things* presents an image of a futuristic dystopia reminiscent of those of science fiction novels, but Auster is not writing about an imagined future that resembles the present, but about a present which has already fulfilled our worst fears about the future; *The Music of Chance* begins as a road novel, but ends as a Kafkaesque parable. As my discussion of each of these novels will show, to identify the presence of elements borrowed from various genres is to isolate only one aspect of each novel, which in its entirety is multi-faceted and resistant to categorisation. Auster deliberately draws attention to these elements the better to expose their conventionality, the way they restrict writing by dictating a strict adherence to certain rules. In 'The Law of Genre', Derrida writes: 'As soon as the word genre is sounded, as soon as it is heard, as soon as one attempts to conceive it, a limit is drawn. And when a limit is established, norms and interdictions are not far behind.'[9] And where norms and interdictions exist, the temptation to break them cannot be far behind either. In the case of 'genre literature', the success of a work depends on a strict observation of the established rules, which create a set of expectations on the reader's part, and it is precisely by failing to meet these expectations that Auster draws attention to his own project, away from formal restrictions and imposed certainties. This deliberate foregrounding of the nature of each novel, which is a feature of postmodernist fiction, serves to question the very nature of writing. Bakhtin's comments are, again, relevant here: 'This ability of the novel to criticize itself is a remarkable feature of this ever-developing genre'.[10] And this ability is nowhere more pronounced than in postmodern, metafictional texts.[11]

In *City of Glass*, the writer-turned-detective seeks to erase his identity, not only to annihilate his former self but actually to divest himself of his

---

9. Jacques Derrida, 'The Law of Genre', trans. Avital Ronell, in *Acts of Literature*, ed. Derek Attridge (London and New York: Routledge, 1992), p. 224.
10. Bakhtin, *The Dialogic Imagination*, p. 6.
11. This is an argument to which I shall return in 'Realities'. Bakhtin goes on to argue that 'Reality as we have it in the novel is only one of many possible realities; it is not inevitable, not arbitrary' (*The Dialogic Imagination*, p. 37). Linda Hutcheon, in *A Poetics of Postmodernism: History, Theory, Fiction* (New York and London: Routledge, 1988) and in her essay 'Discourse, Power, Ideology: Humanism and Postmodernism', in *Postmodernism and Contemporary Fiction*, ed. Edmund J. Smyth (London: B.T. Batsford, 1991), argues that the foregrounding of fictionality is not, as Marxist critics suppose, apolitical, or dehistoricised, since, by drawing attention to its own mode of production, the text makes us aware of 'discourse', which is essentially governed by extra-literary political and economic factors.

very selfhood. In *Ghosts*, the writer, Black, is shot by Blue, the detective-turned-writer. In *The Locked Room*, two writers take the roles of detective and culprit. The latter leaves his life behind, seemingly vanishing into thin air, and the former attempts to track him down. This triple role of the author as detective, criminal, and victim illustrates Auster's complex, and at times conflicting, views on the notion of authorship. Daniel Quinn impersonates a writer called Paul Auster, Blue disguises himself as a Melvillian character who looks like Walt Whitman, while Fanshawe, whose name is borrowed from Hawthorne, goes into hiding and is only willing to communicate through a locked door. The author is thus seen rehearsing various roles through his own characters, attempting to define his own position in relation to the fictions he creates, and is created by; and even though this practice does not erase the presence of the author it questions it, and it keeps it always to the forefront, but always in a doubtful position.

Yea-Saying

The man is only half himself, the other half is his expression.
                                                    Ralph Waldo Emerson

Daniel Quinn, a disillusioned poet turned detective fiction writer who decides to impersonate a private investigator, is assigned a strange case: that of tailing Professor Peter Stillman, a man recently released from prison, who might try to harm his son, Peter Stillman, Jr. Quinn learns that Stillman *père* was once a distinguished scholar who had studied philosophy and religion at Harvard; in an over-zealous attempt to test his hypothesis of a 'natural' language, he had kept his son in complete isolation for nine years, waiting to see what language the boy would learn to speak. Quinn being a man of letters rather than a man of action, his first step is to read Stillman's thesis; the summary we are given is crucial to the narrative on different levels. In the context of the detective story, it sheds light on the culprit's motives, and it helps the investigator to become better acquainted with the way his opponent's mind operates. At the same time, it establishes a link between Auster's own writing and Transcendentalism, especially Emerson's theories of language, while it also places the story in a wider context, since it involves not only issues concerning language, but also their relation to American history and the land's Puritan past.

Stillman's thesis, and later his theories as he explains them to Quinn, play a crucial role in the establishment of a connection between Emerson and Auster. In his double role as madman and prophet, Stillman seems to embody Auster's attitude towards Transcendentalism. Professor Stillman seems like Emerson visiting the twentieth century; he still holds on to his theories, because of rather than despite the fact that he confronts a world in which his Platonic idealism seems to have little relevance, a world in which 'the brokenness is everywhere, the disarray universal' (*CG* 78). The issues dealt with in his book reveal that as a young man Stillman had a completely different vision of his country, and although at the time of writing it he was apparently detached and objective, his subsequent thoughts and actions, as well as his confession to the fabrication of Henry Dark, show clearly how much these theories meant to him. In the first part of *The Garden and the Tower: Early Visions of the New World*, Stillman argues that 'the first men to visit America believed that they had accidentally found paradise, a second Garden of Eden'; '[f]rom the very beginning, according to Stillman, the discovery of the New World was the quickening impulse of utopian thought, the spark that gave hope to the perfectibility of human life' (*CG* 41–42). America, as Gerónimo de Mendieta had prophesied, was destined to become 'a veritable City of God'. However, what Stillman finds after he is released from prison is a City of Glass instead of a City of God; and glass breaks easily. Here is what he tells Quinn: 'I have come to New York because it is the most forlorn of places... You have only to open your eyes to see it. The broken people, the broken things, the broken thoughts' (*CG* 78). His words recall those of the disillusioned Emerson who, in 'The American Scholar', deplores the fact that 'one man', 'this original unit, this fountain of power' has been 'distributed to multitudes', so that '[t]he state of society is one in which the members have suffered amputation from the trunk, and strut about so many walking monsters, – a good finger, a neck, a stomach, an elbow, but never a man' (84). This proposition is central to Emerson's theory, and it is also dealt with in 'Self-Reliance' and 'The Over-Soul'; in all three essays he argues for the existence of a transcendent self, which he calls the 'original unit', and he regards man's union with it as the highest aspiration. Emerson thus subscribes to the Platonic notion of origin, but, in what has come to be identified as a characteristically American optimism, he believes that this union can be achieved in life; as his disciple Thoreau puts it in *Walden*, 'men esteem truth remote, in the outskirts of the system, behind the farthest star, before Adam and after the last man. In eternity there is indeed something true and sublime. But all these times and places and occasions are now and here.'[12] Auster questions not only the accessibility but also the very existence of such an origin, but as I

12. Henry David Thoreau, *Walden* (1854); *The Variorum Walden*, ed. Walter Harding (New York: Twayne, 1962), p. 93. Subsequent references are to this edition.

shall have the opportunity to argue in the next chapter, he does not categorically deny it. Whereas Emerson laments the fragmentation he perceives, and suggests in his writings ways of remedying the problem, Auster can only accept this fragmentation as given. Artistic creation, the text itself in its infinite connections with other texts, and other modes of discourse, is now relied upon to produce signification, rather than to unveil hidden meaning. In other words, Auster accepts the loss of centre and unity, and his task then becomes to find ways of addressing this in its own terms, within its own limitations: 'The question is the story itself, and whether or not it means something is not for the story to tell', warns the narrator in the opening paragraph of *City of Glass* (*CG* 3).

In the second part of his book, Stillman attempts to link the Fall with the Tower of Babel: '[a]ccording to Stillman, the Tower of Babel episode was an exact recapitulation of what had happened in the Garden – only expanded, made general in its significance for all mankind' (*CG* 43). It seems peculiar that Stillman devotes more space to the consideration of the Tower of Babel episode than to the Fall, and indeed his preoccupation with the fall of language is clear throughout this part of his thesis, where he concludes that the story of the Garden records the fall of language as well as the fall of man. If Stillman deplores the fall of man mainly because it entailed the fall of language, then one can see why he regards the Tower of Babel episode as a 'secularised' version of the original fall. For Auster, this is a useful analogy because it draws attention to language, while it also gives him the opportunity to place his own story within a context which encourages an exploration of the contrast between nature as the Promised Land and the city as a place of corruption and disillusionment (this becomes more pronounced in the second part of the Trilogy, *Ghosts*, where Auster takes Walden Pond to the heart of the city). John Irwin sees a very interesting connection between language before and after the Fall, and the contrast between the natural world and the city, when he suggests that

> As opposed to the cosmic tree of life that stood in the center of the natural world of the garden, the tower is the center of an urban world, an artificial world descended from the handiwork of the first city-builder (Genesis 4:17) and first murderer, Cain... the tower, built in the pride of human art, is an attempt to displace heaven and earth, just as the spoken word in its power of arbitrary imposition becomes more important than the thing it links, until in its ultimate abstraction it 'kills' the physical object that it stands for.[13]

13. John Irwin, *American Hieroglyphics: The Symbol of the Egyptian Hieroglyphics in the American Renaissance* (Baltimore and London: Johns Hopkins University Press, 1980), pp. 34–35.

The Tower can be regarded as the ultimate 'empty' signifier, since the thing it stands for is precisely lack of communication, the inability of language to signify or to convey meaning effectively. However, the Tower does convey meaning, even if this is the unavailability of meaning; in the same way, Auster's characters embark on quests, looking for signs in the labyrinthine streets of New York, but it is the telling of the quest that matters rather than the question of whether there is meaning to be found. In a book which, as its title announces, is to a large extent about the city, New York City, the Tower of Babel becomes a potent symbol. The Tower is also alluded to in Auster's pseudonymous detective novel *Squeeze Play*, while his essay on Louis Wolfson is entitled 'New York Babel' (*AH* 26–34). These references to the Tower of Babel place this novel, and much of Auster's writing, within a long tradition of urban writing in America. Like the Tower, the city is a man-made construct, ambitious in its conception but not always fulfilling its intended function. Instead, the city becomes a projection of the mind, a mirror of epistemological uncertainty, and an image of alienation. Such views of the city were already manifesting themselves in nineteenth-century writing, and I shall discuss them at greater length below in 'Nay-Saying'.

Professor Stillman offers what eventually turns out to be his own reading of the Tower of Babel episode in the latter part of his book, where he introduces Henry Dark. Quinn is surprised to learn that Dark was Milton's secretary; after the death of the poet, he went to America, where he published a pamphlet entitled *The New Babel*. 'Written in bold, Miltonic prose, [it] presented the case for the building of paradise in America' (*CG* 46). This new paradise would ultimately restore man to his prelapsarian status, but since Dark did not claim to be a messiah, the only way he thought this could be achieved was by undoing the fall of language, because, if 'man could learn to speak this original language of innocence, did it not follow that he would thereby recover a state of innocence within himself?' (*CG* 47). This was precisely the idea that prompted Stillman to keep his son in isolation for nine years, hoping that the young boy, unsullied by corrupt men and their language, would learn to speak the language of innocence. Later in the novel, Quinn learns that Henry Dark never really existed: Stillman made him up in order to lend his own theories credibility. 'I needed him, you see,' he tells Quinn, 'I had certain ideas at the time that were too dangerous and controversial. So I pretended they had come from someone else. It was a way of protecting myself' (*CG* 80). Needless to say, this is a double-coded remark. Just as Stillman needed Dark, Auster needs Stillman and his fiction-within-a-fiction, Henry Dark. The play of multiple selves and assumed identities in *City of Glass* allows Auster to introduce certain questions into the novel while at the same time retaining a critical distance from them.[14] This can also be seen in those sections of the book which deal with Stillman's thesis: even when it is an account from the Bible, it comes to the reader not as such, but as something that Stillman had included in his study.

Auster leaves little room for doubt that Stillman is a madman; an inspired madman perhaps, but a madman nevertheless. If, as I have suggested, Stillman is a version of Emerson placed in a different context, he is also quite distinct from Emerson; or rather, he personifies the inevitable failure that Auster seems to believe is inherent in any endeavour to gain access to a higher truth through the world of matter. For Emerson, the material world may be emblematic, a sign of the essence which exists behind it, but for Auster the attempt to put back together signifier and signified is not a redemptive act; it is doomed to failure. This becomes clear when Quinn finally confronts Stillman and finds out what the latter's project is. For days Quinn has been following Stillman, who seems to spend most of his time collecting broken, discarded objects from the streets around his hotel. It transpires that his plan is to invent new words for these objects since, having lost their function, they carry a name which does not correspond to their true nature: 'You see, the world is in fragments, sir,' Stillman explains.

> 'Not only have we lost our sense of purpose, we have lost the language whereby we can speak of it... You see, I am in the process of inventing a new language ... For our words no longer correspond to the world. When things were whole, we felt confident that our words could express them. But little by little these things have broken apart, shattered, collapsed into chaos. And yet our words have remained the same. They have not adapted themselves to the new reality. Hence, every time we try to speak of what we see, we speak falsely, distorting the very thing we are trying to represent. It's made a mess of everything.' (CG 76–77)

Stillman thus assumes the role of a new Adam who will give things their 'real' names, thereby restoring mankind to its prelapsarian state.

---

14. It will be recalled that in my introduction I argued that 'The Book of Memory' cannot be read as fiction because the author's artistic dilemmas are not dramatised. That book did address questions of language and signification which also appear in *City of Glass*, but in the latter the dialogue opens up because different ideas are assigned to different characters. Moreover, this practice enables the author to create irony, a quality not present (because not appropriate) in 'The Book of Memory'.

In their studies of Emersonian thinking both Larzer Ziff and John Irwin discuss the connection between Emerson's theory of language and the account of Adam's naming of the beasts in the Book of Genesis: 'And out of the ground the LORD God formed every beast of the field, and every fowl of the air, and brought them unto Adam to see what he would call them: and whatsoever Adam called every living creature, that was the name thereof' (Genesis 2:19-20). Adam's naming of the beasts is open to different interpretations, as Irwin observes. It can simply be a manifestation of human dominance, man being granted a superior status in nature since he has been created in the image of God. This interpretation best illustrates the power human civilisation has always granted the act of naming; however, naming does not necessarily equal knowing, and this is where the second interpretation comes in. This view claims that Adam gave the beasts their 'real' names, the names which were linked to every animal's nature; thus, as Larzer Ziff demonstrates, a leopard was thought to have been called a leopard because of its leopardness,[15] and the name 'leopard' pointed towards the true nature of the animal. Emerson's view of language comes closer to this second tradition, as can be seen from his argument in his famous 1836 essay *Nature*, where he writes:

1. Words are signs of natural facts.
2. Particular natural facts are symbols of particular spiritual facts.
3. Nature is the symbol of the spirit. (48)

According to Emerson's theory, every word is borrowed from material appearance. Thus, he explains, right means straight, and wrong twisted. Nature is a projection, a material image of the human mind, so that 'every appearance in nature corresponds to some state of the mind' (49). Similarly, Stillman writes in his thesis that 'Adam's one task in the Garden had been to invent language, to give each creature and thing its name. In that state of innocence, his tongue had gone straight to the quick of the world. His words had not been merely appended to the things he saw, they had revealed their essences, had literally brought them to life. A thing and its name were interchangeable' (CG 43). Later, in his conversation with Quinn, Stillman almost repeats Emerson's words when he says that 'spiritual matters... have their analogue in the material world' (CG 76). In Emerson's theory, the whole world is seen as emblematic: since the mind is imprinted on the natural world, nature can be read as a

---

15. Larzer Ziff, *Literary Democracy: The Declaration of Cultural Independence in America* (New York: Viking Press, 1981), p. 32.

large hieroglyph, a cipher, and the question of any correspondence between outer shape and inner meaning is one that informs not only *City of Glass* but much of Auster's subsequent writing.

City of Glass contains numerous references to Cervantes's *Don Quixote*; these range from the obvious, such as Daniel Quinn's initials and Paul Auster's theory concerning the authorship of the book, to the obscure, such as the name of Stillman Jr's nurse, Mrs Saavedra, whose husband supposedly recommended the detective Paul Auster to the Stillmans (Saavedra was Cervantes's family name). As I shall argue later, there are parallels between the two books, relating not only to the question of authorship, but also to the 'impossibility' of the second part of the Don's adventures, as well as the narrative of Quinn's investigation. However, Auster explains that the references to *Don Quixote* are also used in order to explore the line that separates madness from creativity (*AH* 271). Stillman Sr is a man who treads the thin line separating the two; during his encounters with Quinn, what emerges is a picture of a man whose deranged rantings conceal elements of wisdom. As stated earlier, his diagnosis of the state of language is correct, but his proposed remedy, the creation of a new language, is clearly insane. In *Nature*, Emerson lamented the corruption of language, noting that 'The corruption of man is followed by the corruption of language... new imagery ceases to be created, and old words are perverted to stand for things which are not; a paper currency is employed, when there is no bullion in the vault. In due time the fraud is manifest, and words lose all power to stimulate the understanding or the affections.' He then went on to claim that 'wise men' can put an end to such corruption: 'wise men pierce this rotten diction and fasten words again to visible things' (51). These wise men are none other than poets. In a passage from 'The Poet' strongly reminiscent of the account of Adam's naming of the beasts in Genesis, Emerson writes: 'the poet is the Namer or Language-maker, naming things sometimes after their appearance, sometimes after their essence, and giving to every one its own name and not another's... The poets made all the words' (271). Therefore, the strength of the poet lies not in original creation (which is what Stillman proposes to achieve) but in the act of discovery, or recovery, of what is already present. As Emerson writes:

> though the origin of most of our words is forgotten, each word was at first a stroke of genius, and obtained currency because for the moment it symbolized the world to the first speaker and to the hearer. The etymologist finds the deadest word to have been once a brilliant picture. Language is fossil poetry... language is made up of images or tropes, which now, in their

secondary use, have long ceased to remind us of their poetic origin. But the poet names the thing because he sees it. (271)

It has been established so far that Stillman is not the poetic genius that Emerson talks about. However, there are other characters in the story who are created so as to lay claim to the title, even if they, too, do not fulfil Emerson's vision. If Stillman Sr is an exaggerated version of Emerson the thinker, then his son is a parody of the Emersonian poet. Peter Stillman, irreparably damaged by his father's cruel experiment, can only express himself with great difficulty. However, here is what he tells Quinn in one of his most eloquent moments: 'I am mostly now a poet. Every day I sit in my room and write another poem. I make up all the words myself, just like when I lived in the dark'; 'I make up words like this all the time. That can't be helped. They just come out of my mouth by themselves. They cannot be translated' (CG 18–19). His are words like 'wimble click crumblechaw beloo. Clack clack... flackle-much chewmanna' – hardly what Emerson would call 'fossil poetry'. In Transcendentalist thought, one has to remove oneself from immediate spatial, temporal and social circumstances in order to achieve contact with the spirit which is man's true essence and identity. Peter Stillman has lived in such conditions but, far from leading to enlightenment, they have resulted in a total breakdown of language and communication.

Of the three major characters in *City of Glass*, Quinn is the only one who can lay claim to the title of a 'real' poet. Early in the story we learn that he had published several books of poetry, plays and critical essays, but had 'quite abruptly' given it all up. 'A part of him had died... and he did not want it coming back to haunt him' (CG 4). Yet there is evidence that Quinn the poet had not really died, and by the end of his bizarre adventure the protagonist will find himself writing 'about the stars, the earth, his hopes for mankind. He felt that his words had been severed from him, that now they were a part of the world at large, as *real* and *specific* as a stone, or a lake, or a flower... Nothing mattered now but the beauty of all this' (CG 130, emphasis added). This description of Quinn's writing is reminiscent of Emerson's notion of 'fossil poetry', and it complicates further the question of where Auster stands in relation to Emersonian theories of language. Arthur Saltzman, one of very few critics to mention Emerson in relation to Auster, reads Quinn as a parody of the Emersonian 'transparent eyeball', while Alison Russell also sees Quinn as a parodic figure, although she discusses this in different terms.[16] In her argument, he is a parody of the romantic hero who, unlike the prototypes he is based on (the heroes of the Romance), fails to achieve the goal of his quest. However, I wish to argue that Quinn is a more complex character who, in his inner struggle between idealism and pragmatism, faith and disillusionment, gives us an insight into Auster's own complex vision, without becoming, I hasten to add, a fictional version of the author himself.

Daniel Quinn is a 'devoted reader of mystery novels': 'What he liked about these books was their sense of plenitude and economy. In the good mystery there is nothing wasted, no sentence, no word that is not significant' (CG 8). Quinn sees in these books the consolation of form; we are given to understand that he clings to them because they create a sense of order and rationality which is the exact opposite of his own life. Having lost his wife and son in an accident, he knows too well that the 'real' world, unlike the 'good mystery', is irrational and unintelligible; or that as the narrator in *The Locked Room* (another version of the investigator) also finds out, 'lives make no sense'. The fact that Quinn gave up writing poetry after his bereavement suggests that his disillusionment with the world extends to words as well. These are facts we learn about Quinn before he even contemplates becoming a private eye; it is therefore quite clear that he is not the naïf hero of the romantic tradition, or the detective who has faith in his powers of deduction, who will set out on a quest knowing that this faith, along with perseverance, will aid in the attainment of his goal. Whatever Quinn ends up thinking and believing is the result of a conscious effort on his part: if he begins to discern a pattern, it is only because he is desperate to convince himself that this pattern exists. Quinn spends many days tirelessly observing and following Stillman, but the supposed criminal appears to do nothing other than wander in the streets collecting broken objects. This is an anti-climax for Quinn, who thought he would be living out one of his fictional detectives' adventures. He wonders whether there is any meaning in his opponent's activity, and he realises that it would be 'much better' to believe that these apparently aimless wanderings really concealed some purpose, some hidden message that he was called upon to decipher. In Emersonian thought nature conveys meaning through shape, and it is to this that

16. Arthur Saltzman, *Designs of Darkness in Contemporary American Fiction* (Philadelphia: University of Pennsylvania Press, 1990), p. 57. Alison Russell, 'Deconstructing *The New York Trilogy*: Paul Auster's Anti-Detective Fiction', *Critique: Studies in Contemporary Fiction*, 31.2 (Winter 1990), p. 71.

Quinn turns in order to discover the hidden truth. He sketches Stillman's itinerary on paper and realises that, each day, his walks seem to spell a different letter of the alphabet, finally spelling the phrase 'The Tower of Babel'. However, even when the letters are set on paper in front of him, Quinn still tries to resist the very interpretation he was hoping for. He reasons with himself, saying that perhaps the letters 'were no letters at all. He had seen them only because he wanted to see them. And even if the diagrams did form letters, it was only a fluke. Stillman had nothing to do with it. It was all an accident, a hoax he had perpetrated on himself' (*CG* 71). Quinn's scepticism echoes Auster's, and it is appropriate that, in a detective story which is no detective story in any traditional sense at all, the private eye has little, if any, faith in patterns, or in the ability of his own interpretative skills to reach an objective truth.

In Emerson's theory, on the other hand, the poet is able to see through appearances so as to create order and generate meaning. In 'The Poet' he writes: 'As the eyes of Lyncaeus were said to see through the earth, so the poet turns the world into glass, and shows us all things in their right series and procession' (270), while in a famous passage in *Nature* he makes the transition from 'I' to 'eye' himself: 'Standing on the bare ground, – my head bathed by the blithe air and uplifted into infinite space, – all mean egotism vanishes. I become a transparent eyeball; I am nothing; I see all; the currents of the Universal Being circulate through me' (39). Malcolm Bradbury and Richard Ruland are right to observe that the Emersonian poet 'may seem to create meaning but actually sees through the surfaces that veil it', since this formulation takes into account Emerson's belief that meaning is embedded everywhere in the material world. 'This stress on seeing, vision, points to one of the many puns transcendentalism used to reconstitute language itself: the poet is a see-er, a prophet who helps us see through our eye, the "I" of our self-reliance'.[17] James Cox's essay 'R.W. Emerson: The Circles of the Eye' offers an insightful analysis of the notion of the 'transparent eyeball', seeing this metaphor not as a static image, but as an act of conversion: 'It is a conversion of the "I" into the Eye, of the self into the Seer'. Cox goes on to argue that 'the metaphor is the symbolic transformation of the subject, the writer, into an identity equivalent to the state of being, a heightened gladness to the brink of fear, which has been experienced on the twilit

---

17. Malcolm Bradbury and Richard Ruland, *From Puritanism to Postmodernism: A History of American Literature* (New York: Viking Penguin, 1991), p. 122.

bare common... But in another sense it is an action, a declaration of change from being to seeing.'[18] As a detective, Quinn also needs to become nothing (for instance, he refrains from any personal judgment when he meets Virginia Stillman) and to see all: quite literally, to watch Peter Stillman at all times, and, in his role as detective, to 'see' the answer, which is traditionally already present but hidden in the mystery narrative. Throughout *City of Glass*, Auster relies on the pun 'private eye/private "I"' to draw attention to the process of generating meaning:

> Private eye. The term held a triple meaning for Quinn. Not only was it the letter 'i', standing for 'investigator', it was 'I' in the upper case, the tiny life-bud buried in the body of the breathing self. At the same time, it was also the physical eye of the writer, the eye of the man who looks out from himself into the world and demands that the world reveal itself to him. For five years now, Quinn had been living in the grip of this pun. (*CG* 8–9)

However, Quinn does not move from 'I' to 'eye'; as he looks 'out from himself into the world', he realises that this outside world does not conceal the hoped-for revelation. The actions that finally lead to his isolation in the Stillman apartment are, if anything, the reverse of the transformation from 'I' to eye. Quinn's progress in *City of Glass* reverses the procedure which moves from self to eye: Quinn pretends to be the private eye, but as the story progresses it becomes increasingly clear that the novel is mainly concerned with his 'I'; the emphasis shifts from action to introspection, from detective story to the existential, or metaphysical, novel. From the early stages of the story, there are already indications that Quinn is fascinated by the case he has been assigned because he sees its relevance to his own life. After hearing Peter's story, Quinn decides to take on the case not only because he finds it intriguing, but because he sees it as a chance to assume the role of the father which was cut short when his own son, also called Peter, died: 'Quinn wanted to be there to stop him [Stillman Sr]. He knew he could not bring his own son back to life, but at least he could prevent another from dying' (*CG* 35). The first notes he makes on the case have very little to do with what one would imagine a detective writes down when he embarks on a new assignment; instead of concentrating on the facts, the clues or the evidence, Quinn tries to identify with his client: 'Little Peter. Is it necessary for me to imagine it, or can I accept it on faith? The darkness. To think of myself

18. James Cox, 'The Circle of the Eye', in *Emerson: Prophecy, Metamorphosis, and Influence*, ed. David Levin (New York and London: Columbia University Press, 1975), p. 123.

in that room, screaming' (CG 39). Stillman Sr's obsessive quest for Adamic language also appeals to Quinn the poet; his successive meetings with his opponent are beyond the call of duty, revealing Quinn's personal interest in the case. When Stillman disappears, and after it has become quite clear that the man has no evil designs on his son, Quinn intensifies his search instead of dropping it. He is no longer the seer, the man whose job is to follow another person and record his moves, to interpret his actions and understand his motives, to create a pattern out of seemingly random facts, to pierce the veil which hides the truth. Instead, he is the man who has to face his own life, assess his achievements and his failures, and think about his future.

The turning point in this transformation occurs when Quinn meets Paul Auster, the supposed detective who turns out to be a writer. Paul Auster stands for everything that Quinn himself could have been: he is a writer, he is happily married, and he has a son who is the same age as Quinn's would have been had he lived. Auster holds up a mirror in which Quinn sees himself as he ought to have been. Quinn no longer looks at the world around him: quite literally, he looks at himself. However, even this encounter with his alter ego does not enlighten Quinn. Since Auster is not a detective after all, Quinn speculates that someone might have tried to play a practical joke on him. Quinn's and Auster's blindness is emphasised when the latter remarks: 'But the fact is, it's not a joke. It's a real case with real people' (CG 96). To complicate matters even further, the character Paul Auster indirectly warns Quinn that he is becoming blind, or at least that he can only see what he chooses to see. His warning, which goes unheeded, comes in the form of an elaborate theory concerning the authorship of Don Quixote. Daniel Quinn observes that he shares the same initials with the Knight of the Sad Countenance, but he fails to realise that, like the Don, he is obsessed with a fiction he has created, and which does not allow him to see clearly any more. Thus, far from becoming someone who is nothing but sees all, Quinn becomes self-obsessed and is only interested in pursuing his own, very personal quest. When he leaves Auster's house, Quinn realises that the tailing job is behind him: 'For the first time since he had bought the red notebook, what he wrote that day had nothing to do with the Stillman case' (CG 108). His obsession, and some unseen force which appears to be manipulating him (and which may or may not be the author who at times can be glimpsed through the cracks in the story), finally leads him to move into the empty Stillman apartment: 'He went to one of the rooms at the back of the apartment, a small space that measured no more than ten feet by six feet. It had one wire-mesh window that gave on to a view of the airshaft, and of all the rooms it seemed to be the darkest' (*CG* 126). With his seemingly voluntary incarceration, Quinn is re-enacting Stillman's experiment; he becomes father and son, observer and participant at the same time, attempting to cancel out the subject/object dichotomy.

On a different ontological level, as far as Quinn's own fictional life is concerned, he changes from detective to poet, from writing about the case he was assigned to writing about the earth and the stars and his hopes for mankind. As the protagonists of the Stillman case disappear one by one, Quinn feels 'sorry that he had bothered to write about the Stillman case at all. For the case was far behind him now, and he no longer bothered to think about it. It had been a bridge to another place in his life, and now that he had crossed it, its meaning had been lost' (*CG* 130). More significantly, though, Auster complicates the issue by having the story told from a 'distorted' perspective, since at the very end it is revealed that the narrator was a friend of Auster's who was given Quinn's notebook: 'I have followed the red notebook as closely as I could, and any inaccuracies in the story should be blamed on me. There were moments when the text was difficult to decipher, but I have done my best with it and have refrained from any interpretations' (*CG* 132). This confession raises a number of questions: for instance, when we are told that Quinn wrote about the stars, the earth, his hopes for mankind, and that his words had been severed from him and were as real and specific as a stone, or a lake, or a flower, how can we know whether this is true? Is it what Quinn actually wrote in his notebook, or is it the narrator's interpretation? Again, the references to *Don Quixote* draw attention to the ontological paradox in the narrative. In the second part of *Don Quixote*, Sancho informs his master that their adventures have been printed under the title of *The Ingenious Gentleman Don Quixote de La Mancha*, but the Don 'could not persuade himself that such a history existed', as indeed it could not. Similarly, the narrator of *City of Glass* 'knows' about dreams that Quinn had and later forgot, a fact which violates the narrative logic of the text. The unnamed narrator concludes his own disclaimer by renouncing the author-character Paul Auster: 'As for Auster, I am convinced that he behaved badly throughout. If our friendship has ended, he has only himself to blame' (*CG* 132). '*Whodunnit*, as the Americans say. In fact, who did it? Not the *crime* but the *text*. The enigma here is not the identity of the criminal, but that of the author.'[19]

19. Roy C. Caldwell, '*New York Trilogy*: Réflections Postmodernes', in *L'Œuvre de Paul Auster: Approches et lectures plurielles*, ed. Annick Duperray (Paris: Actes Sud/Université de Provence, 1995), p. 84.

The same enigma appears in *Blackouts*, a one-act play that was written ten years before the publication of *Ghosts* in 1986. Auster explains that while he was still writing *City of Glass* he began to experience a sense of *déjà-écrit* which made him re-read his old play and turn it into what eventually became *Ghosts*. The basic premise of the plot is already there in the play: Blue is a detective who has been hired to watch Black and write a report; he takes a flat opposite Black's, disguises himself in order to meet his subject, and when he breaks into Black's apartment he shoots him. The action of the play takes place in an office where Blue has come to meet his employer, who turns out to be Black, and there is a third character, Green, who tries to write everything down while employer and employee speak. Towards the end of the play, Green tears up the pages he has written and the audience are left, quite literally, in the dark. Like the novel it eventually became, this play is elliptical; there is no action, and the characters speak in short, cryptic sentences, as if they are conspirators trying to keep their audience in the dark, while there are also conspiracies going on inside the play. The dance of multiple selves, assumed identities and disguises is used in an exaggerated manner in order to highlight ontological concerns; as such, it becomes little more than a metafictional game of characters in search of an author, a fact which may explain Auster's confessed embarrassment with the play. However, he agreed to have it published because he felt it is 'always interesting' to see the source of a literary work.[20] What is also interesting is to see how the emphasis has shifted and how the play was transformed into a novella. I wish to argue that the two major changes that transformed the earlier piece are the inclusion of references to Thoreau's *Walden*, and the specific urban setting of Brooklyn.

Auster paradoxically draws attention to the latter by pretending that it is incidental:

> The address is unimportant. But let's say Brooklyn Heights, for the sake of argument. Some quiet, rarely travelled street not far from the bridge – Orange Street perhaps. Walt Whitman handset the first edition of *Leaves of Grass* on this street in 1855, and it was here that Henry Ward Beecher railed against slavery from the pulpit of his red-brick church. So much for local colour. (*Gh* 136–37)

But if the presence of Ralph Waldo Emerson had to be inferred in *City of Glass*, in *Ghosts* Auster leaves no room for doubt concerning his intentions:

---

20. The play was published for the first time in a French translation by Christine Le Bœuf in *Magazine Littéraire*, 338 (December 1995), pp. 50–58. It is now reprinted in *Hand to Mouth*.

halfway through the story, the narrator remarks that, were the protagonist to read Thoreau's *Walden* 'in the spirit in which it asks to be read,
his entire life would begin to change, and little by little he would come to a
full understanding of his situation' (*Gh* 163). By making the analogy
explicit, Auster is not dictating a forced reading; instead, he opens up
hermeneutic possibilities which relate not only to the story in question, but
also to his novelistic practices in general.

Ghosts is the shortest, and most minimalist, of the three stories in *The
New York Trilogy*. It is, in a sense, a slimmed-down version of *City of
Glass*, as the same questions concerning solitude, language, and the
search for one's identity recur. As in *City of Glass*, the characters in
Ghosts also create fictions and plots and then find themselves trapped in
them. The text is another version of the anti-detective story, one stripped
of all ornament or convention. In the first two paragraphs, Auster manages to dispense with all the conventions of the genre, giving the reader
the bare essentials as if he were writing the summary of a detective story:

> First of all there is Blue. Later there is White, and then there is Black, and
> before the beginning there is Brown... The place is New York, the time is the
> present... The case seems simple enough. White wants Blue to follow a man
> named Black and to keep an eye on him for as long as necessary. (*Gh* 135)

Alison Russell calls this volume 'a "ghost" of *City of Glass* and of the
detective story genre: the "meat" of the text is stripped down to a generic
level, reinforced by Auster's rejection of nomenclature and his use of
Film Noir signifiers'. She also points out that Auster's reductionist technique is deceptive, as it suggests that there will be a solution to the mystery presented in these first few lines.[21] However, as we have now learned
to expect from a Paul Auster novel, the case is not as simple as it seems.
Black and White turn out to be the same person, and Blue is hired so that
Black can watch Blue watching him, Black. The time is both 'the present'
and 3 February 1947, the author's birth date. The verb 'seems', then, in
the phrase 'The case seems simple enough', ought to serve as a warning;
after all, Quinn's assigned case in *City of Glass* seemed simple enough,
but as Auster himself asks, 'What if, in the course of trying to figure it out,
you just unveil more mysteries?' The one thing that will remain stable is
the setting, New York City, a city haunted by the ghosts of American
culture and its own literary past.

21. Russell, 'Deconstructing *The New York Trilogy*', p. 77. As I shall argue in the follow-
      ing section, a similar technique is used by Hawthorne in 'Wakefield', which is another
      strong intertextual presence in the trilogy.

Blue starts working on his case by moving into an apartment opposite Black's. All he has to do is sit by the window, watch the other man through his binoculars, and take notes of everything Black is doing. The case does not seem very promising for a man like Blue who has always enjoyed action: Black seems to spend most of his time sitting at a desk, reading, writing, and occasionally looking out of his window. As early as the fifth page of the story, Blue finds out what Black is reading: '*Walden*, by Henry David Thoreau. Blue has never heard of it before and writes it down carefully in his notebook' (*Gh* 139). Despite having never heard of *Walden*, Blue is engaged in an ironic re-enactment of Thoreau's experiment, as well as being trapped in a book the key to which is *Walden*.

In 1845, Thoreau retired to the woods on the shores of Walden Pond and lived for two years in a cabin he built himself. In his own words:

> I went to the woods because I wished to live deliberately, to front only the essential facts of life... I wanted... to drive life into a corner, and reduce it to its lowest terms, and, if it proved mean, why then to get the whole and genuine meanness of it, and publish its meanness to the world; or if it were sublime, to know it by experience, and be able to give a true account of it in my next excursion. (89)

A scholar and keen naturalist rather than a hermit, Thoreau devoted his time to communion with nature, studying, and recording his thoughts and observations in his journal. A carefully reworked version of this journal was published in 1854, and *Walden* has since reached an almost mythical status not only in literature but also in American culture, as well as being recognised as a work dealing with the stuff of myth: 'the final impression made by *Walden* is that of a myth. In this perspective its basic theme is self-renewal, and its elements are withdrawal from society, isolation, the discipline of poverty, communion with the sacred (nature), and the recovery of a unified and revitalized self.'[22] Auster's story reproduces some of the themes of *Walden*, but with very different results. The figure of the ascetic who withdraws from society to contemplate and write in an attempt to reach a higher truth is here replaced by another 'mythical' figure, one which belongs to the realm of popular culture, namely the hard-boiled detective who lives in a corrupt urban environment and confronts mysteries he is called upon to decipher. The cherished myth of the self-reliant man who finds peace, knowledge and

22. George Hochfield, 'New England Transcendentalism', in *The Penguin History of Literature. 8. American Literature to 1990*, ed. Marcus Cunliffe (Harmondsworth: Penguin, 1993), p. 166.

replenishment in solitude, in nature, and in a spartan lifestyle, is denied to Auster's characters. Where Thoreau reduces his material life to the bare essentials, Auster uses this as a narrative method; replenishment is replaced by economy, by a narrative poverty that reflects the characters' inner life, their emotions, and their inability to understand and interpret what they see.

The story's protagonist is a private eye: the emphasis is once again on the act of seeing and the failure to see through appearances. Unlike Quinn, who is primarily a man of letters, Blue is a 'real' detective fashioned according to the dictates of the school of hard-boiled fiction: 'He likes to be up and about, moving from one place to another, doing things. I'm not the Sherlock Holmes type, he would say to Brown, whenever the boss gave him a particularly sedentary task. Give me something I can sink my teeth into' (*Gh* 139). Blue is also a man not given to introspection, and he does not share Quinn's literary sensibilities – instead, he is a devoted reader of *True Detective*. It is this man of action, who has always believed in the power of rational thought and his ability to separate the essential from the incidental or trivial, and confine himself to 'known and verifiable facts' and solve the mystery, who is assigned the unlikely role of a modern-day Thoreau. Thoreau was very meticulous in his recording of his observations, and *Walden* contains long descriptions of scenes of nature, as well as details of Thoreau's economy. However, Thoreau's is not a record of a mundane life, and none of the descriptions is there for its own sake; the implication is always that there is something more important to be found behind the bare facts. As he writes in *Walden*, 'we inhabitants of New England live this mean life that we do because our vision does not penetrate the surface of things. We think that that *is* which *appears* to be' (93, emphasis in original). Blue, on the other hand, actually takes pride in confining himself to observation and refraining from interpretation: 'His method is to stick to outward facts, describing events as though each word tallied exactly with the thing described, and to question the matter no further. Words are transparent for him, great windows that stand between him and the world, and until now they have never impeded his view, have never even seemed to be there' (*Gh* 146).

Thoreau was a firm believer in the availability of truth in everyday life, arguing that meaning is available in our world if we take the trouble to look for it. One place where truth could be discovered was the woods surrounding Thoreau's cabin: like Emerson, Thoreau saw nature as a hieroglyph, arguing that meaning is embedded in natural forms. In his study of the use of the symbol of Egyptian hieroglyphics in the American

Renaissance, John Irwin focuses on Thoreau's description of a thawing sandbank in *Walden* as representative of his theories concerning nature as well as language, and he concludes:

> Having penetrated the emblematic world of natural forms to discover the inner, unifying form, and then having presented as an analogue of this process the penetration of the language of convention to discover the original language of nature in which words are emblems of things, Thoreau concludes: 'Thus it seemed that this one hillside illustrated the principle of all the operations of nature. The Maker of this earth but patented a leaf. What Champollion will decipher this hieroglyphic for us, that we may turn over a new leaf at last?' The answer to that question is, obviously, Thoreau himself.[23]

Auster does not assume the role of another Champollion who will decipher the Rosetta stone that is the world of observable phenomena, nor does he ascribe this role to any of his characters. By emphasising the parallels between his book and Thoreau's, Auster simultaneously draws attention to himself as author, and renounces the authority associated with that role. As for his characters, whose job it is to decipher clues, they do not fare much better. When Blue sits down to write his first report on Black, he finds out that 'his words, instead of drawing out the facts and making them sit palpably in the world, have induced them to disappear... he discovers that words do not necessarily work, that it is possible for them to obscure the thing they are trying to say' (*Gh* 147–48). What Blue discovers is what Stillman had told Quinn: 'every time we try to speak of what we see, we speak falsely, distorting the very thing we are trying to represent' (*CG* 77). The only explanation that Blue can arrive at is one of negative definition: 'Blue can only surmise what the case is not. To say what it is, however, is completely beyond him' (*Gh* 147). Auster's characters inhabit a fallen world in which words do not correspond to things and surfaces cannot be penetrated; a world defined by absence.

It is appropriate that, in order to describe this fallen world, Auster transports Walden Pond to the heart of the city. Although later novels prove that he never subscribes to a simplistic nature/city innocence/corruption dichotomy, the New York that his characters are placed in is a trap, a claustrophobic maze that offers no hope of redemption. In the final paragraph of the story, after the drama of the confrontation is over, the narrator speculates on Blue's fate. The hero of the hard-boiled

---

23. Irwin, *American Hieroglyphics*, p. 19.

detective novel must be saved, and the narrator imagines this salvation as an escape from the city: 'I myself prefer to think that he went far away, boarding a train that morning and going out West to start a new life. It is even possible that America was not the end of it. In my secret dreams, I like to think of Blue booking passage on some ship and sailing to China' (*Gh* 195–96).

In drawing the parallel between his book and *Walden*, Auster says that *Ghosts* deals with the 'idea of living a solitary life, of living with a kind of monastic intensity', a concept he borrows from *Walden*, but he goes on to add 'and all the dangers that entails' (*AH* 271), which is where he parts company with Thoreau. Thoreau cherished his solitude, which was not only an example of his self-reliance but also the necessary condition for artistic creativity: 'I find it wholesome to be alone the greater part of the time. To be in company, even with the best, is soon wearisome and dissipating. I love to be alone. I never found the companion that was so companionable as solitude' (122). The appeal of such ideas to the author of *The Invention of Solitude* is clear; however, Auster's characters find no delight in solitary pursuits. Blue is overcome by boredom, since all he has to do is sit in his room and watch Black write. As such, he is not only the opposite of Emerson's or Thoreau's poet, the Romantic genius who, in isolation, sees through appearances; he is also an image of the reader reading a modern text which subverts all the conventions of traditional narrative. When Blue starts reading *Walden*, he is soon bored and disappointed. Blue does not even suspect that Thoreau's words are themselves 'hieroglyphics' containing a meaning behind the descriptions of life in the woods:

> He is bored by Thoreau's words and finds it difficult to concentrate. Whole chapters go by, and when he comes to the end of them he realizes that he has not retained a thing. Why would anyone want to go off and live alone in the woods? What's all this about planting beans and not drinking coffee or eating meat? Why all these interminable descriptions of birds? Blue thought that he was going to get a story, or at least have something like a story, but this is no more than blather, an endless harangue about nothing at all. (*Gh* 162–63)

In the third chapter, he finally comes across a sentence that means something to him: 'Books must be read as deliberately and reservedly as they were written – and suddenly he understands that the trick is to go slowly, more slowly than he has ever gone with the words before' (*Gh* 163). We are told that, before *Walden*, all that Blue had ever read was newspapers, magazines and a few adventure novels. Unlike Auster, or Auster's readers for that matter, Blue is the innocent reader, reading for the first time, discovering a world he never knew existed, a world made of words where the point is not whether something happens, but the words themselves. For the first time, Blue reads a book in which things are born in words, where it is not the narrative but the discourse that is important. Blue is also Barthes's reader of realist fiction, the one who reads for the plot: 'read fast, in snatches, some modern text, and it becomes opaque, inaccessible to your pleasure: you want something to happen and nothing does, for *what happens to the language does not happen to the discourse*' (emphasis in original).[24] His inability to understand the book he is reading is a measure of his inability to understand the world, or his own situation. At the same time, the author puts him in a disadvantaged position, since he does not know that he is a character in a book.

In one of the frequent authorial intrusions in the trilogy, Auster has his narrator say that 'were he [Blue] to find the patience to read the book in the spirit in which it asks to be read, his entire life would begin to change, and little by little he would come to a full understanding of his situation – that is to say of Black, of White, of the case, of everything that concerns him' (*Gh* 163). Nevertheless, Blue remains in the dark because he does not 'know' that he is a character in a book the key to which is *Walden*. He does, however, begin to feel a kind of ontological angst:

> He feels like a man who has been condemned to sit in a room and go on reading a book for the rest of his life... But this book offers him nothing. There is no story, no plot, no action – nothing but a man sitting alone in a room and writing a book... But how to get out? How to get out of the room that is the book that will go on being written for as long as he stays in the room? (*Gh* 169)

He also thinks that Black is 'the so-called writer of this book', but later he also considers the possibility of White being the 'real writer'. Auster is here returning to the earlier questions he had tried to probe in *Blackouts*, but they have now become more complex because they need to be considered not only as questions asked by the text, but also in relation to another text which is included in it. What Auster is doing in this story, which he had not done in the play, is to stage, and thus externalise, a dilemma that was central to the thinking of both Emerson and Thoreau: 'Thoreau held and acted upon the Emersonian view that the perceiver

---

24. Barthes, *The Pleasure of the Text*, pp. 12–13.

and the thing perceived, the thought and the world and the object, are
one in the moment of perception and speech'.[25] In his writing, however,
he discovered that the moment of perception and the moment of speech
may not always be readily available in an unadulterated form:

> With thinking we may be beside ourselves in a sane sense... However
> intense my experience, I am conscious of the presence and criticism of a
> part of me which, as it were, is not a part of me, but spectator, sharing no
> experience, but taking note of it; and that is no more I than it is you. When
> the play of life is over, the spectator goes his way. It was a kind of fiction; a
> work of the imagination only, so far as he was concerned. (122)

Charles Feidelson reminds us that Emerson said much the same thing: 'A
poem, a sentence, causes us to see ourselves. I be, and I see my being, at
the same time.'[26] In the case of *Walden*, the 'real' writer is both the man
who lived in the woods and the man who wrote about it. Thoreau may
have come closer to an accurate, or at least honest, description of the
poetic activity than Wordsworth's 'emotion recollected in tranquillity', but
he does stress that the perceived split between subject and object occurs in
'a sane sense'; in other words, there is no denial of the reality of the intense
experience. Auster takes a more literal approach, perceiving the schizophrenic quality inherent in the activity. By assigning the roles of thinking
subject and spectator to different characters, he signals an increased awareness of the fictionality of his creation, while he also questions the notion
of the unified self, or the unity of thought and perception, which both
Emerson and Thoreau embrace. Auster's assignment of the different roles
to different persons, who are not entirely distinct from each other nor a
unified self (Black is not one but several, thinks Blue), allows for an ironic
detachment which is not manifest in Thoreau's writing.

The idea of reading the literature of the past backwards from the present seems reinforced here. In his introduction to *The Random House
Book of Twentieth-Century French Poetry*, Auster writes of the poetry of
Léon-Paul Fargue: 'The poem of witness is at the same time a poem of
remembrance, as if, in the solitary act of seeing, the world were reflected
back to its solitary source and then, once more, reflected outward as
vision' (*AH* 212). Similarly, he writes of Francis Ponge: 'The primary act
of the poet, therefore, becomes the act of seeing, as if no one had ever

25. Charles Feidelson, Jr, *Symbolism and American Literature* (Chicago and London:
    University of Chicago Press, 1953), p. 135.
26. Feidelson, *Symbolism*, p. 136.

seen the thing before' (*AH* 221). The words 'as if' are used in both passages; what is emphasised is not immediacy but a created illusion of immediacy. Were it not for the words 'as if', Auster would have been repeating Romantic theories of poetry, with their emphasis on spontaneity and defamiliarisation. In *Walden* itself, the author tries hard to conceal the artificiality of his writing; *Walden* was carefully worked on and eventually published seven years after the author left the hut by Walden Pond. *Walden* therefore has all the immediacy of a journal, all the poetic beauty of 'seeing things for the first time', while at the same time it is an act of remembrance, a mediated experience 'reflected back to its solitary source and then outward as vision'. But whereas Romantic writers were keen to suppress the process which transforms experience into description, Auster makes this his operative mode. This dual nature of the writer's project is also seen in *Ghosts* when Blue remembers a few sentences from Walden: 'We are not where we are... but in a false position. Through an infirmity of our natures, we suppose a case, and put ourselves into it, and hence are in two cases at the same time, and it is doubly difficult to get out' (*Gh* 168). Blue is trapped in two fictions: the book Paul Auster is writing, and the plot he himself creates in order to understand the case he has been assigned.

Blue and Black, who both sit in their rooms looking at each other and writing, reflect the situation of the author as creator of fictions. On the one hand, he is the one who looks, enquires and records, but he is also the one looking at himself writing. In this sense, Blue and Black are two aspects of the same entity. Forced into solitude and inactivity, Blue, who had always liked to be 'up and about, moving from one place to another, doing things', finds time for introspection. One thing he soon finds out is that, looking at the other man across the street, he sees not only another person but his own self reflected back at him as well: 'For in spying out at Black across the street, it is as though Blue were looking into a mirror, and instead of merely watching another, he finds that he is also watching himself' (*Gh* 144). Blue is watching himself in two ways: since he does not have to follow Black, as he sits in his room he starts thinking about his own life; but he is also watching himself because Black is doing exactly the same thing: like Blue, he sits in a room, takes notes, reads, and looks out of his window. When Blue eventually confronts him, Black explains that his job is to 'watch someone... and send in a report about him every week. Watch this guy and write about him. Not one damned thing more' (*Gh* 180). Again, like Quinn before him, Blue watches another man but can only 'see' himself; what Black does is exactly what Blue himself has been doing, so all the time he was trying to understand what Black was doing he was only trying to understand himself. Both characters try to penetrate surfaces and gain access to something situated outside themselves, but their attempts end in failure. Like the Transcendentalist thinkers whose experiments they re-enact, they withdraw from society, they distance themselves from their immediate temporal, spatial and social surroundings, and yet they fail to reach the hoped-for revelation.

So far I have drawn parallels between *Ghosts* and *Walden*, thus offering one of many possible readings of either book. But as I pointed out in my introduction, *Walden* has now become not just a literary text but a part of American culture, and reading it in such terms opens up many possibilities, enlarging the reading of *Ghosts* itself. Unlike *Blackouts*, which is devoid of any cultural referents, and despite its brevity, *Ghosts* contains many stories-within-stories. The author offers accounts of Blue's reading of publications such as *True Detective* and *Stranger Than Fiction*, past cases that he has solved, and summaries of plots from films he has seen. There is also an account of the history of the construction of Brooklyn Bridge, while Black gives Blue a short lesson in history when he recounts how before paying Walt Whitman a visit Thoreau went to hear Henry Ward Beecher's sermon in Plymouth Church, a place which was also visited by Abraham Lincoln and Charles Dickens. Alison Russell comments:

> In many ways, the second volume of the trilogy offers itself as a collection of the signs that make up American culture, taken from baseball, popular movies, and the canonical texts and authors of nineteenth-century literature. These artifacts of our collective identity haunt the pages of *Ghosts*, raising the issue of whether or not original discourse is possible. Just as language is divorced from the things it signifies, texts themselves become divorced from their creators.[27]

The text signals its awareness of such issues when Blue meets Black dressed up as a tramp he used to know, someone by the name of Jimmy Rose. Jimmy Rose is the eponymous hero of Melville's tale, which charts the rising and falling fortunes of the narrator's friend, but Blue's Jimmy looks like 'an Old Testament prophet', and Black also points out to him that he looks like Walt Whitman. Black tells Blue the story of how Whitman donated his brain to the American Anthropometric Society to be

27. Russell, 'Deconstructing *The New York Trilogy*', p. 78.

measured and weighed; when it arrived at the laboratory, it was accidentally dropped by an assistant: 'It spattered all over the place, and that was
that. The brain of America's greatest poet got swept up and thrown out
with the garbage' (*Gh* 173).[28] Blue, as usual, misses the point of this story,
but its ironies are not lost on the reader. This is a story that deals quite
literally with the death of the author, while the particular choice of
author is also not accidental. Whitman, in many ways the embodiment
of the Emersonian poet, makes his own presence felt very strongly in
his poetry, as the title *Song of Myself* alone indicates. The ideals and
aspirations of the Transcendentalists are reduced to a heap of grey matter
on the floor of a laboratory, and the Romantic genius is shown to be just
another mortal: 'Brains and guts, the insides of a man. We always talk
about trying to get inside a writer to understand his work better. But
when you get right down to it, there's not much to find in there' (*Gh*
175). Another story that Black tells Blue is the plot of Hawthorne's
'Wakefield', which not only foreshadows the third volume of the trilogy,
The Locked Room, but also highlights once again questions of authorship
and authority, while serving to modify Auster's own reading of writers
such as Emerson or Thoreau.

Nay-Saying

Towards the end of *The Locked Room*, the final part of *The New York
Trilogy*, Paul Auster momentarily sheds his fictional mask to inform the
readers that the 'entire story comes down to what happened at the end,
and without that end inside me now, I could not have started this book.
The same holds for the two books that came before it, *City of Glass* and
Ghosts. These three stories are finally the same story, but each one represents a different stage in my awareness of what it is about. I don't claim
to have solved any problems' (*LR* 294). It is true that *The Locked Room*
does not solve any of the problems the three books deal with, but its narrator is clearer in articulating these problems, while the author's position
in relation to them also becomes clearer. The anonymous narrator is not
unlike Quinn or Blue, but he is a more mature version of these two.
During his quest for his childhood friend Fanshawe, he finds out things

---

28. Stephen Jay Gould informs us that Whitman's brain was in fact measured, and found
    to weigh 1.282kg. *The Panda's Thumb* (New York: Norton, 1982), p. 150. Quoted in
    Maria Irene Ramalho de Sousa Santos, 'Plagiarism in Praise: Paul Auster and Melville',
    Revista Portuguesa de Literatura Comparada, 1 (December 1991), pp. 105–14.

that Quinn and Blue were never allowed to discover. As I have argued, they both displayed an increasing scepticism and mistrust concerning the nature of language as well as the nature of the self, the intelligibility of the world and the role of chance and free will, but it remains this narrator's task to articulate these misgivings. In the evocation of Emerson, Thoreau, or even tough-guy crime fiction, Auster allowed fragments of hope or nostalgia to enter the bleak surroundings of his characters' lives, and to modify his own self-consciousness and scepticism; but with *The Locked Room* there is a steady movement towards disillusionment. This final instalment of *The New York Trilogy* ends with the symbolic tearing to pieces of the absent writer's notebook. If this gesture does not imply total erasure, it is not because there is a recovery of meaning, but because uncertainty itself has become the *modus operandi*. As the narrator of *Leviathan* puts it, 'Books are born out of ignorance, and if they go on living after they are written, it's only to the degree that they cannot be understood' (*Lev* 36). It is appropriate that, as the three narratives unfold, providing increasing proof of Auster's position in relation to writing in general and the texts of the past in particular, the final story asks to be read after Nathaniel Hawthorne. Although *Ghosts* provides sufficient proof of its author's interest in Hawthorne, Auster wants to stress the connection in the final volume: 'In *The Locked Room*, by the way, the name Fanshawe is a direct reference to Hawthorne. *Fanshawe* was the title of Hawthorne's first novel. He wrote it when he was very young, and not long after it was published, he turned against it in revulsion and tried to destroy every copy he could get his hands on. Fortunately, a few of them survived' (*AH* 272). *Fanshaw*e, like *The Locked Room*, involves the antagonistic relationship that develops between two close friends, but Auster's story is not a direct rewrite of Hawthorne's. It is the presence of Hawthorne's contribution to American letters, in his reaction to Transcendentalism and certain forms of novel-writing that he developed, which is evident in *The Locked Room*, as well as in Auster's later writing.

A summary of Hawthorne's 'Wakefield' is given in *Ghosts*. 'Wakefield' tells the story of a man who one day leaves his wife and his home pretending that he is going on a journey; instead, he rents a room nearby, and eventually lives there for twenty years, watching his wife unobserved, watching the house he still calls home, her mourning, her recovery, watching what would have been his own life. Then one day he decides to go back, and the story ends as his wife opens the door and lets him in. As a story of a man's inexplicable decision to disappear, 'Wakefield' foreshadows the plot of *The Locked Room*, which chronicles the unnamed narrator's quest for his childhood friend Fanshawe. When Fanshawe disappears, his wife asks the narrator, an old friend of her husband's, to help her find him and as the narrator becomes increasingly involved in his friend's life under the pretence of writing a biography, he is not only interested in finding his friend but also in understanding the motives that led to such a dramatic disappearance. Hawthorne's 'Wakefield' is presented as a story which the narrator remembers reading in an old magazine or newspaper. The plot is summarised in the first paragraph, and over the next few pages the readers are led to believe that they will find answers to the questions raised by such an unusual incident.[29] The narrator does, indeed, start by 'filling in' the plot structure, giving more details about Wakefield and his wife, but when it comes to explaining his hero's motives, or what he was hoping to accomplish, he remains silent. This is characteristic of Hawthorne in two significant aspects. It illustrates his conviction that the 'actual experience of even the most ordinary life is full of events that never explain themselves, either as regards their origin or their tendency',[30] while it also explains his chosen literary practices which stem from such an opinion. By choosing to tell a story which is so mysterious that it defies explanation, Hawthorne builds his story on absence; 'Wakefield' is the story of Wakefield's absence from his own life, or rather, more than the story of Wakefield, it is the story of the failure to write about Wakefield. As meaning is replaced with absence, American literature moves away from Romanticism towards modernity.

Unlike Emerson or Thoreau, Hawthorne did not believe that the writer was the all-seer, the one capable of discovering the truth and making it known to the rest of the world. His was a vision embracing those aspects of life which he felt were destined to remain mysterious and inaccessible. Bradbury and Ruland see Hawthorne as a writer who moves away from Romantic notions: 'Emerson's poet was to be a seer, seeking a clear sign; but Hawthorne's artist is a creature of conscious oppositions. Like many modern writers, Hawthorne was an author who would not claim authority.'[31] This manifests itself in a paradoxical manner in 'Wakefield'. As stated earlier, the narrative begins with the presentation of the entire case; the reader wonders what is left for the story to convey

29. As I have argued, Auster adopts a similar narrative strategy in *Ghosts*.
30. Nathaniel Hawthorne, *The Marble Faun* (1859), ed. Malcolm Bradbury (London: Everyman, 1995), p. 360.
31. Bradbury and Ruland, *From Puritanism to Postmodernism*, p. 149.

when the plot is given away in the opening paragraph. In this respect, what follows is a display of the author's capacity for imaginative creation. Hawthorne deliberately draws attention to his own role, by urging readers to 'Watch him [Wakefield], long enough to see what we have described',[32] by being seen to create the circumstances that surround Wakefield's actions. This, then, is the paradox: Hawthorne casts himself as the puppet master, the manipulator, sole creator of the story of Wakefield's adventures. But by doing so he is admitting that the 'truth' surrounding Wakefield's actions cannot be known. By emphasising his role as author, he does not claim authority, rather he stresses the fact that fictional constructs have the power to deceive. What he ultimately conveys is the knowledge that Wakefield's motives, his thoughts or feelings, can never be known.

Auster does not claim authority either. *The Locked Room* is the story of the failure to write about Fanshawe, who is absent from the text in a more literal way than Hawthorne's Wakefield. The story begins with his disappearance, and his friend's quest comes to an end when he meets Fanshawe, who remains unseen and communicates with him through the door of a locked room. The theme of the missing writer also enables Auster to pose questions relating to the role of the author, while, as in the previous volumes, the quest for another person inevitably turns into a quest for one's own identity and its expression in writing. Throughout the narrative, there are clues pointing to the similarity between the two friends, who may be seen as 'not so much separate characters as two elements of a tandem reality, and neither could exist without the other' (*AH* 83). One day the narrator receives a letter from Fanshawe, who until then was presumed dead; in it, Fanshawe asks his friend to marry his wife and adopt his child, thus effectively appointing him as his 'replacement', or substitute. The narrator also becomes Fanshawe's literary executor, editing his friend's manuscripts for publication. When Fanshawe achieves critical acclaim and commercial success, people in the literary world begin to suspect that Fanshawe does not exist at all, and that the narrator himself has written the books. The boundaries that separate the two men threaten to dissolve, as the narrator contemplates writing books under Fanshawe's name: 'I was not planning to do this, of course, but the mere

32. Nathaniel Hawthorne, 'Wakefield' (1835), repr. in *Selected Tales and Sketches*, ed. Michael Colacurcio (Harmondsworth: Penguin, 1987), pp. 155–56. The texts in this edition are based on those established by the Centenary Edition of Hawthorne's *Works*. Unless otherwise indicated, subsequent references are to the Penguin edition.

thought of it opened up certain bizarre and intriguing notions to me: what it means when a writer puts his name on a book, why some writers choose to hide behind a pseudonym, whether or not a writer has a real life anyway' (*LR* 236). Although the narrator manages to resist this temptation, he accepts a commission to write a biography of Fanshawe, a proposal which he thinks will give him the opportunity to discover his friend's whereabouts and to understand his behaviour. So the man who was at first asked to replace one Daniel Quinn, a private eye who had failed to find Fanshawe, now becomes a literary detective who tries to piece together the fragments of another man's life. But this narrator has serious doubts concerning not so much his own abilities as the very possibility of understanding another person, of putting together the pieces that make up a man's life and his character: 'I was a detective, after all,' he says, 'and my job was to hunt for clues. Faced with a million bits of information, led down a million paths of false inquiry, I had to find the one path that would take me where I wanted to go. So far, the essential thing was that I hadn't found it' (*LR* 282). The narrator is destined not to find this path; instead, in a twist that subverts the rules of the detective genre, it is his absent friend who shows him the way, when he writes to him and arranges for a meeting to take place at 9 Columbus Square on, significantly, April 1st. Continuing the reversal of roles that took place in the previous books, the narrator is summoned by his friend: the culprit finds the detective. So, even if the narrator does manage to have an encounter with Fanshawe, it is not because he has found the right path. Despite his meticulous research into his friend's life, he never comes near an understanding of him. The narrator concludes: 'We exist for ourselves, perhaps... but in the end... we become more and more aware of our own incoherence. No one can cross the boundary into another – for the simple reason that no one can gain access to himself' (*LR* 247).

Writing with the wisdom afforded by retrospection, the narrator warns us from the outset that '[i]n the end, each life is no more than the sum of contingent facts, a chronicle of chance intersections, of flukes, of random events that divulge nothing but their own lack of purpose' (*LR* 217). The narrator of *The Locked Room* will, in his search for his friend, abandon any pretence of being a detective and admit to 'the utterly bewildering nature of human experience': 'Every life is inexplicable, I kept telling myself.' 'No matter how many facts are told, no matter how many details are given, the essential thing resists telling' (*LR* 427). Of course, the narrator's epistemological doubts should not divert attention from the ontological complexities of the text. If Fanshawe remains unknowable, it is not only because the text conveys the message that human nature is unintelligible, but also because Auster chooses not to divulge, or let his narrator acquire, more substantial information about the enigmatic Fanshawe. This deliberate obscuring of the core of the book is a lesson that Auster, along with whole generations of writers, has learnt from Hawthorne; one only has to think of 'The Minister's Black Veil', in which the author deliberately draws a veil over his own story, shielding the thing he is supposed to reveal. In Hawthorne, there is a moral lesson to be learnt from this, as there is in 'Wakefield', which ends with the observation: 'We will not follow our friend across the threshold. He has left us much food for thought, a portion of which will lend its wisdom to a moral; and be shaped into a figure' (158).

Sixteen years later, Hawthorne would give his famous definition of the Romance in his preface to *The House of the Seven Gables* (1851):

> When a writer calls his work a Romance, it need hardly be observed that he wishes to claim a certain latitude, both as to its fashion and material, which he would not have felt himself entitled to assume, had he professed to writing a Novel. The latter form of composition is presumed to aim at very minute fidelity, not merely to the possible, but to the probable and ordinary course of man's experience. The former – while as a work of art it must rigidly subject itself to laws, and while it sins unpardonably so far as it may swerve aside from the truth of the human heart – has fairly a right to present that truth under circumstances, to a great extent, of the writer's own choosing or creation.[33]

The novel as defined here by Hawthorne against the Romance was still in its nascent stages in America, so Hawthorne was probably referring to the realistic novel of writers such as Dickens or Balzac, whose legacy modern writers such as Auster still seek to oppose. It could be argued that the often far-fetched coincidences and extraordinary events that the realists used to bring their stories to a satisfying conclusion did not always 'aim

---

33. Nathaniel Hawthorne, *The House of the Seven Gables*, ed. Allan Lloyd Smith (London: Everyman, 1995), p. 3. Of course, this definition also nods towards the direction of allegory, but Hawthorne's writing always eludes a strict allegorical reading. David Reynolds offers a persuasive account of Hawthorne's practices when he argues that, by using the safe form of allegory, which Hawthorne inherited from the Puritan literary past, he was able to gain a readership that would otherwise be hostile to his subversive imagination. See David Reynolds, *Beneath the American Renaissance: The Subversive Imagination in the Age of Emerson and Melville* (Cambridge, MA, and London: Harvard University Press, 1989). Auster's fiction also has strong allegorical overtones, which I shall discuss in the next chapter, 'Austerities'.

at a minute fidelity to the ordinary course of man's experience', but nevertheless they were used as means of restoring order, creating an intelligible text which would mirror a largely intelligible world, and making the novel conform to the Aristotelian notions of teleology and coherence. In Hawthorne, as in Auster, strange situations are used for different purposes. As Hawthorne admits, he dramatises extraordinary events in order to present the truth under circumstances of his own making; the plotting becomes a means of philosophical investigation rather than a mechanical device, and its open-endedness and deliberate ambiguity distinguish it from the realistic novel and its concern with questions pertaining to social life and its impact on the individual. Auster is also interested in inexplicable events, open-ended structures and the rich possibilities offered by coincidence; he, too, sees it as a way of engaging in a philosophical quest, only the conclusions he draws differ from those of Hawthorne. Auster has been accused of concocting implausible plots driven by coincidences which would never occur in 'real life', which would suggest that Hawthorne's perception of the novel as a genre aiming at 'minute fidelity' still shapes the expectations of many critics. In the romance, on the other hand, Hawthorne saw the freedom to explore the real by way of the invented; if the circumstances are 'of the writer's own choosing or creation', this does not entail that they belong to the realm of the fantastic, or that they renounce any attempt at a representation of a recognisable world.

Although he had once been close to Fanshawe, the narrator now realises that he never really knew his friend. This realisation is also an indication of the author's conviction that the world is unintelligible, but that writing is an attempt to explore the nature of the world. The narrator writes about Fanshawe: 'He was there for you, and yet at the same time he was inaccessible. You felt there was a secret core in him that could never be penetrated, a mysterious center of hiddenness. To imitate him was somehow to participate in that mystery, but it was also to understand that you could never really know him'(*LR* 210). In this comment, the narrator is speaking about his personal experience and his relationship with his friend, but he is also speaking for Auster the author, and the act of writing. Sven Birkerts observes that Auster explores 'the real by way of the invented',[34] and Auster himself acknowledges that the world can be explored through acts of the imagination. As his narrator says, 'Everyone

34. Sven Birkerts, 'Reality, Fiction, and *In the Country of Last Things*', *The Review of Contemporary Fiction*, 14.1 (Spring 1994), p. 67.

knows that stories are imaginary. Whatever effect they might have on us, we know they are not true, even when they tell us truths more important than the ones we can find elsewhere' (*LR 250*). This is not only a celebration of the art of story-telling; it illustrates the author's belief in the power of imaginative creation. In *The Invention of Solitude*, Auster writes: 'Each thing leads a double life, at once in the world and in our minds, and to deny either one of these lives is to kill the thing in both its lives at once' (*IoS 153*). A similar idea is expressed by Hawthorne. In 'The Old Manse', the preface to *Mosses from an Old Manse*, Hawthorne gave a loving description of the house and the surrounding landscape where he lived between 1842 and 1845. Writing about the fishing trips he used to take with his friend Ellery Channing on the river, Hawthorne gives a poetic description of the reflection of the sky and the tree branches in the water, and he asks: 'Which, after all, was the most real – the picture, or the original? – the objects palpable to our grosser senses, or the apotheosis in the stream beneath?'[35] Leaving aside the Romantic implications of Hawthorne's question, and reading it backwards from the present, we find a preoccupation with the nature of representation and the relation between reality and imaginative creation. Throughout his writing, Auster also asks questions about the relationship between 'the original' and its 'picture', but he goes further than Hawthorne in that he believes the picture to be the only means of gaining access to the original. As Malcolm Bradbury writes of Auster, 'to explore the world as a labyrinthine and confused text is still to explore it in some fashion; to reconstruct memory, to master solitude, to find good fortune in the random, to discover the living reflection of things, is to engage in the true act of detection for which the writer is responsible, the detection, out of chaos, of story itself, and ultimately perhaps of reality'.[36]

Jorge Luis Borges also discerns a move away from Romanticism towards modernity in 'Wakefield':

> In that brief and ominous parable, which dates from 1835, we have already entered the world of Herman Melville, of Kafka – a world of enigmatic punishments and indecipherable sins. You may say that there is nothing strange about that, since Kafka's world is Judaism, and Hawthorne's, the wrath and punishments of the Old Testament. That is a just observation, but it applies only to ethics, and the horrible story of Wakefield and many

35. *Nathaniel Hawthorne's Tales*, ed. McIntosh, pp. 280–81.
36. Malcolm Bradbury, *The Modern American Novel* (Oxford and New York: Oxford University Press, 1992), p. 260.

stories by Kafka are united not only by a common ethic but also by a common rhetoric. For example, the protagonist's profound triviality, which contrasts with the magnitude of his perdition and delivers him, even more helpless, to the Furies. There is a murky background against which the nightmare is etched. Hawthorne invokes a romantic past in other stories, but the scene of this tale is middle-class London, whose crowds serve, moreover, to conceal the hero.[37]

'Austerities' will elaborate further on this perceived affinity between Auster and Kafka, but first I would like to remain a little longer with nineteenth-century writers who in many ways prefigure the kind of literature I will be discussing in subsequent chapters.

There is a scene in *City of Glass* in which Quinn goes to Grand Central Station to wait for the arrival of Peter Stillman, Sr. There he sees a poster of a place that could be Nantucket, and he tells himself that he ought to try to see things through Paul Auster's eyes:

> He turned his attention to the photograph again and was relieved to find his thoughts wandering to the subject of whales, to the expeditions that had set out from Nantucket in the last century, to Melville and the opening pages of *Moby Dick*. From here his mind drifted off to the accounts he had read of Melville's last years – the taciturn old man working in the New York customs house, with no readers, forgotten by everyone. Then, suddenly, with great clarity and precision, he saw Bartleby's window and the blank brick wall before him. (*CG* 51–52)

Since Quinn thinks that Paul Auster is a private detective, this reverie means that he fails to see things through Auster's eyes, reverting instead to his own writerly persona. But Paul Auster is also the author of the book, and a multi-faceted (inter)textual event is happening here. The reference to Bartleby foreshadows Quinn's own voluntary incarceration in the Stillman apartment at the end of the book, while the image of the solitary writer working in isolation mirrors not only Fanshawe's fate in *The Locked Room*, but also Auster's own frequent meditations on solitude. As a metafictional comment, this passage invites the reader to construct a hermeneutic hypothesis that takes into account Auster's frequent references to Herman Melville. *Billy Budd*, *Redburn*, 'Bartleby', *Moby Dick*, 'Jimmy Rose', *The Confidence Man*, all are mentioned or alluded to throughout *The New York Trilogy*, and Melville's presence permeates Auster's entire *œuvre*. It can be felt in the visions of dehumanising cities

37. Jorge Luis Borges, 'Nathaniel Hawthorne'; repr. in *Nathaniel Hawthorne's Tales*, ed. McIntosh, p. 410.

in *The New York Trilogy* and *In the Country of Last Things*, in the young artist's claustrophobic room in *Moon Palace*, in *Leviathan* and one man's obsessive struggle against the world and his own conscience which leads to a metaphorical, as well as literal, explosion of America's cherished myths. In the context of *The New York Trilogy*, an intertextual approach which takes into account the references to Melville yields new interpretations of the three stories and provides a new stance from which to examine Auster's relationship with the writings of the Transcendentalists.

Back in Grand Central Station, Quinn is awoken from his reverie by a short, silent man who taps him on the arm. He is a deaf mute who sells pens: 'Stapled to the pen was a little white paper flag, one side of which read: "This good article is the Courtesy of a DEAF MUTE. Pay any price. Thank you for your help"' (CG 52). Coming as it does immediately after the passage on Melville, this little incident clearly echoes the opening of Melville's *The Confidence Man* (1857), where a deaf mute boards the *Fidèle* 'on a first of April' and produces a slate in which he writes messages from the Corinthians.[38] But, as Tony Tanner points out, there is more than one confidence man on board the steamboat, while at the same time it is hard to tell how many of these con men are actually the same man in different guises. Tanner, reading the novel as a book well ahead of its time, observes:

> It is important to recognize that this uncertainty – are they all one, or all different people? – cannot be resolved, since this is central to the novel's deep intention: namely, to question whether man has a core self, whether there is any consistency or continuity-through-change of character; or whether man is indeed serial and partial, a plurality of fragmentary and momentary roles.[39]

It is, of course, the latter that Auster demonstrates in his fiction, from the dance of doubles and substitutions that takes place in *The New York Trilogy* to the character in *Leviathan* who is literally blown to a thousand pieces.

Melville's work was also an attempt to demystify the image of the Emersonian poet, the all-seer, the prophet, and Auster's references to

---

38. At the risk of being led to paranoid interpretation, it is worth mentioning that one of the first reactions from the passengers is to suggest that this man is Caspar Hauser, which is what Quinn also thinks when he meets Peter Stillman, Jr. Moreover, the deaf mute is, like Stillman, dressed all in white.

39. Herman Melville, *The Confidence Man*, ed. Tony Tanner (Oxford and New York: Oxford University Press, 1989), p. xx.

Melville's work serve to counter-balance the references to Emerson, Thoreau and Whitman, to demolish the cherished myths of American literature and also American culture, since these are the authors whose work has achieved the status of cultural symbols. In Chapters XXXVI and XXXVII of *The Confidence Man* Melville satirises both Emerson and Thoreau. The former becomes a 'mystical master' who speaks 'oracularly', while the latter is his disciple, his 'confidential follower', the one who puts the master's teachings into practice. What if we were to read Emerson and Thoreau as they appear in *The New York Trilogy* through Melville? Andrzej Kopcewicz argues that we could then read the Stillmans (who, again, may be one person or two) as confidence men who play a trick on Quinn.[40] But Quinn is also 'Paul Auster' who, on a different ontological level, 'knows' that Quinn is being deceived. He knows that because, like Melville, he recognises the attraction of the teachings of Thoreau and Emerson but at the same time remains sceptical and allows for ambiguity instead of dogma. If Quinn reproduces the divine alphabet with the deaf mute's pen in his notebook, the reader has no access to it and is left to draw his or her own conclusions.

Like Melville, Hawthorne often parodied the ideas of the Transcendentalists; at times this would take the form of a direct response to a text, while at others it would be an exposition of their own views which registered his disagreement, as in 'Wakefield'. David Morse writes:

> as the reader watches Hawthorne watching Wakefield watch... Wakefield seems like a parody of the American writer in the era of Jacksonian democracy, who withdraws from the world in the hope of discovering some imperishable truth but finds not only that the looked-for revelation never comes but that the world could not care less about his ambitions anyway.[41]

A similar fate befalls Fanshawe in *The Locked Room*, who withdraws from his life and then secretly watches his wife and child, sees his book get published, but ends up living alone and dying in the seclusion of a locked room. The red notebook that he leaves behind, which is supposed

---

40. Andrzej Kopcewicz, 'Paul Auster's Masquerades in *City of Glass*', in *American Cultures: Assimilation and Multiculturalism*, ed. Elzbieta H. Olesky (San Francisco and London: International Scholars Publications, 1995), p. 70. Also of interest by the same author is 'The Dark Rooms and Bartleby: An Intertextual Study', in *Canons, Revisions, Supplements in American Literature and Culture*, ed. Marek Wilczynski (Poznan: Bene Nati, 1997), pp. 109–24.

41. David Morse, *American Romanticism. 1. From Cooper to Hawthorne* (London: Macmillan, 1987), p. 189.

to explain the whole mystery, is torn page by page by his friend and ends up in a trash bin at a railway station. Although the narrator cared for Fanshawe a lot more than anyone did for Wakefield, he, too, contributes to his obliteration.

Hawthorne's 'Wakefield' ends with these words: 'Amid the seeming confusion of our mysterious world, individuals are so nicely adjusted to a system, and systems to one another, and to a whole, that, by stepping aside for a moment, a man exposes himself to a fearful risk of losing his place forever. Like Wakefield, he may become, as it were, the Outcast of the Universe' (158). The concept of 'stepping aside' is central to the thinking and practices of the American Romantics, and it is a recurring theme in Auster's fiction as well. For Thoreau, stepping aside means literally leaving everyday life behind and retiring to the woods; it is an occasion for meditation and communion with nature. In Emerson's writing, stepping aside relates to the prophetic vision, the ability to see the grand scheme rather than the fragments that ordinary men perceive. In Auster's fiction, the concept is invested with much greater ambiguity. Quinn steps aside from his own life: first he gives up writing, then he changes his identity, and finally he leaves his apartment to live in a dustbin outside the Stillman apartment, and later inside it as well. Blue and Black lead isolated lives in their apartments, and Fanshawe leaves his entire life behind: his family, his home, his work as a writer, his identity, to the point that he cannot even bear being called by his name. In *In the Country of Last Things*, Anna Blume's journalist brother goes to the nightmarish metropolis and is never heard of again. Marco Stanley Fogg in *Moon Palace* watches his savings dwindle to zero, and when he is evicted he lives as a tramp in Central Park. His grandfather Effing before him claims to have lived as a recluse in the wilderness. Benjamin Sachs in *Leviathan* leaves his writing career, his wife and his friends behind him to meet the woman whose husband he killed, and he becomes a terrorist in a bid to atone for his crime. Jim Nashe quits his job and travels around the country until he meets Pozzi, a meeting that will eventually lead to his imprisonment in the Flower and Stone mansion grounds, while Walt, alias Mr Vertigo, has to undergo a series of humiliating initiation rites which make him feel that he 'was scarcely a hair's breadth greater than nothing, a molecule or two above the vanishing point of what constitutes a human being'. All these characters go too far, and they fail to regain their place in the world; their search for the creative solitude which will lead to revelation often ends in disaster. For Thoreau, as we have seen, stepping aside meant retiring to the woods and leading a self-reliant life of meditation and artistic creativity. For Hawthorne, stepping aside is an act which can have catastrophic results. Although Hawthorne himself lived as a recluse for years, a fact which Auster alludes to more than once, his was not the cherished solitude of Thoreau. As for his characters, if they step aside for a moment, far from reaching a transcendent state of peace and knowledge, they are exposed to terrible risks.

Melville's Bartleby is another character who famously stepped aside and failed to recover. Bartleby is the antithesis of the Thoreauvian ascetic; his withdrawal and passive resistance lead to death and oblivion. Like 'Wakefield', 'Bartleby' is an urban tale; in both stories, the central character suffers the dehumanising effects of the city, becoming literally as well as metaphorically lost in the crowd. For Quinn, this is initially a positive experience:

> Quinn was used to wandering. His excursions through the city had taught him to understand the connectedness of inner and outer. Using aimless motion as a technique of reversal, on his best days he could bring the outside in and thus usurp the sovereignty of inwardness. By flooding himself with externals, by drowning himself out of himself, he had managed to exert some small degree of control over his fits of despair. Wandering, therefore, was a kind of mindlessness. (CG 61)

By the end of his bizarre adventure, though, the situation is reversed. Like Bartleby, Quinn minimises the impact of the outside world when he moves into the Stillman apartment. Instead of 'flooding himself with externals', he now divests himself of them and allows inwardness to overcome him. It is only then, when he has severed his connections with the outside world, that Quinn starts writing again. If, by doing so, he vindicates Bartleby's withdrawal, the text denies the very consolation it is supposed to offer. Paradoxically, Quinn's surge of creativity is absent from the text. What should have been the climax of the story is not there. As Quinn fills the white pages of his notebook, he translates himself into text; when he runs out of blank pages, he disappears.

The blank page is but one manifestation of the emphasis on whiteness which can be seen throughout *City of Glass* and *Ghosts*. When Quinn meets his client for the first time, he is confronted with a ghost: 'Everything about Peter Stillman was white. White shirt, open at the neck; white pants, white shoes, white socks. Against the pallor of his skin, the flaxen thinness of his hair, the effect was almost transparent, as though one could see through to the blue veins behind the skin of his face' (CG 15). As in Melville and the whiteness of the whale, the colour symbolism here is ambivalent. White, as the colour of innocence, marks Stillman as a victim, the victim of his father's cruel experiment. But even though he appears to be transparent, Stillman is in fact impenetrable. Deprived of the faculty of speech, the very man who should be speaking the language of Adam, giving each thing its true name and restoring transparency to a world become opaque, is a cipher himself. In *Ghosts*, a story which is haunted by intertextual ghosts, whiteness and transparency also play an important role. In order to solve the mystery, Blue has to understand that White and Black are the same person. His elusive, secretive employer White does not exist after all; he is quite literally absent, because he is the absence of colour: he is Black.

Whiteness is also the emblem of mystery at the end of Edgar Allan Poe's *The Narrative of Arthur Gordon Pym of Nantucket* (1837), a novel which is alluded to in *City of Glass*, and the Poesque quality of Auster's mysteries is underscored by numerous references throughout the text. Most explicitly, Daniel Quinn writes detective novels using the pseudonym William Wilson; the reference is both to Poe's creation of the detective novel and to the theme of the double that runs throughout the trilogy. However, unlike Poe, Auster is not so much interested in creating the effect of psychological terror that is often found in his predecessor, nor would a psychoanalytical approach be especially fruitful. Auster is interested in the double because of the questions it poses about selfhood, the meaning of 'identity', and whether there can be a separation between the observer and the self observed, while the perils of interpretation also concern both writers.

When Quinn realises that Stillman has been spelling the phrase 'The Tower of Babel' with his steps, he immediately thinks of *Arthur Gordon Pym*:

> Quinn's thoughts momentarily flew off to the concluding pages of *A. Gordon Pym* and to the discovery of the strange hieroglyphs on the inner wall of the chasm – letters inscribed into the earth itself, as though they were trying to say something that could no longer be understood. But on second thought this did not seem apt. For Stillman had not left his message anywhere. True, he had created the letters by the movement of his steps, but they had not been written down. It was like drawing a picture in the air with your finger. The image vanishes as you are making it. (CG 70–71)

Of course, Stillman's letters had been written down: Quinn wrote them down in his notebook, and they are part of the text that makes up *City of Glass*. In this respect, Quinn's limited perception mirrors Pym's, as they are both trapped inside texts of which they are allowed to have only a partial understanding. It is ironic that, although the hieroglyphs that Pym encountered were inscribed into the rock, their concrete presence offered him no insight either: they 'bore also some little resemblance to alphabetical characters, and Peters was willing, at all events, to adopt the idle opinion that they were really such. I convinced him of his error.'[42] Towards the end, however, when Pym has finished his first-person narration, an unnamed narrator appears who informs the reader that the signs were, in fact, hieroglyphs, spelling the phrases 'the region of the south', 'to be shady', and 'to be white'. The narrator ends his 'Note' with the observation that the natives of Tsalal were terrified at the sight of whiteness, since there was nothing white at Tsalal. It is therefore absence that causes terror: the absence of whiteness which represents the unknown to the natives, but also the perfect whiteness of the shrouded human figure that appears at the end of Pym's narrative, literally frustrating any attempt to interpret the incidents related by veiling the story with its ghost-like presence. Absence also characterises both Pym's inability to read the signs he is presented with and the way he vanishes from the text. Both texts tease the reader with the promise of signification, and both authors tease their own characters by not allowing them to penetrate surfaces and appearances.

Arthur Gordon Pym is therefore a lot more apt than Quinn seems to think, but the extent of that novel's relevance cannot be grasped by him because it belongs to the realm of the text, of whose presence Quinn is not aware, not even when he meets 'the writer' Paul Auster. A writer named Poe is also mentioned in Pym's preface to the narrative of his adventures. Mr Poe was the man who undertook to publish Pym's memoir 'under the garb of fiction' in the *Southern Literary Messenger*. When Pym discovered that the public were not fooled by this 'ruse', he decided to conclude the narrative himself, dropping any pretence at fiction-writing. However, in the aforementioned 'Note' that concludes the novel, yet another narrator appears. His identity is not revealed, but he explains that the final pages of Pym's story were lost when the latter died, and Mr Poe declined to write his own conclusion to the story. Since this narrator cannot reconstruct the 'two or three remaining chapters', all he can do is clarify a few points that have escaped the attention of Mr Poe. 'Mr Poe' failed to solve the mystery of Arthur Gordon Pym, while

42. Edgar Allan Poe, *The Narrative of Arthur Gordon Pym of Nantucket*, ed. Harold Beaver (Harmondsworth: Penguin, 1975), p. 225.

'Paul Auster' let Quinn down and 'behaved badly throughout'. In drawing the parallel between the construction of the two texts, it is important to stress that the latter contains the former: another turn of the screw, plunging the reader deeper into the maelstrom of fragmented identities and shifting fields of signification.

The obvious difference between the 'hieroglyphics' that Pym encounters and the ones that Quinn reconstructs is that the former exist in the extremities of the South Pole firmly inscribed in stone, whereas the latter are in a sense invisible, and 'written' on the streets of contemporary New York. But Poe also deals with the attempt to discover meaning in a person's wanderings around the streets of a contemporary metropolis in 'The Man of the Crowd' (1840) where, as in Auster's narrative, the city becomes an image both of the text and of the mental process that fails to solve the supposed riddle. 'The Man of the Crowd' is an anti-detective story. The narrator is a *flâneur* rather than an investigator, and the man of the crowd, like Auster's Stillman, despite being the 'type and the genius of deep crime', does not commit any crime in the story.[43] Poe warns from the outset that the tale does not allow itself to be read, thus producing a story which mocks the reader's desire for closure and interpretation. If one reads the narrator and the man of the crowd as the two elements of the split self, the 'eye' and the 'I', then the nightly wanderings in the dark streets of London become an externalised image, and a textual manifestation, of the mental process. In 'The Book of Memory' Auster also makes the analogy between walking in the city and thinking. The passage is worth quoting in full not only because it deals explicitly with this analogy, but also because, in its density, in the absence of full stops and the use of commas and parentheses, it becomes itself a textual miniature of the process it describes:

> Sometimes it feels as though we are not going anywhere as we walk through the city, that we are only looking for a way to pass the time, and that it is only our fatigue that tells us where and when we should stop. But just as one step will inevitably lead to the next step, so it is that one thought inevitably follows from the previous thought, and in the event that a thought should engender more than a single thought (say two or three thoughts, equal to each other in all their consequences), it will be necessary not only to follow the first thought to its conclusion, but also to backtrack to the original position of that thought in order to follow the second

43. *The Complete Works of Edgar Allan Poe*, ed. James A. Harrison (New York: AMS, 1965), IV, pp. 134–45.

thought to its conclusion, and then the third thought, and so on, and in this way, if we were to try to make an image of this process in our minds, a network of paths begins to be drawn, as in the image of the human bloodstream (heart, arteries, veins, capillaries), or as in the image of a map (of city streets, for example, preferably a large city, or even of roads, as in the gas station maps of roads that stretch, bisect, and meander across a continent), so that what we are really doing when we walk through the city is thinking, and thinking in such a way that our thoughts compose a journey, and this journey is no more or less than the steps we have taken, so that, in the end, we might safely say that we have been on a journey, and even if we do not leave our room, it has been a journey, and we might safely say that we have been somewhere, even if we don't know where it is. (*IoS* 122)

The man of the crowd walks the streets of London in a similar manner: sometimes he walks fast, then he slows down, he pauses and then suddenly rushes, and he repeatedly retraces his own steps throughout the night, until, as day breaks, he reaches once again the street of the D— Hotel where the narrator had first seen him. The observer's interest in this man becomes intense, all-consuming, but then suddenly he grows 'wearied unto death' and decides to drop his quest. If he has learnt anything, it is that 'It will be in vain to follow; for I shall learn no more of him, nor of his deeds.' The story then ends with the same words with which it had begun: 'er lasst sich nicht lesen', it does not permit itself to be read. Like Auster's mental traveller, the narrator has been somewhere, even if he doesn't know where. What the supposed investigator learns at the end of his adventure is that he cannot close the gap between the narrating self and the narrated self: 'Although the stranger's refusal to reveal himself heightens suspense and teases both the narrator and the reader into pursuit, the narrative shows that we can never close the gap between self and other opened up by the sudden appearance of the double.'[44]

This dilemma haunts the entire trilogy, where doubles obsessively pursue one another without ever reaching the hoped-for revelation. The variations on this theme which give each story its own character are rehearsals of narrative viewpoint. *City of Glass* relies on a Chinese-box structure which foregrounds its own epistemological impossibility. *Ghosts* is narrated in the third person by a voice which occasionally reveals its own superior knowledge of the facts surrounding the case. The

---

44. Jonathan Auerbach, *The Romance of Failure: First-Person Fictions of Poe, Hawthorne, and James* (New York and Oxford: Oxford University Press, 1989), p. 32.

story of Fanshawe's disappearance in *The Locked Room* is told in the first person by an unnamed narrator who is the missing man's alter ego.

This dichotomy between subject and object, which is textually manifested in Poe and Auster, is the antithesis of Emerson's 'I be, and I see my being at the same time'. Jonathan Auerbach, who draws attention to another story by Poe, 'How to Write a Blackwood Article', in which the first-person narrator's eyeballs pop from her head onto the ground below, comments:

> the storyteller's 'I' simultaneously plays the part of anguished participant and dispassionate observer, the narrated self who acts in the past and the narrating self who retrospectively analyzes that past action in the present. Unlike the famous transparent eyeball into which Emerson transfigured himself two years earlier in *Nature*, Psyche's eyes do not 'see all' but rather a diminished part, their blind ex-mistress, who now literally remains beside herself.[45]

To paraphrase Borges, in this brief and ominous tale we have already entered the world of Rimbaud's 'je est un autre', of Samuel Beckett's cripples whose literary remains refuse to go away, persisting as the tellers threaten to disappear.

45. Auerbach, *The Romance of Failure*, p. 5.

2

Austerities

Paul Auster has observed that his novels follow a pendular rhythm in which a complex, labyrinthine book is followed by one that is simple in its construction.[1] *The New York Trilogy*, *Moon Palace* and *Leviathan* are all narrated in a complex manner and contain numerous stories within their intricate plots, whereas *In The Country of Last Things* and *The Music of Chance* are characterised by a movement towards lessness. They are what Auster would call 'bare bone narratives', simple stories told in a straightforward manner. This chapter, 'Austerities', as the title suggests, considers the place of these ascetic narratives in Auster's *œuvre*. The most pronounced intertextual presences here are the writings of Beckett, Kafka and Knut Hamsun, while the fairy-tale and the parable are the genres that provide a starting point for Auster's fiction. However, the pendular rhythm that the author identifies can also be detected within *The New York Trilogy* itself, not only in the second story, *Ghosts*, but also in the stripping down of traditional narrative forms (especially the detective novel) which takes place throughout the book. As I argued in the previous chapter, Auster negotiates his own position in relation to nineteenth-century American writing by causing the text to become a field of confrontation for the two opposing trends in the writings of that period. At the same time, though, his own position is also regulated by his reading of modernist literature, and the way it challenged Romantic assumptions as well as realist writing. Therefore, before I examine *In the Country of Last Things* and *The Music of Chance*, I remain with *The New York Trilogy*, this time reading it in relation to Samuel Beckett's *Trilogy*.

If Auster ever came close to experiencing the anxiety of influence, he must have felt it in relation to Beckett. In his own critical work he praises

---

1. Del Rey, 'Paul Auster: Al compas de un ritmo pendular', p. 27. ('It appears that the books I write follow a pendular rhythm: from a very complex one to a very simple one.')

Beckett who, 'Even at his not quite best... remains Beckett, and reading him is like reading no one else... Beckett is not like other writers... beyond Dickens and Joyce, there is perhaps no English writer of the past hundred years who has equalled Beckett's early prose for vigor and intelligence' (*AH* 83–87). In interviews he has admitted that Beckett 'had a tremendous hold over me... the influence of Beckett was so strong that I couldn't see my way beyond it' (*AH* 265). Moreover, it has recently emerged that early in his career Auster sent Beckett copies of his own writing, as well as his translations of poetry by André du Bouchet, which Beckett received favourably.[2] It is therefore surprising, though arguably predictable as well, that there are no direct references to Beckett in *The New York Trilogy*, or indeed in any of Auster's novels. The trilogy, however, is similar both in its formal construction and in its thematic preoccupations to Beckett's *Trilogy* (*Molloy*, 1950; *Malone Dies*, 1951; *The Unnamable*, 1952). The affinity between the two books is discussed in the first part of this chapter, 'The Unnamable', where the title refers not only to Beckett's book but also to *The New York Trilogy*'s resistance to interpretation or categorisation in its relation to the texts of the past.

Professor Stillman, whose theories may be identified with those of Emerson, is transformed from prophet into one of Beckett's existential derelicts. Daniel Quinn, the seeker after truth, in a mockery of his detective investigations ends up living in a dustbin and starving himself the better to keep watch on a man who has already disappeared. Fanshawe, the vanishing author in *The Locked Room*, produces a text in which 'Each sentence erased the sentence before it, each paragraph made the next paragraph impossible' (*LR* 314). This movement towards unburdening and absence is best seen in *Ghosts*, where the formal arrangement of the story mirrors the predicament of the characters and the text. Silence and stasis replace the action required of a detective story, and the plot is reduced to its raw ingredients. *Ghosts* is the closest Auster has come to writing a story in the spirit of the *nouveau roman*, but, when asked if this was deliberate, he replies: 'I have never been interested in the *nouveau roman*, to be honest... The material creates the form.'[3] Of course, that was what Robbe-Grillet also claimed in his manifesto *Pour un nouveau roman*, where he explained that there are not two ways of writing the same book, that art is not 'a more or less highly coloured envelope whose function is to decorate

---

2. James Knowlson, *Damned to Fame: The Life of Samuel Beckett* (London: Bloomsbury, 1996), p. 654. The letters are now in Auster's archive in the Berg collection.
3. Del Rey, 'Paul Auster: Al compas de un ritmo pendular', p. 25.

the author's "message"'.[4] Auster's chosen way of undermining traditional character representation in *Ghosts* is also in keeping with the spirit of the *nouveau roman*, as is his use of the present tense in the narrative. In *Ghosts*, 'the time is the present', and the entire story is told in the present tense, as was Robbe-Grillet's anti-detective novel *Les Gommes* (1953). Paradoxically, the present tense implies an absence: the absence of the past, of referents, of a priori meaning. But Auster's technique of drawing attention to the nature of the text in its relation to other texts cancels out the illusion that the story is a self-contained unit, an act of discovery that coincides with the text. In *City of Glass*, Quinn learned that he could not follow Stillman and write in his notebook at the same time; no matter how adept he became at minimising the distance, there would always be a moment of perception that preceded writing. Even though the story unfolds in the present, the fact that it borrows its structure from the detective novel and the numerous references to texts of the past that it contains bring a sense of the past to what appears to be a non-referential present. Robbe-Grillet stated that the use of the past tense, the novel that began with a 'There was once...' type of narration, presupposed the existence of an already known meaning. Auster's use of the present tense locates meaning in the world of the text, but at the same time this present contains in its fragile, diminished structure the past. Not the past as closure, but as a collection of fragments providing exit-points from a text which threatens to collapse into itself but manages not to do so. As I shall argue in 'The Unnamable', this recovery is typical of Auster's departure from the writings of Beckett.

Auster's preoccupation with diminishing structures, starving protagonists and self-questioning texts is not only an epistemological enquiry, or an aesthetic stance; it is also a manifestation of the way in which he deals with his Jewish identity in his fictions. Auster's interest in modernity is not confined to the fictions of Beckett and Kafka; his critical writings demonstrate an equally strong interest in poetry, from the beginning of the twentieth century through to the present.[5] What emerges from these

4. Alain Robbe-Grillet, *Towards a New Novel*, trans. Barbara Wright (London: Calder and Boyars, 1965), p. 73.
5. Auster's essays, collected in *The Art of Hunger*, first appeared in literary magazines such as *Harper's, Saturday Review, Parnassus, The San Francisco Review of Books* and others. It is interesting to note that Auster was not commissioned to write any of these pieces. He tells Larry McCaffery and Sinda Gregory that he only wrote about writers who interested him, and nearly always suggested the article to the editor of each journal. 'I looked on those pieces as an opportunity to articulate some ideas about writing and literature... All in all, I feel it was a useful apprenticeship' (*AH* 293).

essays, in relation to the theme of narrative impoverishment in the para-
bolic stories that I discuss in this chapter, is the way in which Auster has
chosen to deal with his Jewish identity in his writing. Auster, whose
grandparents were Eastern European Jews, grew up 'as an American boy
who knew less about his ancestors than he did about Hopalong Cassidy's
hat' (*IoS* 28). By his own admission he is not at all a religious person, and
yet he feels that 'Judaism is everything I am, it's where I come from'. 'I
feel very attached to the history of the Jewish people, in all its ramifica-
tions,' he explains, 'but I don't feel any urge to write about Judaism. It's
a part of me which may or may not surface in a book. It's not my princi-
pal source, but rather an element among others which, as much as anything, has left its mark on me.'[6] His essays on Charles Reznikoff, Paul
Celan, Edmond Jabès and Georges Perec may help to illuminate how
Auster has negotiated his Jewish identity and his secular upbringing in his
own work. In his essay 'The Decisive Moment', Auster discusses the
poetry of Charles Reznikoff, whose interest in Judaism is much more
pronounced than Auster's own, and he concludes: 'America is
Reznikoff's present, Judaism is his past. The act of immersing himself in
Jewish history is finally no different for him than the act of stepping out
into the streets of New York. In both cases, it is an attempt to come to
terms with what he is. *The past, however, cannot be directly perceived: it
can only be experienced through books*' (*AH* 45, emphasis added).
Auster's writing always emphasises the fact that the past is experienced
through books. Marco Stanley Fogg, the protagonist of *Moon Palace*,
inherits 1,492 books from his uncle and reads them in random order as
his uncle's fragmented life-story: 'reading the same words, living in the
same stories, perhaps thinking the same thoughts. It was almost like following the route of an explorer from long ago, duplicating his steps as he
thrashed out into virgin territory' (*MP* 22). And when Anna Blume finds
a group of Jews in hiding in the country of last things, she finds them in
the city's library, which they have chosen as their sanctuary. When Fogg
runs out of money, first he uses the books as furniture, and then he sells
them in order to buy food; books, writing and survival are also closely
linked in *In the Country of Last Things*.

As I argued in the introduction, another writer who has been instrumental in shaping Auster's preoccupation with the act of writing and the
nature of the novel is Edmond Jabès. Auster reads Jabès as a writer whose

6. Gérard de Cortanze, *La Solitude du labyrinthe: essai et entretiens* (Paris: Actes Sud,
   1997), pp. 93–94.

Jewish identity is inseparable from his identity as a writer. Of Jabès's *Book of Questions*, Auster remarks that

> the question is the Jewish Holocaust, but it is also the question of literature itself. By a startling leap of the imagination, Jabès treats them as one and the same... *The Book of Questions* came into being because Jabès found himself as a writer in the act of discovering himself as a Jew... To Jabès, nothing can be written about the Holocaust unless writing itself is first put into question. If language is to be pushed to the limit, then the writer must condemn himself to an exile of doubt, to a desert of uncertainty. What he must do, in effect, is create a poetics of absence. (*AH* 107, 114)

In the Country of Last Things and *The Music of Chance* also put writing itself into question, but they do so in a more conventional manner than *The Book of Questions*. One of the ways in which Auster creates his own 'poetics of absence' is through the use of allegorical elements. Allegory can be said to be a genre of absence, since what it deals with is literally not there in the text. However, this absence is not assumed to be recoverable in any unambiguous way. By using allegory as one element among many, Auster evades interpretative restrictions and replaces certainty with doubt, and forced readings with polysemy. In doing so, as I shall argue, the writer not only manages to address his Jewish identity in secular terms, but he also allows the narrative itself to become an act of redemption. The ever-diminishing structures that he takes from modernism do not lead to negation because the writing of the story, the text, provides its own affirmation, becomes a kind of replenishment in itself.

'A Hunger Artist', the second part of this chapter, examines how Auster deals with his Jewishness in literary terms. In his second novel, *In the Country of Last Things*, Auster puts into practice what he had written about Jabès and Reznikoff, and the question of the Holocaust becomes one with the question of writing. Although this book is not allusive like *The New York Trilogy*, the fact that its roots may be found in the literary as well as in 'real life' manifests itself in various ways. The novel opens with the image of a city which belongs to the realm of dystopia: 'These are the last things,' the narrator writes, 'A house is there one day, and the next day it is gone.' The weather, as in much science-fiction writing, 'is in constant flux. A day of sun followed by a day of rain, a day of snow followed by a day of fog, warm then cool, wind then stillness, a stretch of bitter cold' (*CLT* 1). What follows, however, is a depiction of a city that is as much a self-conscious collage of literary cities as it is disturbingly recognisable in historical terms: the country of last things is Leningrad under siege, the Warsaw ghetto, and present-day New York City. The story is narrated in the laconic, staccato voice of a young woman; it is sparse, devoid of all ornament, and it imparts a sense of urgency in the face of impending doom. Anna Blume keeps a journal, and the act of writing it helps her to cope with the hardships she experiences. But as she is the narrator of the novel, Anna's writing also becomes *voice*, the voice of a Scheherazade who speaks in order to remain alive. The theme of survival is prominent in the book and it is closely linked with Auster's use of the theme of hunger. Anna Blume's emaciated prose reflects the hunger that afflicts both the inhabitants of the country of last things and their real-life counterparts in Leningrad or the Warsaw ghetto. At the same time, the narrator's survival depends as much on the act of narration as it does on material sustenance: in order to remain alive, Anna 'translates' herself into the voice of the text, staving off hunger by substituting the secondary function of the mouth for the primary one. Through his use of hunger as trope, Auster writes a book that explores both historical trauma and the formal possibilities of the novel itself; he combines his interests in a concurrent investigation of the world and the word. His deliberate paring-down of narrative, the textual starvation which questions the boundaries between self and text, constitute both an attempt to represent the unrepresentable world of historical nightmare and a manifestation of his continuing interest in modernist modes of writing.

In the context of the author's interest in modernist fiction, 'A Hunger Artist' also examines the relation of *In the Country of Last Things* to Kafka's 'A Hunger Artist' and Knut Hamsun's *Hunger*. Auster's novel reveals a fascination with paradox, and its roots are traced to the inherent contradiction between hunger and survival that dominates both Kafka's and Hamsun's texts. This interest in paradox can, among other things, be read as the author's struggle to write literature after the Holocaust. In his discussion of Reznikoff's poetry, Auster writes:

> The Holocaust, which is precisely the unknowable, the unthinkable, requires a treatment beyond the facts in order for us to be able to understand it – assuming that such a thing is even possible. Similar in approach to a 1960s play by Peter Weiss, *The Investigation*, Reznikoff's poem rigorously refuses to pass judgement on any of the atrocities it describes. But this is nevertheless a false objectivity, for the poem is not saying to the reader, 'decide for yourself', it is saying that the decision has already been made and that the only way we can deal with these things is to remove them from their inherently emotional setting. The problem is that we cannot remove them. This setting is necessarily the starting point. (*AH* 50)

Auster's writing has always been interested in the problematic process of addressing 'reality' and drawing the line between fact and fiction, and his comments on Reznikoff's poetry show that his abiding interest in paradox as well as his self-questioning texts and his intellectual puzzles are not manifestations of depthless, dehistoricised fiction that concerns itself with its own process of enunciation. Instead, these themes and techniques very often constitute attempts to speak the unspeakable and represent the unknowable. Auster's textual practices openly acknowledge his debt to other authors, and the writer is seen to experience the past through books. However, this is not only in recognition of the discursive nature of history and the importance of reading fictions within a broader cultural intertext, but also because Auster does not separate his interest in literature from his quest to address the historical past, a quest which leads him to explore his own Jewish heritage.

In addition to its connection with history and modernity, the issue of narrative starvation which manifests itself in the laconic telling of the story is also related to Auster's confessed admiration of fairy-tale narratives:

> In the end, though, I would say that the greatest influence on my work has been fairy tales, the oral tradition of story-telling. The Brothers Grimm, the Thousand and One Nights – the kinds of stories you read out loud to children. These are bare-bone narratives, narratives largely devoid of details, yet enormous amounts of information are communicated in a very short space, with very few words. (*AH* 304)

In the Country of Last Things in many ways resembles a fairy-tale. The telling of the story is, in its sparseness, reminiscent of that genre, where 'only what is essential to the plot is mentioned; nothing is stated for its own sake, and nothing is amplified... The abstract stylization of the folk tale gives it luminosity and firm definition.'[7] This is a method also used by Kafka and, in him as in Auster, the clarity imparted by this simple narration underscores the strange and often terrifying nature of the events related. The actual story told in *In the Country of Last Things* also complies, up to a point, with Vladimir Propp's definition of the wondertale: 'A wondertale begins with... a desire to have something, and develops through the hero's departure from home and encounter with the donor who provides him with a magic agent which helps the hero to find the object of the search. The tale also includes a combat with an adversary, a

---

7. Max Lüthi, *The European Folktale: Form and Nature*, trans. John D. Niles (Philadelphia: Institute for the Study of Human Issues, 1982), p. 36.

return and a pursuit.'[8] All of these functions are to be found in the novel, except for the actual accomplishment of the task. Anna Blume does not find her brother, but 'the object of the search' is attained in a different way. Unlike fairy-tales, this story is told in the first person, and in this respect the telling of the story becomes the heroine's accomplishment.

Auster sees *The Music of Chance* as another story with fairy-tale elements, and this novel shares with *In the Country of Last Things* a simple plot and an austere narrative tone. What they also have in common is a preoccupation with the individual's struggle against unseen powers, and strong allegorical overtones. The presence of 'Wakefield' in *Ghosts* and *The Locked Room* had already established a connection with allegory, and now Hawthorne is alluded to once more. *In the Country of Last Things* takes its epigraph from Hawthorne's 'The Celestial Rail-Road', an ironic rewrite of *Pilgrim's Progress* which evades a strict allegorical reading. In Auster's appropriation of Hawthorne we recall once again Borges, who drew the parallel between the works of Hawthorne and those of Kafka. The term 'Kafkaesque' is one that easily springs to mind in relation to *The Music of Chance* but, as I shall be arguing, to read *The Music of Chance* as a 'Kafkaesque' story is not merely to point to the fact that the protagonist finds himself at the mercy of powers he cannot fully comprehend. The link is much deeper, and it refers to the ideological, philosophical, and aesthetic assumptions in the work of the two writers.

The title of the final part of this chapter, 'Wall Writing', of course suggests that *The Music of Chance* is a novel about the building of a wall, but this wall is also to be read as a multi-faceted metaphor. Auster's active intertextual strategies are examined in relation to the image of wall-building, while the same chapter also considers the act of writing as equivalent to the arduous task of building a wall. This orderly activity is also read in contrast with the randomness of chance, which shapes the protagonist's life. Throughout *The Music of Chance*, Auster in fact worries at the borders that separate the random from the predetermined, the accidental from the carefully designed. This is mirrored in the two parts into which the narrative is divided. In the first one, a kind of road narrative, Nashe travels around the country with no destination in mind, and this random movement gives him the illusion of freedom. As soon as he steps into the Flower and Stone mansion, though, movement comes to a

---

8. Vladimir Propp, *Morphology of the Folktale*, trans. Laurence Scott, ed. Louis A. Wagner (Austin and London: University of Texas Press, 1968), p. 7.

stop. When he becomes a prisoner, he discovers that he needs to reconcile freedom and responsibility. As the narrative charts his attempts to do that, the question that arises concerns 'the extent to which everything is plotless or totally plotted: whether one lives in a world of hermetic containment in complete meaning, or in a world of undifferentiation and pure randomness'.[9]

Just before the fateful game of poker, Nashe spends a night in a hotel where he reads Rousseau's *Confessions*:

> Just before he fell asleep, he came to the passage in which the author is standing in a forest and throwing stones at trees. If I hit that tree with this stone, Rousseau says to himself, then all will go well with my life from now on. He throws the stone and misses. That one didn't count, he says, and so he picks up another stone and moves several yards closer to the tree. He misses again. That one didn't count either, he says, and then moves still closer to the tree and finds another stone. Again he misses. That was just the final warm-up toss, he says, it's the next one that really counts. But just to make sure, he walks right up to the tree this time, positioning himself directly in front of the target. He is no more than a foot away from it by now, close enough to touch it with his hand. Then he lobs the stone squarely against the trunk. Success, he says to himself, I've done it. From this moment on, life will be better for me than ever before. (*MC* 53)

Nashe is amused and at the same time embarrassed in the face of what he thinks of as 'naked self-deception' (*MC* 54). Presumably this refers to Rousseau's decision to regard the earlier attempts as warm-ups, and to move closer to the tree in order to hit his target. However, it is an even greater self-deception to invest the throwing of the stone with such significance in the first place, but this is a decision that goes unchallenged in the narrative. Perhaps the implication here is that, if one sets out to investigate the workings of chance, one must arbitrarily posit a point that exists outside, is taken to be other than, chaos and meaninglessness. That this choice must be arbitrary is taken for granted, but this does not have to be a cause for despair. Within *The Music of Chance*, Auster uses two images that relate to chaos and order: playing poker and building a wall. But which is orderly, and which chaotic? A game of cards is largely a matter of chance, but players can improve their chances by studying and practising; the whole point of a game of cards is to defeat the random.

9. Tim Woods, '*The Music of Chance*: Aleatorical (Dis)harmonies within "The City of the World"', in *Beyond the Red Notebook*, ed. Barone, p. 149.

Arthur Saltzman makes the analogy between playing cards and writing when he draws attention to Pozzi's words:

> Once your luck starts to roll, there's not a damn thing that can stop it. It's like the whole world suddenly falls into place. You're kind of outside your body, and for the rest of the night you sit there watching yourself perform miracles. It doesn't really have anything to do with you anymore. It's out of control, and as long as you don't think about it too much, you can't make a mistake. (*MC* 136–37)

Saltzman compares this passage with Auster's comments on the writing process: 'It's a funny thing… but I'm not actually in control of what I'm doing. I think a lot of writers feel this way.'[10] Auster had rehearsed the author's dilemma in *The Invention of Solitude*, where he wrote:

> Like everyone else, he craves a meaning. Like everyone else, his life is so fragmented that each time he sees a connection between two fragments he is tempted to look for a meaning in that connection. The connection exists. But to give it a meaning, to look beyond the bare fact of its existence, would be to build an imaginary world inside the real world, and he knows it would not stand. At his bravest moments, he embraces meaninglessness as the first principle, and then he understands that his obligation is to see what is in front of him (even though it is also inside him) and to say what he sees. (*IoS* 147)

To embrace meaninglessness, however, need not lead to utter negation. As Auster's later novelistic career would prove, the imaginary world inside the real one does stand. It may be fragile, arbitrarily chosen, but fiction can also become a redemptive site, an agent of recuperation. This is what the poetry of Jacques Dupin has taught Auster: 'The gods have vanished, and there can be no question of pretending to recover the divine logos. Faced with an unknowable world, poetry can do no more than create what already exists. But that is already saying a great deal. For if things can be recovered from the edge of absence, there is the chance, in so doing, of giving them back to men' (*AH* 182). The novels I shall discuss in 'Austerities' illustrate how Auster effects such a recovery, rescuing both his protagonists and his own fictional structures from the edge of absence.

---

10. Arthur Saltzman, *The Novel in the Balance* (Columbia: University of South Carolina Press, 1993), p. 81.

The Unnamable

And on the threshold of being no more I succeed in being another.

Samuel Beckett

When Quinn realised that Peter Stillman had been spelling the phrase 'The Tower of Babel' in the streets of New York, his 'mind dispersed. He arrived in a neverland of fragments, a place of wordless things and thingless words' (*CG* 72). This neverland of fragments is Molloy's native town in Samuel Beckett's *Molloy*, a town whose name Molloy cannot remember: 'I had been living so far from words so long, you understand, that it was enough for me to see my town, since we're talking of my town, to be unable, you understand... Yes, even then, when already all was fading, waves and particles, there could be no things but nameless things, no names but thingless names.'[11] Exiled in this world of brokenness, knowing that it is impossible to re-attach words to things or to abstract ideas, the author needs to create a space where writing can still be justified or made possible. As Auster writes of Charles Reznikoff, the 'act of writing... is a process by which one places oneself between things and the names of things, a way of standing watch in this interval of silence' (*AH* 35). This interval of silence is also where Beckett locates the text. As Georges Bataille comments, 'it could even be that *literature* already has fundamentally the same meaning as silence, but it recoils before the last step that would constitute silence'.[12]

The analogies between Auster's *New York Trilogy* and Beckett's *Trilogy* are not as immediately apparent as the parallels between *Ghosts* and *Walden*, for example. However, both Arthur Saltzman and Steven Connor have drawn attention to them, although only the former has attempted to examine the relation between the two works.[13] Although both writers call their works trilogies, they both subvert the notion of the traditional trilogy. Where one would expect a gradual dénouement, a movement towards closure and resolution, both trilogies begin as quest narratives which are soon sabotaged; each new narrative seems to multiply the questions raised and reveal more angles, more ways of looking at

11. Samuel Beckett, *The Beckett Trilogy: Molloy, Malone Dies, The Unnamable* (London: Picador, 1979), pp. 30–31. Subsequent references are to this edition, with page numbers given parenthetically. The three texts are abbreviated as follows: *Ml*: *Molloy*; *MD*: *Malone Dies*; *TU*: *The Unnamable*.

12. Georges Bataille, 'La Vérité dont nous sommes malades', in *Les Critiques de notre temps et Beckett*, ed. Dominique Nores (Paris: Garnier, 1971), p. 45.

13. Connor, *The English Novel in History 1950–1995*. Saltzman, *Designs of Darkness*.

the same problems, more complications. Furthermore, the narratives in both trilogies are only loosely connected; if characters reappear, or situations are repeated, they seem more like fragments of a dream, vague and half-remembered. *City of Glass* is, like *Molloy*, a quest narrative, a distorted detective story. In both cases, what starts as a quest for another person turns out to be a search for one's own identity; the theme of the double, present in both narratives, underscores the increasing uncertainty of the two detectives concerning their own sense of self, while the fact that they both write reports about their undertaking raises the more complex issue of the search for one's identity in writing.

Ghosts marks a shift from movement to stasis in the trilogy: whereas Stillman and Quinn wander the streets of New York, Blue and Black sit in their rooms and look at each other through their windows. Similarly, whereas both Molloy and Moran sit in their rooms and write about their wanderings in the countryside, Malone sits in a room and writes about sitting in a room and waiting to die. 'While waiting I shall tell myself stories', he writes (*MD* 165). As for Blue, he 'now begins to advance certain theories. More than just helping to pass the time, he discovers that making up stories can be a pleasure in itself' (*Gh* 144). At the same time, he begins to experience a paralysis of the will, not unlike Malone's physical deterioration: 'This, too, is troubling him, for he cannot remember a time in his life when he has been so reluctant to do a thing he so clearly wants to do. I'm changing, he says to himself. Little by little, I'm no longer the same' (*Gh* 145–46).

The Locked Room is the final part of *The New York Trilogy*, and yet the narrative does not come nearer to any kind of solution. The enigmatic Fanshawe and his mysterious disappearance only create yet another riddle, another question that the anonymous narrator will puzzle over but will be unable to understand and explain. As the narrator searches for his lost friend, he has trouble distinguishing himself from him. When he feels tempted to usurp Fanshawe's identity, does he realise that this would be an act that would transform the story's narrator into a vanished writer? The Unnamable claims authorship of *Molloy* and *Malone Dies*, as well as nearly everything else that Beckett has written. A more modest authorial intervention takes place in *The Locked Room* when it is admitted that 'the three stories are finally the same story' (*LR* 294). When the narrator tears up the vanished author's notebook page by page, bringing the trilogy to its close, his action recalls the Unnamable's question: 'Is not this rather the place where one finishes vanishing?' (*TU* 269).

It is doubtful that Auster modelled his entire trilogy on Beckett's. Despite the analogies I have just outlined, there is not a strict one-to-one correspondence between each of the parts in the two works, although Beckett's presence is strongly felt throughout *The New York Trilogy*. Arthur Saltzman writes of *City of Glass*:

> The case itself is a protracted version of the anxious queries of Beckett's Unnamable: 'where now? who now?'... The absurd dance of detective and detected in *City of Glass* parallels that of Beckett's *Molloy*, in which Moran is first professionally, then psychologically, and finally physically absorbed by Molloy. As his mission disintegrates into arbitrariness, Moran learns that coming too close to Molloy (like Stillman, a sort of walking lacuna) exiles him from the brisk certainties of selfhood, and this enterprise leaves such 'deep lesions' in his identity that he becomes unrecognizable to himself outside of his imitations of the actions and eccentricities of the man he is merging into. [14]

Daniel Quinn undergoes a multiple identity crisis in the course of the narrative. He publishes detective novels under the pseudonym William Wilson, and his fictional detective is called Max Work. Quinn has a complicated relationship with these personae: 'Over the years, Work had become very close to Quinn. Whereas William Wilson remained an abstract figure for him, Work had increasingly come to life. In the triad of selves that Quinn had become, Wilson served as a kind of ventriloquist. Quinn himself was the dummy, and Work was the animated voice that gave purpose to the enterprise. If Wilson was an illusion, he nevertheless justified the lives of the other two' (*CG* 6). However, there is more than a triad of selves at play here. William Wilson's name, by recalling Poe's story of the double, implies further fragmentation, both intra- and intertextual. No less deliberate a choice, the name Work connotes not only the active agent in Quinn's detective stories, but also the notion of the literary work. Quinn, the supposed author of Work, becomes a dead medium through which the voice of the work may be heard. But this is a voice that readers of *City of Glass* do not hear, since Quinn's novels are both inside the text and absent from it. This dizzying *mise-en-abîme* widens to include other ontological spheres as the narrative progresses. Not content with his triad of selves, Quinn also takes on the identity of one Paul Auster, a supposed detective who is really a writer. When he meets Peter Stillman, he introduces himself as Daniel Quinn, but also as Henry Dark and Peter Stillman, Jr. This profusion of confused identities leads him to write in his notebook:

> And then, most important of all: to remember who I am. To remember who I am supposed to be. I do not think this is a game. On the other hand, nothing

14. Saltzman, *Designs of Darkness*, pp. 58–59.

is clear. For example, who are you? And if you think you know, why do you keep lying about it? I have no answer. All I can say is this: listen to me. My name is Paul Auster. This is not my real name. (*CG* 40)

The preoccupation with words and naming permeates Beckett's trilogy. It evokes only to shatter the dream of objective unity, and it serves as a constant reminder of the linguistic and textual prison Beckett's characters are trapped in. Quinn's identity crisis is precipitated by his adoption of a series of aliases, while in *Molloy* characters also seek – and often fail – to define themselves through naming: 'My name is Moran, Jacques. This is the name I am known by. I am done for. My son too. All unsuspecting... His name is Jacques, like mine. This cannot lead to confusion' (*Ml* 85). The two Stillmans in *City of Glass* also share the same name. Stillman Jr tells Quinn:

> I am Peter Stillman. I say this of my own free will. Yes. That is not my real name. No... For thirteen years the father was away. His name is Peter Still- man too. Strange, is it not? That two people can have the same name? I do not know if that is his real name. But I do not think he is me. We are both Peter Stillman. But Peter Stillman is not my real name. So perhaps I am not Peter Stillman, after all. (*CG* 15, 18)

Peter is the man who should be speaking the language of Adam, but as Romantic notions of organic unity are seen to collapse, he is left only with the notion that this is how things should be. In Peter's damaged world, there is no distinction between name and identity: because he does not know his 'real name', he is unsure of his own identity. He has the assumptions and aspirations but none of the powers of the poetic genius that his father, and Emerson before him, had dreamed of. This evocation of a Romantic past, coupled with the creation of a literary trope that parodies it, can be found in Beckett as well as in Auster. Sylvie Debevec Henning discerns in Beckett a desire for subjective oneness, which is constantly challenged: 'Romantic aspects do exist in Beckett and constitute a definite tendency perceptible in both his critical essays and his literary work. His subjects... often retreat into solitary chambers to savor solipsistic pleasures and sorrows. Another tendency exists, how- ever, and counters the first with parody and irony.'[15] Quinn, Blue and Fanshawe all retreat to solitary chambers but fail to reach the hoped-for revelation. Malone is another character who retires to his room and

---

15. Sylvie Debevec Henning, *Beckett's Critical Complicity: Carnival, Contestation, and Tradition* (Lexington: University of Kentucky Press, 1988), p. 2.

delivers a long, self-questioning monologue. Early in his narrative, though, he shatters any illusions of transcendence: 'What matters is to eat and excrete. Dish and pot, dish and pot, these are the poles' (*MD* 170). A similar incident of disillusionment is related in *Ghosts*, when Black tells the story of how Thoreau and Bronson Alcott went to visit Whitman, who welcomed them with a full chamber pot right in the middle of his room: 'the two New Englanders found it hard to keep talking with a bucket of excrement in front of them' (*Gh* 175).

Young Peter Stillman is the character who best embodies Auster's mistrust of Romantic theories of language and the self. His story, as he tells it to Quinn, may be described using the Unnamable's words: a story dominated 'by affirmations and negations invalidated as uttered, or sooner or later? Generally speaking. There must be other shifts. Otherwise it would be quite hopeless. But it is quite hopeless' (*TU* 267). Like Beckett's narrating voices, Peter's voice is obsessive, self-questioning and self-negating:

> I am Peter Stillman... Yes. That is not my real name. No. Of course, my mind is not all it should be. But nothing can be done about that. No...You sit here and think: who is this person talking to me? What are these words coming from his mouth? I will tell you. Or else I will not tell you. Yes and no... This is what is called speaking. I believe that is the term. When words come out, fly into the air, live for a moment, and die. Strange, is it not?... I am the last of the Stillmans... There are no others. I am the end of everyone, the last man. So much the better, I think. (*CG* 15–19)

Stillman *père* wanted his son to be Adam, but instead he turned him into the last of the Stillmans: 'The poet, who is the first man to be born, is also the last. He is Adam, but he is also the end of all generations: the mute heir of the builders of Babel' (*AH* 35). Peter, for nine years literally, and then only figuratively, lives in the prison house of language. The question that is being asked here is whether the self can be separated from its representation in language, whether thought exists outside words. The self can only be defined in language, but this imposes the restriction of speaking in a shared code which by definition excludes the possibility of talking about the self. Ross Chambers identifies this dilemma as Beckett's main concern in *The Unnamable*:

> In order to speak the language of the 'I', [the Unnamable] would have to invent a new language, outside time and space. But while waiting, not knowing any words other than the useless words of a common language, it can only bait itself, accomplishing its 'pensum', its absurd but inevitable

task, condemned to name itself in a language which has no words for it, and condemned never to cease its attempts until it wins, and so condemned to an eternal *wordy-gurdy* from which it is impossible to escape.[16]

In *The Unnamable*, and in *City of Glass*, this dilemma is rehearsed as soliloquy, but in *Ghosts* it is dramatised in the split selves of Blue and Black who watch each other and take notes. Black tells Blue:

> No, Blue, I've needed you from the beginning. If it hadn't been for you, I couldn't have done it.
> Needed me for what?
> To remind myself of what I was supposed to be doing. Every time I looked up, you were there, watching me, following me, always in sight, boring into me with your eyes. You were the whole world to me, Blue, and I turned you into my death. You're the one thing that doesn't change, the one thing that turns everything inside out. (*Gh* 194)

'Thus the world reveals itself as theatre where the other does not exist for me except in *representation*, where I am not myself except by the role imposed upon me by the other's gaze.'[17] Black's words imply that subject and object cannot coincide in language. The moment the self is uttered, it loses its selfhood, it becomes other. As Blue finds out 'to enter Black, then, was the equivalent of entering himself... Just look at him, Blue says to himself. He's the saddest creature in the world. And then, the moment he says these words, he understands that he's also talking about himself' (*Gh* 190–91). Similarly, Moran, who writes a report of his quest for Molloy, ends up wondering whether the latter exists at all. Beckett identifies this dichotomy as a central concern in Proust: 'Nor is any direct and purely experimental contact possible between subject and object, because they are automatically separated by the subject's consciousness of perception, and the object loses its purity and becomes a mere intellectual pretext or motive.'[18] This, however, is not only a problem concerning language. Beckett is also referring to the philosophical problem of (self-)consciousness, which is an epistemological matter. Malone, whose voice is also the text, brings the two problems together when he says: 'I wonder if I am not talking yet again

16. Ross Chambers, 'Destruction des catégories du temps', in *Les Critiques de notre temps et Beckett*, ed. Nores, pp. 96–97.
17. Valéry Hugotte, 'Paul Auster ou l'art de la fugue', *Esprit*, 10 (1994), p. 43. I shall return to the question of the spectator (or reader) as witness in 'A Hunger Artist'.
18. Samuel Beckett, *Proust and Three Dialogues* (1931; London: Calder and Boyars, 1965), p. 74. Auster quotes Beckett's essay on Proust in 'The Book of Memory' (*IoS* 138).

about myself. Shall I be incapable, to the end, of lying on any other subject?' (MD 174).

The New York Trilogy, like Beckett's *Trilogy*, charts an epistemological enquiry that cannot be separated from questions of identity and language. *City of Glass* relies heavily on the conventions of the detective novel, and *Molloy* retains a few elements from the genre in the character of Moran. Both narratives chronicle the investigators' initial mistrust of, and eventual loss of faith in, patterns, discerned or imposed. When Quinn agrees to take the job offered by Virginia Stillman, he sees himself as a detective, and tries to think and act like his fictional hero, Max Work. Soon, however, he realises that the conventions he has been employing in his writing do not apply to his own world. When he goes to the railway station to wait for Stillman, he sees two men who could be the person he is supposed to tail. He realises that there is no way of knowing which one to follow, and his decision is based on impulse rather than reasoning. The process of disillusionment starts here, as Quinn realises that 'there was no way to know: not this, not anything' (CG 56). In the second part of *Molloy*, Moran's narrative reveals him initially as a methodical, meticulous man who trusts his own reasoning powers. However, during his quest for Molloy, he will also lose his faith in patterns and their ability to convey meaning, and he will learn to question the possibility of signification. On his way back home after his unaccomplished mission, during which he seems to have reached a new level of self-awareness, Moran thinks of his bees, whose dance he had always observed and attempted to explain. After trying out various theories, he came to understand that none of them could really explain the bees' dance:

> And I said, with rapture, Here is something I can study all my life, and never understand. And all during this long journey home, when I racked my mind for a little joy in store, the thought of my bees and their dance was the nearest thing to comfort. For I was still eager for my little joy, from time to time! And I admitted with good grace the possibility that this dance was after all no better than the dances of the people of the West, frivolous and meaningless. (Ml 156)

Moran, like his creator, knows that there is comfort to be found in the belief that the world does convey meaning, and that the patterns he observes are not random and meaningless. Equally, however, he experiences joy at the recognition of non-signification, the admission of randomness and chaos. Similarly, when Quinn is confronted with the apparently aimless pattern of Stillman's daily walks, he is desperate to believe that they are not meaningless: 'How much better it was to believe that all his steps were actually to some purpose' (*CG* 61). After their failed quests, both characters paradoxically reach a new level of self-knowledge. Moran says that he no longer recognises his face, but feels he has a clearer sense of his identity than ever before (*Ml* 156), while Quinn forgets his case, gives up trying to make sense and solve the mystery, and learns to accept even the invisible helper who brings him food in his empty room. If their creators allow these characters a brief respite from their gropings in the dark, they do so only to the extent that this justifies their own writing. The patterns that Moran and Quinn are confronted with *are* the meaning, just as the texts the two writers produce are the only possible answer to the questions they raise. Beckett's words on Joyce seem apt here: 'Here is the savage economy of hieroglyphics.'[19]

Malone experiences a similar moment of joy in his narrative when he manages to retrieve his notebook, which has fallen to the ground:

> And I rejoiced... at the thought that I now knew what I had to do, I whose every move had always been a groping... And here again naturally I was utterly deceived, I mean in imagining I had grasped at last the true nature of my absurd tribulations, but not so utterly as to feel the need to reproach myself with it now. For even as I said, How easy and beautiful it all is!, in the same breath I said, All will grow dark again. (*MD* 206)

And it will, indeed, grow dark again because Malone 'depends for his existence on the act of narration'.[20] But Malone exists both as narrating self and as narrated self, and in his latter capacity he depends on the author who writes him, and the text he is written into. This emphasis on the textuality of the narrative can also be seen in *City of Glass*. Towards the end of the book, when he writes in the Stillman apartment, Quinn begins to wonder what will happen when his red notebook runs out of paper. 'The last sentence of the red notebook reads: "What will happen when there are no more pages in the red notebook?"' (*CG* 131). Quinn only exists as long as the words he writes exist, and when he does run out of paper he simply disappears from the page himself. Malone translates himself into text, and as he does so his pencil grows smaller: 'my little pencil dwindles, inevitably, and the day is fast approaching when nothing

---

19. Beckett uses the phrase to describe *Finnegans Wake* in *Our Exagmination Round His Factification for Incamination of Work in Progress* (1931). Quoted in Ihab Hassan, *The Literature of Silence: Henry Miller and Samuel Beckett* (New York: Alfred Knopf, 1967), p. 121.
20. Hassan, *The Literature of Silence*, p. 161.

will remain but a fragment too tiny to hold' (*MD* 204). The characters who write in their notebooks have an identity not only as long as they write but also as long as they are being written by their creators. When Malone loses his pencil, he has to stop writing for two days, of which, he thinks, 'nothing will ever be known' (*MD* 204). But what Malone's fictional status prevents him from knowing is that these are not so much days of which nothing will be known as days which never were.

The complicated relationship between author and character, between text and voice, leads both trilogies to their inconclusive endings. Although indeterminacy is what they have in common, their differences are no less pronounced. *The New York Trilogy* ends with the disappearance but not the death of the writer Fanshawe. The narrator reads his friend's notebook and finds that, as in the narrative of *The Unnamable*, 'each sentence erased the sentence before it, each paragraph made the next paragraph impossible' (*LR* 314). But this is how Auster effects his recovery: the actual *text* of that notebook is absent from the narrative, replaced here by the narrator's comment that Fanshawe 'had answered the question by asking another question, and therefore everything remained open, unfinished, to be started again' (*LR* 314). Auster, who at first could not see his way beyond Beckett, has now found a way out: Beckett has been written into his text, but he has been placed in a larger framework. Haunting *The New York Trilogy* with its conspicuous absence, Beckett's *Trilogy* is made to produce signification, even if it cannot provide answers.

Recovery, for Beckett, can only be situated, if at all, outside the text. The Unnamable hovers between the states of being and non-being throughout, its voice persisting, trying to revise the fragments of its previous existence as it is seen to negate them, and uttering its famous last words: 'I can't go on, I'll go on' (*TU* 382). 'Beckett has not put aside his obligation to keep trying the art of the impossible', Ihab Hassan writes. Asked why he continued to write when he had lost faith in the ability of language to convey meaning, Beckett replied: 'Que voulez-vous, Monsieur? C'est les mots; on n'a rien d'autre.'[21] Words are all that remain for Anna Blume, the narrator-protagonist of *In the Country of Last Things*. As her body starves, and her narrative is threatened, her task is to translate her being into text in order to survive. As her narrative becomes an effort to preserve words before they disappear along with the objects they were once attached to, the text itself sustains her and ensures her continuing existence.

21. Hassan, *The Literature of Silence*, pp. 137–38.

A Hunger Artist

An article in the *Magazine Littéraire* offers ten key words which could be used to describe Auster's *œuvre*. The headings read: *the fall, America, the father, Brooklyn, the room, the frontier, man without God, coincidence, inheritance, the wall*.[22] Paul Auster would not be displeased with the ten key words; after all, he has remarked that all his books are really the same book, 'the story of my obsessions… the saga of the things that haunt me' (*AH* 285). Although his novels display a remarkable diversity concerning the genres he works with, the characters he creates and the stories he tells, there are certain themes that inform his entire *œuvre*. Lists are important as much for what they exclude as for what they include, and this one has one grave omission: the theme of hunger, which runs throughout Auster's writing. In *City of Glass*, Quinn leaves his apartment and goes to live in a dustbin, the better to watch the man he is supposed to protect; as he has to keep watch twenty-four hours a day, he learns to live on the minimum amount of food, barely keeping himself alive. In *In the Country of Last Things*, there is a food shortage in the entire city, and those people who do not die of starvation are reduced to talking about food, the description of long, elaborate meals being the closest they can get to nourishment. Marco Stanley Fogg, the protagonist of *Moon Palace*, is an impoverished student who survives on next to nothing and nearly dies of exhaustion and starvation, until he is rescued by his friends. Jim Nashe in *The Music of Chance* does not go hungry, but he does manage to eat away the entire inheritance left by his father, thus ending up imprisoned in the Stone and Flower mansion. These images of starvation are used for various purposes. They may underscore the protagonists' moral or psychological degradation, or they may be used for social critique, while they also function as metaphorical or metafictional elements reflecting the author's views concerning language and narrative.

Starvation becomes a major theme in Auster's 1988 novel *In the Country of Last Things*. The book comes to the reader in the form of a long letter written by the protagonist, Anna Blume, who has gone to an unnamed metropolis in search of her missing journalist brother. Her search proves futile, and as she realises that there is no escape from this nightmarish city, her letter chronicles her struggle for survival and her attempts to retain her humanity while adjusting to her new circumstances. The country of last things is a city in a state of terminal decay. All services

22. Gérard de Cortanze, 'Les Romans en dix mots-clés', *Magazine Littéraire*, 338 (December 1995), pp. 43–48.

have been disrupted, people live in extreme poverty, and the city appears to be run by opportunists, black marketeers and ruthless officials. Most inhabitants live as scavengers and sleep rough, while mass suicide has become a familiar phenomenon. Anna's journal/letter becomes not only a document of this desolation, but also a means of survival, a way of maintaining her humanity amidst the corruption of every value she grew up with. Paul Auster is eager to emphasise that this is not a futuristic novel:

> I feel that it's very much a book about our own moment, our own era, and many of the incidents are things that have actually happened... Admittedly, the book takes on these things from a somewhat oblique angle, and the country Anna goes to might not be immediately recognizable, but I feel that this is where we live. It could be that we've become so accustomed to it that we no longer see it. (*AH* 275)

The working title of the novel was *Anna Blume Walks Through the Twentieth Century* and many scenes in the book do, indeed, recall some of the more horrific events in recent Western history. In this context, and considering Auster's Jewish identity, the theme of hunger is first of all used as a realistic theme. It is the hunger of the people in the ghettos, in concentration camps, in cities under siege or occupation. Anna's depiction of the country of last things is especially reminiscent of life in the Warsaw ghetto; various critics have drawn this parallel, and the incident of Anna's encounter with the Jews who are hiding in the library reinforces the connection. Like the ghetto, this city has guarded exits, and a wall is being built around it, the 'Sea Wall Project'. People cannot leave, but new ones are always coming in: 'People die, and babies refuse to be born... And yet, there are always new people to replace the ones who have vanished. They pour in from the country and the outlying towns, dragging carts piled high with their belongings... all of them hungry, all of them homeless' (*CLT* 7). Toshia Bialer, an eyewitness of the transfer of the Jews to the ghetto, described the following scene: 'Try to picture one third of a large city's population moving through the streets in an endless stream, pushing, wheeling, dragging all their belongings... Pushcarts were about the only method of conveyance we had.' [23] The dead of the

---

23. Abraham Lewin, *A Cup of Tears: A Diary of the Warsaw Ghetto*, trans. Christopher Hutton, ed. Antony Polonsky (Oxford: Blackwell, 1988), p. 6. I have also consulted Yisrael Gutman, *The Jews of Warsaw 1939–1943*, trans. Ina Friedman (Brighton: Harvester, 1982), and Rotem Simha, *Memoirs of a Warsaw Ghetto Fighter*, trans. and ed. Barbara Harshav (New Haven and London: Yale University Press, 1994). Auster himself quotes Israel Lichtenstein's 'Last Testament from the Warsaw Ghetto' (*IoS* 83–84).

country of last things are stripped naked by scavengers if they die in the streets, and the corpses are taken to crematoria, also known as Transformation Centers. Disposing of these corpses is the most important task of the government in a city so over-populated. Overpopulation was a big problem in the Warsaw ghetto, where one third of the city's inhabitants were crammed into 2.4 per cent of the area of Warsaw. In Auster's city 'there is no such thing as a vacancy' (*CLT* 8), and people not only live but also die in the streets. The worst problem, however, in this imaginary city as in the ghetto, is hunger. Food was rationed in the ghetto, allowing people a mere 184 calories' worth of food a day, a situation which led to smuggling, and ultimately to the death from malnutrition of more than 65,000 Jews in the space of sixteen months. In the country that Anna goes to 'People are so thin… they are sometimes blown away' (*CLT* 3); food shortages are frequent, and there are many 'private sellers' who bribe the police in order to sell food outside the 'municipal markets'.

The fact that the novel is written in the form of a diary, coupled with the protagonist's name, inevitably invites the reader to draw analogies with Anne Frank's diary, a book which Auster admits has 'meant a lot' to him.[24] The diary form gives the novel an air of authenticity, the appearance of a first-hand account of events that 'really occurred', but always inevitably filtered through the personality of the diarist, his or her interpretation of, and reaction to, events. Life in the Warsaw ghetto, for example, is well documented, mainly thanks to the efforts of the historian Emmanuel Ringelblum who created a secret archive while there, but also through the private diaries of many of the inhabitants; as Ringelblum himself observed, 'everyone wrote' in the ghetto. Among those diarists was Chaim Kaplan who, before being transported to his death in Treblinka, wrote one last entry in his diary: 'If I die – what will become of my diary?' – a question that lends a wholly different perspective to the textual anxieties of Quinn or Malone. By using the diary form, Auster creates a text which merges the theme of survival with the formalist questions his writing addresses; the diary here becomes not only personal testimony or a record of survival, but also a means of survival.

Although it has already been mentioned that many of Auster's protagonists starve themselves at some point in the story, Anna Blume is in one significant way different from them. Unlike Quinn, Blue, the narrator of *The Locked Room,* or Nashe, she does not choose to undergo hardship;

---

24. Del Rey, 'Paul Auster: Al compas de un ritmo pendular', p. 26. ('Ese es un libro que ha significaso mucho para mi.')

Anna is a victim of circumstances. Where the other books focus on the male protagonists' self-destructive propensities, this one concentrates on the way Anna learns to cope with the grim reality around her. The reiteration of motifs familiar from this book's predecessor, *The New York Trilogy*, takes the 'games of inner brinkmanship', as Auster describes them, and places them in a world where they are also externalised as the forces of history. However, Auster considers this novel to be an optimistic one; as he points out, the anonymous narrator who introduces the story and appears two or three times in the course of the narrative is used as a device aimed at showing that Anna's letter 'somehow or other' reached its destination (*AH* 311). The stress, in other words, is placed on recovery, symbolised here by the letter reaching its recipient.

In his depiction of a city in ruin, Auster offers a critique of Western civilisation. This country of last things is what remains of the affluent society; the junk, the crumbling buildings, the vanishing words all create a sterile urban landscape which is the result of hundreds of years of civilisation. In this context, starvation is the result of consumerism and its excesses. But it becomes itself a kind of excess, an excess of want, of need. The breakdown of the social fibre in this country is followed by moral collapse; the hungry city-dwellers do not hesitate to steal, kill, rob the dead. In the frightening scene where Anna is lured into a butcher's shop, she learns that even people have become a commodity, reduced to pieces of meat to be sold in the black market. Auster says that this is based on a true story which took place during the siege of Leningrad, while the garbage collection system is based on the real system used in Cairo (*AH* 314–15). But as in all his books, Auster approaches the real by way of the invented, offering a stylised narrative, a text which is as concerned with its own mode of production as it is with its relation to the 'real'. The city where Anna lives is not only a collage of actual cities, but also a version of the city as it appears in Auster's other novels. In a passage reminiscent of *City of Glass*, Anna writes: 'That is what the city does to you. It turns your thoughts inside out' (*CLT* 2). However, whereas Quinn cherishes the opportunity to forget his troubles by being lost in the streets, and learns much later, to his own cost, that the city is a confusing site of shifting signifiers, Anna knows from the outset that she is exposed to danger: 'In the city, the best approach is to believe only what your own eyes tell you. But not even that is infallible. For few things are ever what they seem to be, especially here, with so much to absorb at every step, with so many things that defy understanding' (*CLT* 18–19).

Like Peter Stillman, Anna becomes a scavenger, but she does not share his aspirations:

> As an object hunter, you must rescue things before they reach this state of absolute decay. You can never expect to find something whole – for that is an accident, a mistake on the part of the person who lost it – but neither can you spend your time looking for what is totally used up. You hover somewhere in between, on the lookout for things that still retain a semblance of their original shape – even if their usefulness is gone. (*CLT* 36)

Anna rescues things by writing her letter/journal. She accepts the 'brokenness', and puts things back together not by inventing a new language for them, but by turning them into the text of testimony. 'It's not just that things vanish,' she writes, 'but once they vanish, the memory of them vanishes as well' (*CLT* 87). As the country of last things threatens to become a place of wordless things and thingless words, the pressure mounts for Anna to preserve not only the words but her own identity, which is constructed through words, through voice:

> It is a slow but ineluctable process of erasure. Words tend to last a bit longer than things, but eventually they fade too, along with the pictures they once evoked. Entire categories of objects disappear... and for a time you will be able to recognize those words, even if you cannot recall what they mean. But then, little by little, the words become only sounds, a random collection of glottals and fricatives, a storm of whirling phonemes, and finally the whole thing just collapses into gibberish. (*CLT* 89)

But if Auster, through Anna, diagnoses this breakdown, he does not renounce the possibility of signification. Rather, he questions its availability in any form other than the collection of fragments that keep his protagonist alive, and the words that make up her textual identity. When Anna takes refuge in the National Library she finds out that, although there are hundreds of thousands of volumes in it, the system of classification has been disrupted: 'When you consider that there were seven floors of stacks, to say that a book was in the wrong place was as much as to say that it had ceased to exist. Even though it might have been physically present in the building, the fact was that no one would ever find it again' (*CLT* 115). It is against such odds that Auster's narrators and characters have to struggle, but occasionally there is a breakthrough which saves them from the threat of extinction.

The country of last things is a land ridden with paradox. Some of its inhabitants experience happiness while they are waiting to die in the Euthanasia Clinics. Others join the Assassination Clubs which promise 'a quick and violent death in the not-too-distant future', and while waiting for their assassination they are 'filled with a sense of life' (*CLT* 15). Scavengers need a cart to collect rubbish, but they can only afford one if they have collected enough garbage. Among the semi-allegorical trials that the inhabitants have to endure, hunger is the hardest. *In the Country of Last Things* takes its epigraph from Hawthorne: 'Not a great while ago, passing through the gate of dreams, I visited that region of the earth in which lies the famous City of Destruction.' This quote is taken from 'The Celestial Rail-Road' (1843), a story which ostensibly takes the form of a latter-day *Pilgrim's Progress*, but, as is often the case in Hawthorne, never quite assumes the allegorical qualities normally associated with the genre.[25] Once again, by inviting comparisons with Hawthorne's work, Auster asks that his story be read within a certain context, but by using the ambiguous work of his predecessor he is also renouncing the very authority he appears to invoke. The allegorical overtones of *In the Country of Last Things* do not require an authorial intervention in order to be identified, but by drawing attention to their nature, which owes as much to Kafka as it does to Hawthorne, Auster makes visible his effort to insert himself into a literary continuum and at the same time to shift the centre away from the author as originator towards a wider intertext and a reminder of the fact that he is aware of the fictionality of his work. Hunger, as I shall argue, is both an intertextual event and a metafictional device.

Auster's 1992 essay collection is appropriately called *The Art of Hunger*. The title derives from his essay on Knut Hamsun's novel *Hunger*, while there is the obvious allusion to Kafka, who is also examined in this volume. In one of his very first essays, written in 1970, when he was a young man of 22 who had not started writing prose, Auster reads *Hunger* as a novel that marks the beginning of modernity:

> It is a work devoid of plot, action, and – but for the narrator – character. By nineteenth-century standards, it is a work in which nothing happens. The radical subjectivity of the narrator effectively eliminates the basic concerns of the traditional novel... Historical time is obliterated in favor of inner duration. With only an arbitrary beginning and an arbitrary ending, the novel faithfully records the vagaries of the narrator's mind, following each thought from its mysterious inception through all its meanderings, until it dissipates and the next thought begins. (*AH* 10)

25. In it, Hawthorne also continues his satire of Emerson and his disciples with the figure of the German-born 'Giant Transcendentalist' who lives in the cave previously occupied by Pope and Pagan in *Pilgrim's Progress*.

In this short description, Auster identifies some of the major concerns and techniques of the modernist novel. Starvation is the theme of Hamsun's novel, but it is also an image of the stripping-down of traditional realist convention. However, literary innovation by definition belongs to a limited period of time. Auster's own books are often more traditional in that they respect certain narrative conventions for which a writer such as Hamsun shows total disrespect, but what survives in Auster's own fiction is the way in which his chosen themes are inextricably linked with his narrative strategies.

Hunger chronicles the struggles of a young man who chooses to starve and yet wants to remain alive: 'He goes hungry, not because he has to, but from some inner compulsion, as if to wage hunger strike against himself... His fast is... a contradiction. To persist in it would mean death, and with death the fast would end. He must therefore stay alive, but only to the extent that it keeps him on the point of death' (*AH* 13). Most of Auster's male protagonists wage hunger strike against themselves like Hamsun's (anti-)hero. Each in his own different way denies himself what was once thought necessary or held dear. Their self-destructive propensities, however, do not amount to a desire for annihilation. The paradox that Auster sees in *Hunger* is one that can be found in his own work where in their self-denial, and their attempts to go on when they can't go on, his characters test the limits of their own individuality. To hunger voluntarily is also to seek to define the boundaries that separate self and other and this, too, is a paradox: 'you don't begin to understand your connection to others until you are alone, the more deeply you plunge into a state of solitude, the more deeply you feel that connection... In other words, we learn our solitude from others. In the same way that we learn language from others' (*AH* 308–309). In one short sentence, Auster links the paradoxical nature of solitude and identity with language. Similarly, when he writes of *Hunger* that 'the idea of ending is resisted in the interests of maintaining the constant possibility of the end' (*AH* 13), he is referring not only to the hero's predicament, but also to the writer's. He reads this process of deferral and displacement in *Hunger*:

> Something new is happening here, some new thought about the nature of art is being proposed in *Hunger*. It is first of all an art that is indistinguishable from the life of the artist who makes it. That is not to say an art of autobiographical excess, but rather, an art that is the direct expression of the effort to express itself. In other words, an art of hunger: an art of need, of necessity, of desire... It is an art that begins with the knowledge that there are no right answers. For that reason, it becomes essential to ask the right

questions. One finds them by living them. To quote Samuel Beckett: 'What I am saying does not mean that there will henceforth be no form in art. It only means that there will be a new form, and that this form will be of such a type that it admits the chaos and does not try to say that the chaos is really something else... To find a form that accommodates the mess, that is the task of the artist now.' (*AH* 18–19)

Of Beckett's own work, he writes: 'The key word in all this, I feel, is dispossession. Beckett, who begins with little, ends with even less. The movement in each of his works is toward a kind of unburdening, by which he leads us to the limits of experience – to a place where aesthetic and moral judgements become inseparable' (*AH* 87). Paradoxically, Beckett chose to 'accommodate the mess' in ever-diminishing or collapsing structures, until he reached a form of extreme poverty and irreducible minimalism in his later works, stopping just one step before silence. Although it never assumes Beckettian proportions, the idea of narrative starvation, of textual asceticism, is one that Auster employs in *In the Country of Last Things*.

Auster concludes his essay on Hamsun by drawing parallels with Kafka's 'A Hunger Artist', another powerful modernist text which deals with hunger. Kafka's tale is written in a simple, almost child-like manner reminiscent of fairy-tale narratives, and the innocence and clarity of the narrating voice create throughout a tone that is amusing and terrifying at the same time. It is, again, a story devoid of plot and action and, like *Hunger*, it is, rather, a story about inaction. The hunger artist is a circus freak displayed in a cage, and the crowds come to observe him and marvel at what he does not do. Kafka teases his readers with nods towards a possible allegorical meaning, using strong religious overtones, but in the end he mocks the very desire for signification: just before he dies, the hunger artist admits that the only reason he would not eat was because he could not find the food he liked. With this anti-epiphanic revelation, the writer refuses to give meaning to his stories, unless the only meaning is the realisation that there is no meaning, like the hunger artist's starvation which signifies nothing but itself and its own lack of purpose. Fasting is often associated with the desire for spiritual purification, and in the character of the hunger artist Kafka mocks this desire for transcendence, or the belief that it can be found in fiction. There is one aspect of Kafka's story which is especially relevant to Auster's project: there are watchers appointed by the public to oversee the artist's fast and to make sure he does not eat in secret (and, in deadpan style, we are told that these are 'usually butchers, strangely enough'). However, even they cannot keep watch all the time, so that the artist is 'bound to be the sole completely satisfied spectator of his own fast'.[26] This is a paradox because, at the same time, the possibility of being a hunger artist relies on the existence of spectators. 'The moral seems to be that it is not by food that we survive but by the gaze of others; and it is impossible to live by hunger unless we can be seen or represented doing so.'[27] An analogy with writing begins to emerge here: it is a solitary activity, but it also depends on the interaction with the reading public.[28] In the context of *In the Country of Last Things*, it is significant that, although Anna is essentially keeping a journal, she writes it in the form of a letter. The writer, at her most solitary, needs to imagine herself as other; the gesture implies an acknowledgment of the fact that even writing about oneself is an act of representation in which, inevitably, the self becomes other. The moment the self is articulated, it is mediated through the written word, and it ceases to be pure subject; representation is by its very nature alienating, and the moment something is conceived in words it becomes subject and object at the same time. Hence Auster's frequent quoting of Rimbaud's dictum 'je est un autre'. In Beckett's *Molloy*, the character Molloy, who undergoes a series of hardships that reduce him to a near invalid, keeps a supply of stones in his pockets which he frequently sucks. This gesture has attracted much interest and various interpretations from critics, which I shall not be concerned with here, but one thing it does recall is Rimbaud's hunger poems. In 'Fêtes de la faim' (1872), and again in 'Faim' (1873), another existential vagabond says: 'Si j'ai du goût, ce n'est guère/Que pour la terre et les pierres.'[29] Maud Ellmann reads this appetite as a metaphor for writing:

> To write, for Rimbaud, is to hunger, and it is only through a diet of stone-
> crop that the poet can accede to the inhuman solitude of art. This visionary
> hunger also resembles the miraculous abstinence of the medieval saints, for
> whom to fast was not to overcome the flesh so much as to explore the limits

26. Franz Kafka, 'A Hunger Artist', in *The Penal Colony: Stories and Short Pieces*, trans. Willa and Edwin Muir (New York: Schocken, 1961), pp. 244–46.
27. Maud Ellmann, *The Hunger Artists: Starving, Writing and Imprisonment* (London: Virago Press, 1993), p. 17.
28. Auster has also dealt with this issue in *Ghosts*, where Black tells Blue that he needed him, because he needed to be watched while he was writing.
29. Arthur Rimbaud, *Œuvres Complètes*, ed. Rolland de Reneville and Jules Mouquet (Paris: Pléiade, 1963). The standard translation for this is 'I only find within my bones a taste for eating earth and stones.' *Complete Works*, trans. Paul Schmidt (New York and London: Harper & Row, 1975).

of corporeality, where humanity surrenders to a bodiliness so extreme that it coalesces with the bestial or divine.[30]

As I shall argue, Auster also explores the limits of corporeality through Anna's hunger, but within a different context, one that is secular and primarily concerned with the nature of fiction writing: as Anna starves and her voice thrives, the subject becomes text.

Ellmann reads 'A Hunger Artist' in much the same way that Auster reads Hamsun's *Hunger*: 'As the hunger artist starves his flesh, so Kafka emaciates the prose, supplanting the fat novel of the nineteenth century with the skeletal apparatus of a writing machine.'[31] One only has to think of the works of Proust, Joyce, or Mann to realise that this is just one tendency in modernist writing, but it is, clearly, the one to which Auster is most attracted. This paring-down strategy that reveals both epistemological uncertainties and an increasing preoccupation with the form of the novel and its mode of production can be seen in Kafka and in Beckett (and later inherited in the works of the *nouveau romanciers*), and it is developed thematically in *In the Country of Last Things*. The difference, however, is that Auster does not inherit his precursors' anti-humanist tendencies. If physical starvation threatens his characters' lives, emotional starvation keeps them alive. If it is necessary for survival, it is in anticipation of a future of replenishment. When Sam and Anna are reunited, the former explains how he managed to survive away from the library and away from her:

> 'I gave up trying to be anyone,' he said. 'The object of my life was to remove myself from my surroundings, to live in a place where nothing could hurt me anymore. One by one, I tried to abandon my attachments, to let go of all the things I ever cared about. The idea was to achieve indifference, an indifference so powerful and sublime that it would protect me from further assault... To want nothing, I kept telling myself, to have nothing, to be nothing. I could imagine no more perfect solution than that. In the end, I came close to living the life of a stone.' (*CLT* 162–63)

Yet this is a temporary stage in his life; as soon as he is reunited with Anna, he regains his humanity, he is reborn. Auster describes the poetic process in similar terms: 'the poetic operation becomes a process whereby he [poet Jacques Dupin] unburdens himself of his garments, his tools, and his possessions, in order to assume, in nakedness, the fullness of being' (*AH* 180). In narrative terms, Auster in his own work associates

30. Ellmann, *The Hunger Artists*, p. 13.
31. *The Hunger Artists*, p. 66.

nakedness with fullness: 'I want my books to be all heart, all center, to
say what they have to say in as few words as possible' (*AH* 305).

In *City of Glass* narrative economy was the quality that appealed to
Quinn in detective novels:

> What he liked about these books was their sense of plenitude and economy.
> In the good mystery there is nothing wasted, no sentence, no word that is
> not significant... Everything becomes essence; the centre of the book shifts
> with each event that propels it forward. The centre, then, is everywhere, and
> no circumference can be drawn until the book has come to its end. (*CG* 8)

As I argued above, the same is true of fairy-tales, but whereas in those
narratives, as in the detective novel, paucity of discourse is a means of
investing every word with significance and sparseness is used to acceler-
ate the plot, in *In the Country of Last Things* the emphasis lies precisely
on the discourse, and the teller.

If Anna's narrative resembles a fairy-tale, the author reserves for her
the role of Scheherazade. Anna is writing under pressure: 'These are the
last things, she wrote. One by one they disappear and never come back.
I can tell you of the ones I have seen, of the ones that are no more, but I
doubt there will be time. It is all happening too fast now, and I cannot
keep up' (*CLT* 1). Like the narrator of *The Arabian Nights*, who has to
keep telling stories in order to survive, knowing that the end of her narration will be the end of her life, Anna has to write before it is too late.
Her physical existence may not be threatened inside her fictional world,
where her narrative becomes a means of survival, but when the journal
ends so does the novel. Anna Blume feels compelled to write before it is
too late; Effing dictates his obituary/autobiography from his deathbed;
Peter Aaron races against time to write his dead friend's story before the
police identify the body. This compulsion to write, the sense of urgency
which transforms writing into the sole means of survival, is one that
Brian McHale identifies as a trait of modernist writing. In *Postmodernist
Fiction* he writes:

> The modernist and late-modernist death-bed monologue not only continues
> and transforms the Victorian death-scene tradition, it also revives a much
> older *topos* of death and fiction, that of *les hommes-récits*, story-persons.
> The phrase is Tzvetan Todorov's; he is thinking of characters such as, clas-
> sically, Sheherazade, whose existence, inside as well as outside the fictional
> world, depends upon their continuing to tell stories. As long as she produces
> narrative discourses, Sheherazade lives; at the moment her discourse falters
> or stops, she will die. Here, quite graphically, life has been equated with

discourse, death with the end of discourse and silence. Essentially this is also the situation of the death-bed monologuists Ivan Ilych, Malone, Artemio Cruz, and the others: as long as the thread of their discourse continues to spin out, they are alive; at the moment this thread breaks, and they lapse into silence, they are dead.[32]

In McHale's formulation, speech is equated with life for the fictional characters he examines; in this it becomes the equivalent of eating in real life, where nutrition, the primary function of the mouth, is necessary for survival. Maud Ellmann points out that '[the] belief that words can take the place of food goes back as far as the Old Testament... where we are told that God humbled his people and suffered them to hunger so that they might know that "man doth not live by bread only, but by every *word* that proceedeth out of the mouth of the LORD doth man live". "If you follow this truth," Saint Catherine wrote, "you will have the life of grace and never die of hunger, for the Word has himself become your food."'[33] In a sense, the starving Anna is also given a new lease of life thanks to the word. Isabel, the woman who had rescued her from the hostile streets, eventually fell ill and lost her power of speech. Anna then bought her a notebook and some pencils so she could write down what she had to say, but Isabel died before she could use the notebook much:

> If I had not found these things in my bag the other day, I don't think I would have started writing to you. But there was the notebook with all those blank pages in it, and suddenly I felt an overwhelming urge to pick up one of the pencils and begin this letter. By now it is the one thing that matters to me: to have my say at last, to get it all down on these pages before it is too late. I tremble when I think how closely everything is connected. If Isabel had not lost her voice, none of these words would exist. Because she had no more words, these other words have come out of me. I want you to remember that. (*CLT* 79)

Anna is effectively nourished and kept alive by her own words, which in turn are inherited from, and thus can be said to feed on, someone else's words which have been lost to her.

The Art of Hunger contains an essay on the American writer Louis Wolfson in which Auster examines the link between food and speech. Wolfson was a schizophrenic who refused to speak, or even listen to, the English language. He would sometimes write in French, or invent a language of

---

32. Brian McHale, *Postmodernist Fiction* (London and New York: Routledge, 1987), p. 228.
33. Ellmann, *The Hunger Artists*, p. 22.

his own, using elements from French, German, and Hebrew. In his book *Le Schizo et les Langues*, Wolfson talks about what he calls his 'language disease', and he also records his obsession with food: even during his bulimic bouts, he takes care not to read the English labels on the food packages, and he makes sure that the food enters his mouth without first touching his lips, as this might expose him to contamination. Auster concludes: 'There is a fundamental connection between speaking and eating, and by the very excessiveness of Wolfson's experience, we are able to see how profound this relationship is. Speech is a strangeness, an anomaly, a biologically secondary function of the mouth, and myths about language are often linked to the idea of food' (*AH* 32–33). Connections between language and food can be found in Auster's writing, too. In *In the Country of Last Things*, Anna writes:

> Food, of course, is one of the favorite subjects. Often you will overhear a group of people describing a meal in meticulous detail, beginning with the soups and appetizers and slowly working their way to dessert, dwelling on each savor and spice, on all the various aromas and flavors, concentrating now on the method of preparation, now on the effect of the food itself, from the first twinge of taste on the tongue to the gradually expanding sense of peace as the food travels down the throat and arrives in the belly... If the words can consume you, you will be able to forget your present hunger and enter what people call the 'arena of the sustaining nimbus'. There are even those who say that there is a nutritional value in these food talks – given the proper concentration and an equal desire to believe in the words among those taking part. (*CLT* 9–10)

Here Auster takes McHale's proposition one step further, and considers the possibility of food and speech actually coinciding. As words become substitutes for food, representation replaces reality and becomes autonomous, self-referential. The blurring of the distinction between language and reality is also emphasised in the currency the inhabitants of the country of last things use, the glot. The glot is a minimal unit of language; money, like language, is meaningless in itself and only acquires meaning through transaction; they both work on the principle of deferral, but in the process they become detached from the thing they are supposed to stand for.

In *City of Glass*, Quinn also goes hungry, and this is what he finds out:

> Quinn learned that eating did not necessarily solve the problem of food. A meal was no more than a fragile defence against the inevitability of the next meal. Food itself could never answer the question of food: it only delayed the moment when the question would have to be asked in earnest. The

greatest danger, therefore, was in eating too much... His ambition was to eat as little as possible, and in this way to stave off his hunger. In the best of worlds, he might have been able to approach absolute zero, but he did not want to be overly ambitious in his present circumstances. Rather, he kept the total fast in his mind as an ideal, a state of perfection he could aspire to but never achieve. (CG 114)

In the light of Auster's own comments on the relation between food and language, this passage can be read as an expression of his views concerning the nature of language and writing. Just as food does not answer the question of food, language does not answer the question of language, since it is an autonomous, self-referential system. Like food, language works on the basis of deferral, and the linguistic equivalent of Quinn's desire to approach absolute zero would, of course, be silence. Silence is the ideal that Beckett strives to achieve; as he famously put it, all language is an excess of language. The 'state of perfection' (Quinn's fast, the writer's silence) is one that cannot be reached because the attainment of this goal would defeat its own purpose. Jim Nashe, the protagonist of *The Music of Chance*, confronts similar dilemmas. Although he is free of the historical traumas that direct Anna's life, he is trapped in capitalist structures that promise freedom but deliver imprisonment; he is both trapped and liberated by money, as well as by chance, or fate, and the novel charts this modern Sisyphus's attempts to exit the plots and fictions in which he allows himself to be caught.

Wall Writing

After the austerity of *In the Country of Last Things*, the pendulum swung to the exuberance of *Moon Palace*, and then back to sparseness with *The Music of Chance*, in which asceticism characterises both the narrative mode and the protagonist's predicament. The title of the novel itself, however, contains a contradiction, pitting control against chaos, and order against shapelessness. Music, like language, is a unique, original arrangement of available sounds; when it is composed, the sounds are represented by an arbitrary system of signs which stand for, but do not coincide with, the notes that make up a piece of music. Chance, on the other hand, is meaningless and unpredictable, and therefore the title aptly demonstrates Auster's attempt to 'accommodate the mess'. In the narrative this is reflected in the protagonist, who tries to make sense of his own life while he is engaged in a controlled, structured activity. But rather than treating the two categories as irreconcilable opposites, Auster proposes a synthesis which is not an intellectual compromise. He puts this succinctly in *White Spaces*, where he writes that 'randomness does not, in itself, preclude a meaning' (*GW* 82).

The Music of Chance is again fairy-tale-like in both its plot and the way it is told. The author explains:

> When I was about two-thirds of the way through the first draft, it occurred to me that the story had the same structure as a fairy tale. Up until then, I had only thought about the book in concrete terms, the reality of the action. But if you reduce the book to its skeleton, then you wind up with something that resembles a typical story by the Brothers Grimm, don't you? A wanderer stumbles onto an opportunity to make his fortune; he travels to the ogre's castle to test his luck, is tricked into staying there, and can win his freedom only by performing a series of absurd tasks that the ogre invents for him. (*AH* 319–20)

However, this simple narrative frame conceals a number of subtle intricacies. The fairy-tale hero is Jim Nashe, a divorced fireman who unexpectedly inherits a large sum of money after the death of his estranged father. Nashe quits his job and begins a journey across America, driving his red Saab with no fixed route or destination. As he eats away the inheritance, he begins to realise that he is 'stuck, that if something did not happen soon, he was going to keep on driving until the money ran out' (*MC* 19). At this point, fate intervenes in the form of Jack Pozzi, a badly beaten-up hitchhiker whom Nashe picks up on the road. From this moment on, a number of shifts occur in the novel: one is a narrative shift, as the book switches from what reads like a conventional road narrative to an intense meditation on chance, free will, freedom and responsibility, enacted within confined spaces, in sharp contrast with the first part of the narrative. Nashe's fortune shrinks at an unpredictable rate as he loses the rest of his money, as well as his freedom. Action is replaced by stasis, and several characters whom Nashe meets and interacts with in the first part of the book disappear. Auster, discussing Beckett's 'dispossession', comments: 'Beckett, who begins with little, ends with even less. The movement in each of his works is toward a kind of unburdening, by which he leads us to the limits of experience' (*AH* 87). Here Auster can be seen to attempt something similar, as a material and narrative *dénuement* forms the basis of his novel. Nashe prepares for his journey by ridding himself of his possessions, and even the trivial tasks of moving out of a house are invested with an importance that illustrates Nashe's symbolic erasure of his former identity in the hope of replenishment and rebirth:

For the next five days, he took care of business, calling up his landlord and telling him to look for a new tenant, donating furniture to the Salvation Army, cutting off his gas and electric service, disconnecting his phone. There was a recklessness and violence to these gestures that deeply satisfied him, but nothing could match the pleasure of simply throwing things away... There was a certain pain involved in these transactions, but Nashe almost began to welcome that pain, to feel ennobled by it, as if the farther he took himself away from the person he had been, the better off he would be in the future. He felt like a man who had finally found the courage to put a bullet through his head – but in this case the bullet was not death, it was life, it was the explosion that triggers the birth of new worlds. (*MC* 9–10)

But this is where Auster differs from Beckett: he strips Nashe of everything he possesses, everything he is, in order to allow him to be reborn. This element of hope has little in common with conventional happy endings, but it still manages to afford Auster's characters a positive aspect: Quinn, alone and naked in an empty room, writes poems 'as real and specific as a stone, or a lake, or a flower'; the narrator in *Ghosts* imagines Blue sailing to China; Anna Blume walks towards freedom; and Fogg finds his vocation as an artist after he has lost everything else in his life. The words he speaks could apply to the protagonist of *The Music of Chance* as well: 'Perhaps that was all I had set out to prove in the first place: that once you throw your life to the winds, you will discover things you had never known before, things that cannot be learned under any other circumstances' (*MP* 58).

The Music of Chance shares with *In the Country of Last Things* more than a linear, straightforward plot and a fable-like quality. Both represent Auster's attempt to explore 'the power of fiction and the fictions of power'.[34] *In the Country of Last Things* charts an individual's struggle against a totalitarian state; in a city where resistance is futile, Anna Blume strives to retain her humanity, to keep her personality intact when everything around her is falling apart. The main means of achieving this is the writing of her journal, the creation of fiction. This is especially apt since one of the main problems Anna faces is telling reality from appearances; the country of last things is in a state of constant change, as what is there one moment is gone the next, and names for things disappear with the things themselves. She fights this loss of words with her own words, replenishing an ever-diminishing fiction. Unlike Anna Blume, Nashe makes a calculated decision to relinquish responsibility: 'Without the slightest tremor of fear, Nashe closed his eyes and jumped' (*MC* 1). As a

34. Woods, '*The Music of Chance*', p. 143.

result of this recklessness, he finds himself imprisoned in the Flower and Stone mansion and, paradoxically, it is this confinement that will allow him to exercise self-discipline and gain his freedom. When he is invited by Pozzi to escape, he explains: 'I promised myself I'd see it through to the end. I'm not asking you to understand it, but I'm just not going to run away. I've done too much of that already, and I don't want to live like that anymore' (*MC* 166).

Auster considers the issue of freedom to be 'the true subject of the book' (*AH* 319). However, as in all of Paul Auster's books, ethical questions and moral dilemmas are never far removed from a concern with the nature of writing. As Tim Woods argues, the 'struggles against the restrictions of individual freedom often result in specific epistemological and ontological anxieties, frequently precipitating crises of confidence in what separates reality from appearance for the various protagonists'.[35] The characters' struggle against authority operates on two levels: within the fictional world of the text, characters have to overcome difficulties imposed on them by other characters, or by the circumstances they find themselves in. At the same time, their predicament is also related to their status as fictional characters who are manipulated by the author, the orchestrator of the fictional world. When Nashe begins his travels, he feels that he is free from all responsibility, but it is an irony that it was an unpredictable event (his father's inheritance) rather than his own actions that allows him his freedom. When he picks up Pozzi, he has reached a point at which he actually wants fate to intervene and take control of his life. Thus he finds himself agreeing to bet all his money on the game of poker that Pozzi is going to play with Flower and Stone. Nashe not only relinquishes responsibility by putting his money on a bet, he is also absorbed in Pozzi's story, he becomes part of this stranger's plot. Later, when they are reduced to living in a trailer in the Flower and Stone mansion grounds and building a wall in order to pay off their debt and win their freedom, they both become trapped in yet another plot. Once they have finished building the wall, Nashe and Pozzi have cleared their debt, but they are still penniless. They ask their supervisor, Murks, if they could work for a few more days in order to earn some money and, to their surprise, they find that this decision has already been made for them. Murks presents them with a contract that has already been drawn up:

> That was what was so strange about it. They hadn't even come to a decision until last night, and yet here were the results of that decision already

35. Woods, '*The Music of Chance*', p. 143.

waiting for them, boiled down into the precise language of contracts. How was that possible? It was as if Flower and Stone had been able to read their thoughts, as if they had known what they would do before they knew it themselves. (*MC* 151)

In the film of *The Music of Chance*, Stone is seen adding bricks to the wall within his City of the World which contains a miniature of the mansion and its grounds, a powerful image that reinforces the *mise-en-abîme* elements in the book as well as the feeling of manipulation by an unseen authority that runs throughout the novel. 'This submission of agency, the recourse to fate and the implied unalterable succession of events, opens another theme that preoccupies the writing of Auster: self-determination, inevitability, agency and chance.'[36]

The Music of Chance may resemble a fairy-tale but, as usual, Auster borrows from other genres as well, only to subvert them and frustrate the readers' expectations. Nashe starts out as the main character in a road narrative and, as Auster continues to explore, and explode, the cherished myths attached to the American dream, his protagonist experiences what he perceives as total liberty and self-sufficiency; his travels become not so much journeys of self-discovery as assertions of his individuality, his freedom from spatial and temporal boundaries:

> Speed was of the essence, the joy of sitting in the car and hurtling himself forward through space. That became a good beyond all others, a hunger to be fed at any price. Nothing around him lasted for more than a moment, and as one moment followed another, it was as though he alone continued to exist. He was a fixed point in a whirl of changes, a body poised in utter stillness as the world rushed through him and disappeared. The car became a sanctum of invulnerability, a refuge in which nothing could hurt him anymore. As long as he was driving, he carried no burdens, was unencumbered by even the slightest particle of his former life. That is not to say that memories did not rise up in him, but they no longer seemed to bring any of the old anguish. (*MC* 11–12)[37]

In *America* (1986), Jean Baudrillard discusses driving across the American desert:

> Speed creates pure objects. It is itself a pure object, since it cancels out the ground and territorial reference-points, since it runs ahead of time to annul

36. Woods, '*The Music of Chance*', p. 144.
37. The description of the car as a 'sanctum' is reminiscent of Auster's frequent descriptions of the room as a place of introspection. In *Leviathan*, for instance, Aaron's room is a 'sanctuary of inwardness'. I offer a fuller discussion of this in the next chapter.

time itself, since it moves more quickly than its own cause and obliterates that cause by outstripping it. Speed is the triumph of effect over cause, the triumph of instaneity over time as depth, the triumph of the surface and pure objectivity over the profundity of desire. Speed creates a space of initiation, which may be lethal; its only rule is to leave no trace behind. Triumph of forgetting over memory.[38]

This is the kind of transcendence that Nashe aspires to, but the illusion of freedom, his attempt to obliterate causality, space and time is doomed to failure. As he flees his former life and imagines himself free, he is driving towards the Flower and Stone mansion where he will be imprisoned. He is trapped inside a plot that moves towards a predetermined conclusion, and what he imagines to be his freedom is the result of a series of events that started with the death of his father. The narrator warns from the outset that 'it all came down to a question of sequence, the order of events', and with this phrase Auster not only announces a major theme in the novel, the debate about free will and determination, but he also foregrounds his own role as artificer. The novel is a pseudo-first-person narrative, a structure which echoes the thematic preoccupation of the novel. Auster relies on a double-coded discourse that imparts a sense of doom and marks Nashe as a captive long before he becomes one physically. A good example of how this operates is the phrase '[driving] became... a hunger to be fed at any price': it describes Nashe's feeling of compulsion, but the reader is also reminded of Auster's fascination with paradox, which begins with his reading of Hamsun's *Hunger*. Baudrillard again: 'And the crucial moment is that brutal instant which reveals that the journey has no end, that there is no longer any reason for it to come to an end.'[39] In his travels, Nashe is caught in a self-referential, sealed world; he has to feed his hunger for driving, but since this can only work if he never reaches a destination, he is condemned to drive on, always moving towards a destination that necessarily recedes as he approaches it. Auster's characters imagine, or try to find, ways of escaping from the fictions they create, as well as the ones they feel they are trapped in. This in turn re-enacts the author's own dilemma, and his ways of coping with the knowledge of being trapped in the prisonhouse of language:

> language and the writer are caught... between the dream of nominalism, a one-for-one fit between word and its thing-like meaning and the arbitrariness

38. Jean Baudrillard, *America*, trans. Chris Turner (New York and London: Verso, 1988), p. 6.
39. Baudrillard, *America*, p. 10.

and *différance* announced by structuralism and post-structuralism. The individual is similarly thrown between a desire for unity and the play of multiple selves. Often these alternatives are enacted in the individual's location and bearing in physical space, in box-like rooms or in perambulations across the city or journeys across and out of the country: a seeming analogue of the life of a writer's language upon the page and across languages and literatures.[40]

The contrast between journeys and confined spaces, which is also an important feature of *Moon Palace*, serves many different purposes. On the simplest level, it stands for Nashe's changing fortunes, his movement from freedom to captivity, from self-determination to submission. However, such binary oppositions are not relied upon to carry the whole semantic weight of the novel. As Peter Brooker observes, this contrast is also a metaphor for the act of writing, the interplay between the personal, the intense concentration on the part of the writer (and, in this case, the asceticism of the resulting text as well), and the metaphorical journey of his imagination, as well as across literatures, his appropriation of the work of other writers.

In most of Auster's novels, the difference between journeys and enclosed spaces is clearly defined, but in *The Music of Chance* the two categories are more ambiguous as they merge into one another. As already mentioned, Nashe's car becomes a sanctum, and he is paradoxically stationary and isolated while he is covering long distances. The nature of his confinement is equally ambivalent. Although he lives in a trailer, most of the day is spent in the open air where he is engaged in physical activity; he may have signed a contract with Flower and Stone, but, to all intents and purposes, he is a prisoner. This ambiguity suggests that solitude is a state of mind, and the ghost of Thoreau comes back to haunt *The Music of Chance*, too: 'Solitude is not measured by the miles of space that intervene between a man and his fellows.'[41] In a rare moment of serenity, Nashe observes the natural world around him and notes the changing of the seasons:

Sparrows, cardinals, chickadees, blue jays. Those were the only birds left in the woods now. And crows. Those best of all, Nashe felt. Every now and then, they would come swooping down over the meadow, letting out their strange, throttled cries, and he would interrupt what he was doing to

40. Peter Brooker, *New York Fictions: Modernity, Postmodernism, The New Modern* (London and New York: Longman, 1996), p. 145.
41. *The Variorum Walden*, ed. Harding, p. 123.

watch them pass overhead. He loved the suddenness of their comings and
goings, the way they would appear and disappear, as if for no reason at all.
(*MC* 202)[42]

This passage can be read as an indication of Nashe's ironic (and, to an
extent, unwilling) re-enactment of Thoreau's retreat and his observations
of nature, and the underlying melancholy captures both the yearning for
something that is lost, and an acute awareness of the impossibility of
repeating it. But this passage is also significant in another way, as a subtle
form of defamiliarisation is evident in the form of the narrative. Auster
here allows the distance between narrator and protagonist to be min-
imised, until the two become almost indistinguishable and the third-person
voice is rendered inaudible. The grammar of alienation continues to operate here: the 'I' in *In the Country of Last Things* presupposed the existence
of a 'you', while here 'he' approximates 'I' in ways so subtle as to be nearly
imperceptible.[43]

Although *The Music of Chance*, in common with most of Auster's writing (with the possible exception of *The New York Trilogy*), is not overtly
metafictional, the writer remains aware of, and continues to signal, the
fictionality of his writing. Like *Ghosts*, *The Music of Chance* was inspired
by a play that Auster had written before he turned to fiction. *Laurel and
Hardy Go to Heaven* is a one-act play that was written between 1976 and
1977. There is very little action as two characters, operating under
instructions from some unseen authority, build a wall on the stage and
talk to each other as they do so, trying – and failing – to discover the
meaning of their appointed task. By the end, the wall is high enough to
conceal them from the audience, and the play ends with the stage instruc-
tion 'Silence. Total darkness' (*HM* 166). This is a play that is very conscious of its own nature, since it is based on the premise of a reversal of
tradition. Where realist theatre seeks to remove the 'fourth wall', Auster
puts that wall back, by means of his characters, in the most literal sense.
Not only does he thus reject conventional representation, he creates a
piece in which this rejection becomes the action of the play. Such overt

42.   It is worth noting here that the presence of the crows, with the associations of death
      they carry, renders an otherwise idyllic scene ominous, while it is also interesting that
      Nashe likes the suddenness of their movements. Even in captivity, he is still fascinated
      by the workings of chance and continues his own struggle with the forces of contin-
      gency and the dream of controlling his life.
43.   The narrative deception in *The Music of Chance* works so effectively that in 'Paul
      Auster ou l'art de la fugue', Valéry Hugotte refers throughout to Nashe as the narra-
      tor of the novel.

gestures may be absent from *The Music of Chance*, but the wall remains a central image that reflects both the structure and the thematic preoccupations of the novel.

Before they start the game of poker, Flower and Stone show Nashe and Pozzi around the house and talk about their new status as millionaires. Among other things, they mention a trip to Ireland, during which they bought a fifteenth-century castle destroyed by Oliver Cromwell, dismantled it and shipped it to the United States. Rebuilding it was dismissed as impractical, as there were too many stones missing and, besides, they would have 'to mix in new materials with the old. And that would defeat the purpose' (MC 85). Flower explains what they plan to do with the stones instead:

> 'Rather than try to reconstruct the castle, we're going to turn it into a work of art. To my mind, there's nothing more mysterious or beautiful than a wall. I can already see it: standing out there in the meadow, rising up like some enormous barrier against time. It will be a memorial to itself, gentlemen, a symphony of resurrected stones, and every day it will sing a dirge for the past we carry within us.' 'A Wailing Wall,' Nashe said. (MC 86)

Nashe's analogy, however, is not very apt. The Wailing Wall is what remains of an existing monument, whereas this wall is the monument dismantled in order to be reconstructed. It 'is "postmodern" in that the ruins of the old castle appear to become something new even if possessing a non-usable function. To borrow Fredric Jameson's terms, the wall is postmodern because it is a pastiche of its origins.'[44] By rebuilding the castle as a wall, Flower and Stone effectively erase its meaning and negate its history, but to say that the wall has no function is to talk about the world within the novel, the fictional world of Stone, Flower, Nashe and Pozzi. Within the novel that Paul Auster has written, the wall is far from being a self-referential construct of no use.

The term 'pastiche' comes charged with Jameson's critique of the depthlessness and ahistoricity of postmodernism, but this wall is also a pastiche in a more 'neutral' sense: it can be read as the sum of other walls. It is the wall built on stage in Auster's early play, the wall which recurs as an image in Auster's poetry, and Kafka's *Great Wall of China*. The presence of Kafka is felt throughout the novel: Nashe and Pozzi find themselves trapped in a situation they cannot fully comprehend or control, in the manner of many a Kafka hero; like Kafka's works, *The Music of Chance* is written with a clarity that underscores, rather than subtracts

44. Woods, '*The Music of Chance*', p. 153.

from, the terrifying content of the book. Above all, however, it is the image of wall-building and its unseen connections with authority and fate that provide a link between the two writers. Paul Bray points out that *The Music of Chance* is 'Kafkaesque, not in the superficial sense of uncanny bureaucratic entanglements but in the Kierkegaardian sense of a divine order that eludes human comprehension. There is this major difference: where Kafka and Kierkegaard hypothesize a deity essentially separate from humankind, Auster posits a kind of cosmic current.'[45] This cosmic current is chance – or fate – and far from being separate from humankind, it is built into everyday life.

Kafka's story *The Great Wall of China*, which is probably a fragment of a larger project that was never completed, is narrated in the first person; the narrator records what he knows of the process of building the wall, and offers his own thoughts and comments. He begins by describing 'the principle of piecemeal construction' that was applied:

> gangs of some twenty workers were formed who had to accomplish a length, say, of five hundred yards of wall, while a similar gang built another stretch of the same length to meet the first. But after the junction had been made the construction of the wall was not carried on from that point, let us say, where this thousand yards ended; instead the two groups of workers were transferred to begin building again in quite different neighbourhoods. Naturally in this way many great gaps were left... In fact it is said that there are gaps which have never been filled in at all.[46]

The wall in its entirety would represent the divine law that Kafka's characters seek to lead their lives in accordance with. But they are prevented from catching a glimpse of that order by being assigned small tasks; the little knowledge they are offered comes in a fragmented fashion, thus ensuring that they will never see the whole. In 'Franz Kafka: On the Tenth Anniversary of his Death' Walter Benjamin writes: 'Kafka... could have defined organization as destiny. He faces it not only in the extensive hierarchy of officialdom in *The Trial* and *The Castle*, but even more concretely in the difficult and incalculable construction plans whose venerable model he dealt with in *The Great Wall of China*.' Benjamin goes on to discuss the principle of piecemeal con-

45. Paul Bray, 'The Currents of Fate and *The Music of Chance*', *The Review of Contemporary Fiction*, 14.1 (Spring 1994), p. 83.
46. Franz Kafka, *The Great Wall of China and Other Pieces*, trans. Edwin Muir (London: Martin Secker, 1933), p. 136.

struction, and he concludes: 'This organization resembles fate.'[47] It is to such an incomprehensible fate that Nashe abandons himself at the beginning of his adventures, but the task of building the wall, which he receives as a punishment for his excesses, becomes not an impediment but his only hope of coming to an understanding. In other words, Auster replaces Kafka's pessimism with a more pragmatic approach: Nashe will never discover meaning in its entirety, and he does not even seek to do so. The wall he builds is already 'deconstructed' and stripped of its own signification; but by putting together those discontinuous fragments he will attain some level of awareness, which will in turn allow him to take control of his life and exit the tight structure of the fiction in which he is trapped.[48]

Rosemary Jackson observes that *The Great Wall of China* 'constructs fragments which will never add up to a whole meaning, for its human subjects do not understand "the empire" which rules them';[49] but it is equally the case that the fragments will not add up to a whole meaning because we are dealing with a modernist text which questions its own ability to convey meaning. If this fragmentation was a novel proposal when put forward by modernist writers, Auster arrived on the literary scene late enough to accept it as a given. The wall, which becomes a paradigm of fragmentation, a collection of free-floating signifiers, can only be reassembled randomly. But just because its components are dispersed and have to be put back together with no recourse to a master-plan, it does not mean that they cannot be used to build a wall. The new wall that Nashe and Pozzi erect is, first of all, stripped of its primary function: this is a wall that neither encloses nor shuts out; although it is an emblem of confinement, this wall does not confine. Unlike the Statue of Liberty in *Leviathan*, which is the locus of conflict and as such contains the key to Sachs's later development, this wall allows signification to be dispersed rather than concentrated.

47. Walter Benjamin, 'Franz Kafka: On the Tenth Anniversary of his Death', in *Illuminations*, trans. Harry Zohn, ed. Hannah Arendt (London: Fontana, 1973), p. 119. Auster called his own essay on Kafka 'Pages for Kafka: On the Fiftieth Anniversary of his Death' (*AH* 23–25).
48. Although the novel is 'open-ended' and it is up to the reader to decide whether Nashe survives the crash, in the film version Nashe is seen walking along the road, like Pozzi at the beginning, and offered a lift by a man played by Paul Auster himself. So the author saves his character, after all.
49. Rosemary Jackson, *Fantasy: The Literature of Subversion* (London and New York: Methuen, 1981), p. 161.

In *Laurel and Hardy Go to Heaven*, the stones the two workers have to lift are extremely heavy, but there is a suggestion that their weight depends on Laurel and Hardy's state of mind. Nashe and Pozzi are also faced with an arduous task, as ten thousand stones sit in the meadow, and they have to put one on top of another. 'Those stones had been standing inside me for years', Auster remarks (*AH* 319). This is a reference not only to the earlier play, but also to the act of writing as perceived by Auster. He explains how writing *The Music of Chance* was 'a very wrenching experience... utterly grueling and exhausting' (*AH* 311). In his poetry as well as in this novel, images of stones and wall-building are made to stand for the difficult task of composition, of writing as the painstaking arrangement of words. In the poem 'Interior' (1972–75), he writes: 'A voice that speaks to me/only of the smallest things./Not even things – but their names./And where no names are – /of stones' (*GW* 31). The connection between names and stones resurfaces in *The Music of Chance*: every night, Nashe writes down the number of stones he has added to the wall. What begins as a list of numbers soon acquires a new meaning for him, as he senses that 'it was fulfilling some inner need, some compulsion to keep track of himself and not lose sight of where he was. By early December, he began to think of it as a journal, a logbook in which the numbers stood for his intimate thoughts' (*MC* 203). In another poem, 'Disappearances' (1975–77), a similar connection may be found: 'For the wall is a word. And there is no word/he does not count/as a stone in the wall' (*GW* 64). To liken writing to the building of a wall is to treat it as a physical activity, as the act of putting one word after another. But whereas in the poetry the act of ordering words becomes the subject-matter of the poems, the novel asks more complex questions about whether the ordering of words proceeds according to a plan, as well as whether it reflects such a plan that is seen to pre-exist. In order to deal with these questions, Auster makes a covert analogy between writing and music.

After Pozzi's disappearance, Nashe asks for an electronic keyboard, and the piece of music he finds himself playing most often is 'The Mysterious Barricades' by François Couperin:

> It took just over two minutes to perform, and at no point in its slow, stately progress, with all its pauses, suspensions, and repetitions, did it require him to touch more than one note at a time. The music started and stopped, then started again, then stopped again, and yet through it all the piece continued to advance, pushing on toward a resolution that never came. Were those the mysterious barricades? Nashe remembered reading somewhere that no one was certain what Couperin had meant by that title. Some scholars

interpreted it as a comical reference to women's underclothing... while others saw it as an allusion to the unresolved harmonies in the piece. Nashe had no way of knowing. As far as he was concerned, the barricades stood for the wall he was building in the meadow, but that was quite another thing from knowing what they meant. (*MC* 181)

Like this piece of music, the narrative advances towards its inconclusive ending, putting one word after another, just as Nashe puts one stone on top of another. If scholars read the title of Couperin's composition as a reference to its unresolved harmonies, then it follows that the lack of resolution is deliberate: unresolved harmonies exist in 'The Mysterious Barricades' because unresolved harmony is what the music conveys. Similarly, *The Music of Chance* asks questions concerning the nature of chance and its relation to patterning and structures.

This question is further explored in the image of another elaborate structure, Stone's miniature model of the City of the World:

'Willie's city is more than just a toy,' Flower said, 'it's an artistic vision of mankind. In one way, it's an autobiography, but in another way, it's what you might call a utopia – a place where the past and future come together, where good finally triumphs over evil. If you look carefully, you'll see that many of the figures actually represent Willie himself... That's what you might call the private backdrop, the personal material, the inner component. But all these things are put in a larger context. They're merely an example, an illustration of a man's journey through the City of the World. Look at the Hall of Justice, the Library, the Bank, and the Prison. Willie calls them the Four Realms of Togetherness, and each one plays a vital role in maintaining the harmony of the city. If you look at the Prison, you'll see that all the prisoners are working happily at various tasks, that they all have smiles on their faces. That's because they're glad they've been punished for their crimes, and now they're learning how to recover the goodness within them through hard work. That's what I find so inspiring about Willie's city. It's an imaginary place, but it's also realistic. Evil still exists, but the powers who rule over the city have figured out how to transform that evil back into good.' (79–80)

During the game of poker, Nashe goes to take a closer look at this miniature city, and breaks off the figures of Flower and Stone. When Pozzi finds out, he claims that at that precise moment his luck turned and he began to lose the game: 'You tampered with the universe, my friend,' he tells Nashe, 'and once a man does that, he's got to pay the price' (*MC* 138). Nashe, who only tampered with a man-made model of a world after all, tries to convince Pozzi of the absurdity of his superstition:

You want to believe in some hidden purpose. You're trying to persuade yourself there's a reason for what happens in the world. I don't care what you call it – God or luck or harmony – it all comes down to the same bullshit. It's a way of avoiding the facts, of refusing to look at how things really work… We're just a pair of know-nothings, you and I, a couple of dunces who got in over our heads. (*MC* 139)

Of the two dunces, Nashe is the one who survives until the end of the novel. Auster continues to negotiate the Romantic faith in the subject and its relation to the world, in individual creativity and fulfilment on the one hand, and a distinctly modernist sense of the loss of a centre. One after another, his protagonists abandon themselves to the world at large in the hope of attaining a universal truth, of discovering a governing principle that will impart sense to their lives and actions; they all fail to do that, although they do discover a personal truth to live by: the reality of the fictions they create.

Something 'quite disturbing', 'utterly uncanny' happened the day Auster finished writing *The Music of Chance*: the Berlin Wall came down. 'There's no conclusion to be drawn from this,' he remarks, 'but every time I think of it, I start to shake' (*AH* 284). Auster's interviewer, Sinda Gregory, reads in this episode Borgesian overtones of fictions seeping into the world, and even if this coincidence is, by definition, meaningless, it nevertheless helps to highlight the author's critique of capitalism and the power of money, inherent in both the structure and the subject matter of *The Music of Chance*. Tim Woods has convincingly read the novel as a critique of the ideology of American capitalism, noting that 'the extent to which money controls and coerces is one of the more insidious issues at stake in the novel'.[50] If we remain with the image of the wall, it becomes clear that the central position that this trope occupies in the book, and of course the references to Kafka, invite a reading that would seek to combine the more abstract meditations on chance, fate, order and chaos with a concurrent investigation of the material forces and the attendant ideologies that shape notions such as agency or free will. The principle of piecemeal production that Benjamin reads in Kafka's text, for example, resembles not only fate, but also the worker's alienation from production which makes ideological control possible. Similarly, in Stone's City of the World model, realms of social activity are clearly demarcated; each one exists in isolation, with no indication of a cause-and-effect relationship, thus excluding the possibility of *narrative*, of a discourse that would

50. Woods, 'The Music of Chance', p. 150.

reveal any sense of an underlying political or social structure. For instance, the Prison in the model exists because 'Evil still exists'.

Flower's collection of memorabilia is no less ideologically suspect. It comprises a random collection of objects such as the telephone that had once sat on Woodrow Wilson's desk, a half-smoked cigar belonging to Winston Churchill, a pair of spectacles worn by Voltaire.

> In the weeks and months that followed, he [Nashe] often found himself thinking back to what he had seen there, and it stunned him to realize how many of the objects he could remember... It was all so random, so misconstrued, so utterly beside the point. Flower's museum was a graveyard of shadows, a demented shrine to the spirit of nothingness. If those objects continued to call out to him, Nashe decided, it was because they refused to divulge anything about themselves. It had nothing to do with history, nothing to do with the men who had once owned them. The fascination was simply for the objects as material things, and the way they had been wrenched out of any possible context, condemned by Flower to go on existing for no reason at all: defunct, devoid of purpose, alone in themselves now for the rest of time. It was the isolation that haunted Nashe, the image of irreducible separateness that burned down into his memory, and no matter how hard he struggled, he never managed to break free of it. (MC 83–84)

Nashe himself is subsequently 'wrenched out of context', condemned to an activity that is 'devoid of purpose', thus becoming part of his captor's meaningless, dehistoricised collection, but at the same time he is also sucked into Stone's project, as 'the ideologies that are theorized and conceptualized in the model are reproduced practically in the meadow' where his work is seen by the two millionaires, and Pozzi, more as punishment than as the paying off of a debt.[51] The third-person foreshadowing in the above-quoted passage from the novel also *repeats* – and thus underscores – the notions of captivity and control, effected in formalist terms as the narrator (and by implication the author) traps the character inside the plot, which is another kind of sustained discourse. The relationship between the construction of fiction and the discourse that shapes the 'real' world, and the place of the individual amid such structures, are issues which are more explicitly dealt with in the two novels I examine in the next chapter, *Moon Palace* and *Leviathan*.

51. Woods, 'The Music of Chance', p. 153.

3

Realities

The fall of the Berlin Wall may have given *The Music of Chance* a resonance that the author himself could not have anticipated, but in much of
his fiction Auster deliberately explores the boundaries between the 'real'
and the 'fictive'. As I have discussed in previous chapters, *The New York
Trilogy* is as much about the literary ghosts that haunt the modern city as
it is about the experience of living in it, while *In the Country of Last
Things* presents a collage of cities which have witnessed the progress and
the horrors of the twentieth century. These novels may have revealed a
bias, on my part as well as Auster's, towards the 'literary' rather than the
'factual', but they have never been totally detached from the real world.
After all, as I have argued, the notion of the intertext is not limited to
literary works but embraces processes of fiction-making which have not
always been recognised as such. The interaction between the 'real' world
of history and politics and the world of fiction is given a more prominent
position in *Moon Palace* and *Leviathan* and, in a different way, also in *Mr
Vertigo*. Although all three are complex narratives encompassing stories
within stories, and covering a large time-span that is signposted through
references to historical events, the effect is not one of all-inclusiveness.
Paradoxically, this panorama of historical and political events is not meant
to represent an attempt at mimesis, but serves rather to emphasise subjectivity. In other words, these are narratives that may appear to be 'grand'
in scale but which seek not to assert their authority, but rather constantly
to put it in question. As Chantal Coulomb-Buffa states in relation to *Moon
Palace*, Auster's writing 'keeps questioning the infinite power of text to
generate itself and the impossibility to [sic] reach any original truth'.[1]

1. Chantal Coulomb-Buffa, 'Réconciliation dans *Moon palace* de Paul Auster', *Révue
   Française d'Etudes Américaines*, 62 (November 1994), p. 404. [Epigraph in English
   translation.]

Moon Palace is a novel that could be described, in Linda Hutcheon's terms, as historiographic metafiction. She uses the term to refer to novels which display an awareness of the process of fiction-making, whether that fiction be the novel itself or another kind of narrative:

> In most of the critical work on postmodernism, it is narrative – be it in literature, history, or theory – that has usually been the major focus of attention. Historiographic metafiction incorporates all three of these domains: that is, its theoretical self-awareness of history and fiction as human constructs (historio*graphic meta*fiction) is made the grounds for its rethinking and reworking of the forms and contents of the past.[2]

Hutcheon cites Larry McCaffery, who offers Márquez's *One Hundred Years of Solitude* as an example of this kind of writing: 'It has… become a kind of model for the contemporary writer, being self-conscious about its literary heritage and about the limits of mimesis… but yet managing to reconnect its readers to the world outside the page'.[3] This is also the case in *Moon Palace* which, like Márquez's novel (though not in the magic-realist tradition), puts the emphasis on story-telling but allows for a broader definition of 'story' itself. What postmodern writing does, Hutcheon goes on to argue, is 'to contest the very possibility of our ever being able to *know* the "ultimate objects" [in Fredric Jameson's terms] of the past. It teaches and enacts the recognition of the fact that the social, historical, and existential "reality" of the past is *discursive* reality.'[4] In Auster's fiction, the emphasis is always on subjectivity which stems from the loss of faith in grand, totalising narratives; his interest in the process of myth-making, which in America is more closely tied to history than elsewhere, constitutes an acknowledgment of the 'made-upness' of the past. By rejecting notions of authenticity, or unadulterated reality, the author is seen to question not only the status of the past he inherits, but also his own contribution, his own interaction with the world around him.

Novels such as *Moon Palace* or *Leviathan* not only stress the subjective aspect of the author's creation; they also remind us that the past itself can only be known through narrative, even if that narrative is historiographical rather than fictional. To recognise that historiography is essentially a literary activity is not to deny the reality, or the importance, of the events it describes. When, in 1977, E.L. Doctorow stated that there is 'no fiction or nonfiction as we commonly understand the distinction: There is

2. Hutcheon, *A Poetics of Postmodernism*, p.5.
3. *A Poetics of Postmodernism*, p. 5.
4. *A Poetics of Postmodernism*, p. 24.

only narrative',[5] he was not denying the importance of historiography and claiming the superiority of fiction. Although he modestly added that this was 'a novelist's proposition, I can see that very well', historian Hayden White had already taken a similar view with his influential book *Metahistory* (1973). A few years later, in an essay tellingly entitled 'The Historical Text as Literary Artifact', he argued:

> The older distinction between fiction and history, in which fiction is conceived as the representation of the imaginable and history as the representation of the actual, must give place to the recognition that we can only know the *actual* by contrasting it with or likening it to the *imaginable*... all narrative is not simply a recording of 'what happened' in the transition from one state of affairs to another, but a progressive *redescription* of sets of events in such a way as to dismantle a structure encoded in one verbal mode in the beginning so as to justify a recoding of it in another mode at the end... it may be observed that if historians were to recognize the fictive element in their narratives, this would not mean the degradation of historiography to a status of ideology or propaganda. In fact, this recognition would serve as a potent antidote to the tendency of historians to become captive of ideological preconceptions which they do not recognize as such but honor as the 'correct' perception of 'the way things really are'. By drawing historiography nearer to its origins in literary sensibility, we should be able to identify the ideological, because it is the fictive, element in our own discourse.[6]

Although Auster's interest in the discursiveness of the past places him within the context of historiographic metafiction, broadly defined, it should be stressed that his version of history, or even of mythology, differs from that of other American authors who may be more easily identified as exponents of this tendency. For instance, he may share with writers such as Robert Coover or E.L. Doctorow a 'postmodernist' view of history, but his is a stylised version of history which is always subordinate to the artistic, aesthetic concerns of his texts. In Coover's *The Public Burning*, for example, political history forms the basis of the novel. The execution of Julius and Ethel Rosenberg is rewritten as circus entertainment, as an orgiastic, carnivalesque fantasy that shows no respect for recorded events. The limits and conventions of historiography are exposed through Coover's use of official documentation, newspaper reports and other sources, while the relationship between the real and the fictive is problematised as historical

---

5. E.L. Doctorow, 'False Documents', in *Poets and Presidents: Selected Essays 1977–1992* (London: Macmillan, 1993), p. 163.
6. Hayden White, *Tropics of Discourse: Essays in Cultural Criticism* (Baltimore: Johns Hopkins University Press, 1978), pp. 98–99.

figures and imaginary characters occupy the same ontological sphere in the novel. Again, in Doctorow's *Ragtime*, historical persons not only interact with fictional characters but are also involved in events in which they did not participate in real life, with sometimes comical results. It is the absence of such parodic intentions that sets Auster's texts apart.

Moon Palace asks forcefully to be read within a specific context. It opens with the words 'It was the summer that men first walked on the moon. I was very young back then, but I did not believe there would ever be a future' (*MP* 1). The effect achieved here is twofold: on the one hand, it is announced from the outset that this is a book set in a specific historical time; on the other hand, we are introduced to a narrator who is seen to be choosing to relate his story to the events of this time. The man who utters these words, who traces the beginning of his artistic development to the time of the first moon landing, is called Marco Stanley Fogg, or MS for short. His initials draw attention to the fact that he is a textual construct, a paper character, but, as I explain at length in the first part of this chapter, 'Inventing America', they also draw attention to the subjectivity of the story: this character is a blank page on which 'history', his country's as well as his own, is written, on which facts converge to create an individual. Similarly, the name Marco Stanley Fogg serves a variety of purposes, which will also be examined at some length. As the narrator rather needlessly explains, 'Marco... was for Marco Polo...; Stanley was for the American journalist who had tracked down Dr Livingstone "in the heart of darkest Africa"; and Fogg was for Phileas, the man who had stormed around the globe in less than three months' (*MP* 6). The narrator, then, is a quester, but his quest does not involve the discovery of real worlds, or universal, extratextual truths; it is a personal quest that leads him to discover his own artistic sensibilities, which in turn allow him to write the story that makes up the novel *Moon Palace*. And since this artistic aesthetic had to be discovered before he could begin his narrative, he is allowed to select the factors which shaped him.

Auster told Gérard de Cortanze: 'I feel in permanent conflict with the United States... I am not the only one... The United States is nothing like other countries; it's an invented, "discovered" country.'[7] The theme of discovery, so prominent in the novel, concerns not only the narrator's discovery of his father's identity and his artistic sensibilities, but also a discovery of his country, especially the construction of its history and its

---

7. De Cortanze, *La Solitude du labyrinthe*, p. 95.

geography. The exploration of space, as I shall argue in 'Inventing America', plays a major role in *Moon Palace*.

Fogg is an orphan; his parentless condition may be read as a parody of the heroes of nineteenth-century novels, but at the same time it also highlights his quest for legitimacy. In order to attain his artistic identity, Fogg first needs to solve the mystery of his paternity. This task is an image of the author's practice in his engagement with the world, literary or otherwise. Auster incorporates history in his fiction, but at the same time he also writes himself, and his plots, into history. He is seen to acquire his genealogy.

Moon Palace is narrated in the first person, and it concerns the events in the life of the protagonist narrator, but the centre of the novel is given over to another character and his story. This shift in point of view serves to question the objectivity of the telling: since this is a story within a story, the fact that the narrator has chosen not to relate it in his own words is indicative of his doubts concerning its truthfulness. This fact in turn is reinforced by the actual story told. Effing's story cannot be verified; not only are there no witnesses, but the very place where much of it is supposed to have happened no longer exists. At the same time, this is also the story of how a man reinvented himself, and a story set in an already much-mythologised land, the Wild West. It is no accident that it is this story, whose fictional truthfulness even the narrator cannot guarantee, that contains references to real, historical figures. Effing begins his narration by recalling his visit to the Columbian Exposition in Chicago in 1893; it was there that he first met Tesla, who had discovered alternating current. Years later, he met him again, only this time his childhood hero had become a beggar. Effing claims he was also acquainted with Ralph Blakelock and Thomas Moran, and considers the latter to have been his mentor. Andrew Addy comments: 'intrusions of the real world into the world of *Moon Palace* creates [sic] an ambivalence towards notions of fictionality, of story, and of fact'.[8]

Just before he begins telling his story, Effing asks Fogg to go to the Brooklyn Museum and look at *Moonlight*, a painting by Ralph Albert Blakelock. Two years before the publication of *Moon Palace*, Auster had written about that painting in *Art News*, and some of his words are attributed to Fogg in the novel:

> It is a small picture that measures only 27 by 32 inches, and at first glance it seems almost devoid of color: dark brown, dark green, the smallest touch of

8. Andrew Addy, 'Narrating the Self: Story-Telling as Personal Myth-Making in Paul Auster's *Moon Palace*', *Q/W/E/R/T/Y*, 6 (1996), p. 157.

red in one corner... A perfectly round full moon sits in the middle of the canvas – the precise mathematical center, it seems to me – and this pale white disk illuminates everything above it and below it... I was only guessing, of course, but it struck me that Blakelock was painting an American idyll, the world the Indians inhabited before the white men came to destroy it.[9]

Echoing his creator, Fogg looks at this non-realistic painting, and observes that perhaps 'this picture was meant to stand for everything we had lost. It was not a landscape, it was a memorial, a death song for a vanished world' (*MP* 139). It is only after he has come to this realisation that he can begin to listen to Effing's story which, appropriately enough, is also meant to be his obituary. Like that obituary, the painting is not only an elegy for a lost world but also an unrealistic, exaggerated version of a world which is known mainly through its representations. Just as the moon in Blakelock's painting occupies the centre of the canvas, Effing's narrative occupies the centre of the novel. In the heart of the book lies the suggestion that 'to re-write or to re-present the past in fiction and in history is, in both cases, to open it up to the present, to prevent it from being conclusive and teleological'.[10] My discussion of Effing's obituary, and Auster's *Moon Palace*, will attempt to demonstrate that 'the interaction of the historiographic and the metafictional foregrounds the rejection of the claims of both "authentic" representation and "inauthentic" copy alike, and the very meaning of artistic originality is as forcefully challenged as is the transparency of historical referentiality'.[11]

Questions of authenticity are also raised in *Leviathan*, a novel which tells the story of Benjamin Sachs, an author who gives up writing in order to become a terrorist and urge America to change its ways. The second part of this chapter, 'Exploding Fictions', argues that the bias in favour of story-telling is once again evident here. This story is narrated in the first person by another writer who is the protagonist's best friend: the writer's engagement in the real world turns into another writer's plot, while the whole situation also recalls Auster's own earlier *The Locked Room*. The Statue of Liberty, which is the central image in the book, is associated throughout with personal experience, but it is replicas of the statue that the phantom of liberty attacks – representations of symbolic value rather than the real thing.

9. Paul Auster, 'Moonlight in the Brooklyn Museum', *Art News*, 86.7 (1987), p. 105.
10. Hutcheon, *A Poetics of Postmodernism*, p. 110.
11. *A Poetics of Postmodernism*, p. 110.

Benjamin Sachs is portrayed by his friend as a self-mythologiser. Born on 6 August 1945, Sachs refers to himself as America's first Hiroshima baby, the 'original bomb child':

> he used to claim that the doctor had delivered him at the precise moment Fat Man was released from the bowels of the *Enola Gay*, but that always struck me as an exaggeration... it was no more than a bit of innocent mythologizing on his part. He was a great one for turning facts into metaphors... By gorging himself on these facts, he was able to read the world as though it were a work of the imagination, turning documented events into literary symbols, tropes that pointed to some dark, complex pattern embedded in the real. (*Lev* 23–24)

The point is that Sachs is, inevitably, shaped by cultural as well as historical events: 'If I had to sum up his attitude toward his own beliefs,' Aaron writes, 'I would begin by mentioning the Transcendentalists of the nineteenth century. Thoreau was his model' (*Lev* 26). Like his fictional creation, Auster himself reads the world as a work of the imagination, and he foregrounds this activity by writing about the world in terms of the imagined and the personal. My discussion of *Leviathan* explores the paradox of a fictional writer whose desire to step into the real world and act is shaped by his reading of books.

MS Fogg is another self-mythologiser whose identity is closely related to books, and this fact is repeatedly emphasised in his own narrative. When he goes to college, he takes with him 1,492 books that belonged to his uncle. These are kept in boxes, and he uses them as furniture for his apartment:

> My friends found it a bit odd, but they had learned to expect odd things from me by then. Think of the satisfaction, I would explain to them, of crawling into bed and knowing that your dreams are about to take place on top of nineteenth-century American literature... In point of fact, I had no idea which books were in which boxes, but I was a great one for making up stories back then, and I liked the sound of those sentences, even if they were false. (*MP* 2–3)

However, what begins as a casual link, and a little harmless self-mythologising, reveals its true import in Fogg's life when he has to sell the books in order to survive: 'The room was a machine that measured my condition: how much of me remained, how much of me was no longer there. I was both perpetrator and witness, both actor and audience in a theater of one. I could follow the progress of my own dismemberment. Piece by piece, I could watch myself disappear' (*MP* 24). Fogg is connected to the world through books, and as he gradually loses them, his very existence is threatened. Looking at his life in retrospect, Fogg realises that he saved himself 'through the minds of others' (*MP* 1). As a metafictional comment, this can be taken to highlight the fact that Fogg is a character in the book who exists as long as there are readers whose minds 'save' him. However, within his own world as well he is saved by story-telling, first of all by being hired to record Effing's story. Andrew Addy observes that 'it is the act of story-telling that builds the connections between people, creating shared experience, shared memories, and it is these connections that fend off the isolation and despair of the kind felt by Marco in Central Park and by Effing in the Utah desert'.[12]

It is too late for Peter Aaron to save his friend with stories, but he, too, attempts to fend off despair, to fill in the gap left by his best friend's death by telling his story. Benjamin Sachs's main problem seems to be that he cannot decide whether to be a writer or a political activist. In a similar way, the book can be said to be poised halfway between the personal and the political, but the two issues are united through a wider frame of reference, the emphasis on representation. Sachs blows up replicas of the Statue of Liberty, thus exploding one of his country's foremost symbols, but the myth he cannot blow to pieces is his own, the solipsistic system of his personal myth-making. It is left up to others to save him: Aaron does so by writing his account of the events that led up to the fatal explosion, while the artist Maria Turner performs a similar function by allowing him to see himself through the eyes of others, by representing him in her art. Needless to say, neither of these processes can lead to redemption: if they offer salvation for Sachs, it is to the extent that they allow him to become part of a larger structure, a bigger system of reference. The narrator of *The Locked Room* claimed that 'No one can cross the boundary into another – for the simple reason that no one can gain access to himself'. Mark Osteen suggests that *Leviathan* revises this position 'by suggesting that only through others can one gain access to the locked room of self'.[13] This room is also the book, and the world. As Peter Aaron puts it, 'Everything is connected to everything else, every story overlaps with every other story' (*Lev* 51). It is this connectedness that Auster continues to explore in *Moon Palace* and *Leviathan*.

12. Addy, 'Narrating the Self', pp. 155–56.
13. Mark Osteen, 'Phantoms of Liberty: The Secret Lives of *Leviathan*', *Review of Contemporary Fiction*, 14.1 (Spring 1994), p. 90.

Inventing America

What is man if the signs that predate him have such power?
                                                    Jean Baudrillard, America

While he was still working on *Moon Palace*, Paul Auster described it to
Joseph Mallia as a 'kind of *David Copperfield* novel' (*AH* 276), a description that is as misleading as it is useful. The plot does, indeed, have a
Dickensian backbone: it tells the story of Marco Stanley Fogg, of
unknown paternity, orphaned at eleven when his mother is killed in an
accident. Marco spends his adolescence with his slightly eccentric uncle
Victor, and when he, too, dies, he is left to fend for himself. From now
on, he will experience a series of extraordinary adventures, in the course
of which he will fall in love, come into an inheritance, and discover the
secret of his paternity. In this sense, Auster could have described his book
as a *Tom Jones* kind of novel, and although either of these descriptions
may apply to the plot, they tell us little about the novel that finally became
Moon Palace. With this book, Auster continues the investigation he
started in his earlier novels, and the question of identity is once again
prominent here, although this time it is addressed in different terms. As I
have argued, in *The New York Trilogy* identity was perceived mainly as a
linguistic construct, whereas in *In the Country of Last Things* the narrating voice was the unifying and sustaining force of the individual. In *Moon
Palace*, Auster considers a wider intertext and addresses the question of
identity taking into account not only linguistic but also socio-historical
factors. Although the novel shares many themes and concerns with
Auster's earlier books, it is the first in which the author engages in questions pertaining to American history and mythology, and the first to offer
an extensive exploration of the American landscape and cityscape. Fogg
is modelled on the picaresque hero, and as the plot follows his adventures
and peregrinations, it charts the birth of an artist who is struggling to find
his own voice and his place in the world, to make sense of his own life
and understand the role of art. This course involves the discovery of his
genealogy as well as a confrontation of socio-historical reality.

Moon Palace is saturated with references to historical events, which are
often used to establish the chronology of the narrative. The story begins
with the phrase 'It was the summer that men first walked on the moon',
and the action unfolds during a specified period designated by important
events in America's history; unlike *Ghosts*, for example, where 'the time
is the present', but it is also 3 February 1947. Fogg's story begins with the
Apollo moon landing, an event which signals the beginning of a new era,

but which fails to live up to its promise. Looking back, Fogg recalls a time of unrest and discontent rather than hope: 'Those were difficult days for everyone, of course. I remember them as a tumult of politics and crowds, of outrage, bullhorns, and violence. By the spring of 1968, every day seemed to retch forth a new cataclysm. If it wasn't Prague, it was Berlin; if it wasn't Paris, it was New York. There were half a million soldiers in Vietnam. The president announced that he wouldn't run again' (*MP* 25). There are also references to the New York City blackout, the Chicago Eight, the Black Panther trial and the Kent State massacre, and throughout his narrative Fogg keeps track of the progress of two baseball teams, the Cubs and the Mets.[14] Finally, throughout the novel there are numerous references to Columbus, and the idea of crossing frontiers. Auster explains: 'First there's Columbus, then there was the discovery of the West, then finally there is outer space: the moon as the last frontier' (*AH* 317). The moon, however, may not be the last frontier. After the conquest of space, there is still inner geography to explore. Salman Rushdie writes:

> The historian F.J. Turner's 'frontier thesis' – the idea that a country born with the urge to push a frontier westwards has needed, constantly, to find new frontiers, ever since it reached the Pacific – has long been a useful lens through which to view American history. The space race is only one subject which the thesis illuminates. In the last two decades many Americans have turned inwards in search of that new frontier.[15]

Jean-François Chassay, who draws attention to this passage by Rushdie, writes of *Moon Palace*:

> Opening the novel with this phrase ['It was the summer that men first walked on the moon'] indicates the importance given to the *American Dream* (and thus to American history), since it returns to the myth of the frontier. After having crossed this ultimate frontier of space, what is left to do?... It's this other 'ultimate frontier', that of his consciousness, that Fogg must confront.[16]

Fogg's story does, indeed, record a journey of discovery; the young protagonist embarks on a quest for his own identity, as well as for that of his country, and the two quests are often hard to tell apart.

14. Auster, himself a baseball fan, observes that the sport is very closely linked with American history. See de Cortanze, *La Solitude du labyrinthe*, p. 92.
15. Salman Rushdie, 'In God we Trust', in *Imaginary Homelands: Essays and Criticism 1981–1991* (London: Granta, 1991), p. 390.
16. Jean-François Chassay, '*Moon Palace*: le palimpseste historique', in *L'Œuvre de Paul Auster*, ed. Duperray, pp. 218–19.

Although *Moon Palace* is a quest narrative, there is not a fundamental truth waiting to be discovered by the narrator/protagonist. The sense of indeterminacy, which is a manifestation of epistemological as well as ontological uncertainty, is underscored by the fact that the plot relies heavily on coincidence. Chance and coincidence play a big role in all of Auster's fiction, and he has been accused of concocting implausible plots driven by the forces of contingency. However, Auster considers this to be realistic. As he explains:

> When I talk about coincidence, I'm not referring to a desire to manipulate. There's a good deal of that in bad eighteenth- and nineteenth-century fiction: mechanical plot devices, the urge to tie everything up, the happy ending in which everyone turns out to be related to everyone else. No, what I'm talking about is the presence of the unpredictable, the utterly bewildering nature of human experience. From one moment to the next, anything can happen. Our life-long certainties about the world can be demolished in a single second. In philosophical terms, I'm talking about the powers of contingency. Our lives don't belong to us, you see – they belong to the world, and in spite of our efforts to make sense of it, the world is a place beyond our understanding. We brush up against these mysteries all the time. The result can be truly terrifying – but it can also be comical. (*AH* 279)

The author acknowledges the similarity between *Moon Palace* and the plots of nineteenth-century novels, calling his own book a kind of *David Copperfield* novel, but at the same time the narrator himself pokes fun at it when he remarks that he sobbed himself to sleep at night 'like some pathetic orphan hero in a nineteenth-century novel' (*MP* 5). In a wider context, what Auster questions is the conventions of nineteenth-century realism, especially its reliance on linearity and causality. A related issue here is his questioning of the validity of these concepts when they are applied to another form of narrative, i.e. history. Early in the novel, Marco finds out that 'Causality was no longer the hidden demiurge that ruled the universe: down was up, the last was the first, the end was the beginning. Heraclitus had been resurrected from his dungheap, and what he had to show us was the simplest of truths: reality was a yo-yo, change was the only constant' (*MP* 62).

Although there are many references to historical events, history is not treated as a plot which complies with Aristotelian notions of unity of time and place, or a narrative with a recognisable beginning, middle and end. Steven Weisenburger remarks:

causal history tumbles aside; it is too fragile, too limited to fully *do* contemporary work. It cannot function as a reality principle for postmodern
theaters of action. The more open the perceptible universe is to fluctuation
and coincident innovation, the less useful are metaphors about genealogy
and progressive growth... any conception of events as 'plot'... must be
ceaselessly reinvented on the basis of contingent potentials.[17]

In interviews, Auster has said much the same thing, albeit on a personal
level: 'no life unfolds in a straight line. We are always prey to everyday
uncertainties... And our lives are made up of random events.'[18] Jean-
François Chassay attempts to synthesise the personal and the larger
forces of history when he compares *Moon Palace* to *The Education of
Henry Adams*. He reads *The Education* as a *Bildungsroman*, since it is an
autobiography written in the third person, and hence made to read like
fiction. He also points out that through Adams's ancestry, as the grandson and great-grandson of American presidents, his life is inexorably
linked with the history of his country.[19] Adams breaks his links with his
family by rejecting their values and Fogg has no links with his family
through accident, and it is due to this orphaned state that the two heroes
set out to discover the American country and its landscape. In both cases,
the personal and the universal merge, while the world, and history, are
seen as multiple, contradictory, chaotic. The obvious difference, of
course, is that *Moon Palace* is a work of fiction. It does deal with history,
with journeying across the country and attempting to decipher it, but it
also addresses questions of representation and signification. Although
Chassay's comparison would probably collapse upon closer scrutiny, it is
useful to the extent that it emphasises the link between the protagonist
and his country, his identity and his heritage.

Fogg's quest for an identity is to a large extent a quest for authority,
which manifests itself as a search for the missing father. At the beginning
of his story, he knows nothing of his father. His uncle Victor, who brings
him up, is far from being a paternal source of authority: 'He [Victor]
knew that fatherhood was beyond him, and therefore he treated me less
as a child than as a friend, a diminutive and much-adored crony' (*MP* 6).
The next father-figure in Fogg's life is Thomas Effing, an unlikely mentor
for the young adventurer who never suspects that the old man is actually
his grandfather. After Effing's death, Fogg meets the old man's son,

17. Steven Weisenburger, 'Inside *Moon Palace*', *The Review of Contemporary Fiction*,
    14.1 (Spring 1994), pp. 74–75.
18. De Cortanze, *La Solitude du labyrinthe*, p. 84.
19. Chassay, '*Moon Palace*', pp. 223–24.

Solomon Barber, who had always believed his own father dead. By that time, Fogg himself is hoping to become a father, but his girlfriend Kitty has an abortion, which leads to their separation. The dance of dead fathers and lost sons comes to a dramatic climax when Barber reveals himself as Fogg's father. The recognition scene takes place in a cemetery where Fogg is visiting his mother's grave; when the truth is revealed, a fight ensues and Barber falls into a freshly dug grave. He survives long enough for the two to be reconciled, and with his death Fogg's quest draws to an end. Having filled in the blanks of his family history, he now takes full control of his own life, and embarks on his final journey of discovery across the desert. It is here that he will finally reach adulthood and make peace with himself.

The theme of the father–son relationship dominates Auster's *œuvre*. It begins, as we have seen, with the first part of *The Invention of Solitude*, 'Portrait of an Invisible Man', where Auster recounts the painful process of coming to terms with his estranged father's death, and meditates on his own role as a father. In *City of Glass*, Quinn has lost his son in an accident, and Stillman has abused his with his cruel experiment. Fanshawe's father in *The Locked Room* is 'a silent man of abstracted benevolence' (*LR* 218) whom Fanshawe watches die slowly and painfully, whereas in *The Music of Chance* Nashe becomes a surrogate father for the younger Pozzi but is unable to save his life. In *Moon Palace*, Marco discovers not only who his true father was, but also his past in a wider sense, through the stories that Effing tells him and through the journey he undertakes to test the veracity of his grandfather's story. 'So the importance of filiation, evident since *The Invention of Solitude*, no longer concerns only the genetic father but also the "Fathers of the Nation".'[20] Chantal Coulomb-Buffa also draws attention to Fogg's orphaned state, and concludes that, since his life lacks the structure provided by family ties, Fogg is determined by larger cultural forces: 'His belonging to the world is governed by representations, by the cultural fictions which are imposed on him; his reality is constructed by fiction in fiction'.[21] As an orphan, Fogg craves a sense of belonging, and, before he finds his own identity, he tries to see if he can belong to the world at large. He puts himself through a series of tests, having decided to 'drift along with the flow of the universe'. As he explains, 'Our lives are determined by manifold contingencies... Two years ago, I decided to give up

20. Chassay, '*Moon Palace*', p. 216.
21. Coulomb-Buffa, 'Réconciliation dans *Moon palace* de Paul Auster', p. 410.

the struggle... because I thought that by abandoning myself to the chaos of the world, the world might ultimately reveal some secret harmony to me, some form of pattern that would help me to penetrate myself' (*MP* 80). But even as he abandons himself to the world, he goes on creating his own myth, and his rejection of familiar comforts turns him into another hunger artist. He pretends that his increasing poverty is a lifestyle choice: when he has his phone disconnected because he can no longer afford it, he pretends that he is resisting 'the death of human contact' (*MP* 26), and when he refuses every job opportunity that is offered to him, and decides to do nothing to help himself, he still tries to account for his actions in terms of aesthetics: 'This was nihilism raised to the level of an aesthetic proposition. I would turn my life into a work of art, sacrificing myself to such exquisite paradoxes that every breath I took would teach me how to savor my own doom' (*MP* 21). Writing about this period of his life in retrospect, he concedes that the elaborate myth he constructed around himself was a manifestation of his desire for a sense of belonging. When Uncle Victor leaves, Marco inherits his tweed suit, which he wears all year round even though suits 'were hardly in fashion for undergraduates':

> At moments of stress and unhappiness, it was a particular comfort to feel myself swaddled in the warmth of my uncle's clothes, and there were times when I imagined the suit was actually holding me together, that if I did not wear it my body would fly apart. It functioned as a protective membrane, a second skin that shielded me from the blows of life... What my friends didn't know, of course, was that I wore it for sentimental reasons. Under my nonconformist posturing, I was also satisfying the desire to have my uncle near me. (*MP* 15–16)

Later, when he gets the job with Effing, he is given his predecessor's tweed overcoat: 'I found it eerie to walk around in it, knowing that it had belonged to a man who was now dead... Whenever I put it on, I couldn't help feeling that I was stepping into a dead man's body, that I had been turned into Pavel Shum's ghost' (*MP* 120). As Fogg drifts along with the flow and wears other people's clothes, he is trying to have an identity inscribed on the blank page that is his self. Yet, as a fictional creation, his identity is already determined by the author, and especially by Auster's choice of name for his character. The name Marco Stanley Fogg reveals a very specific aspect of his nature, his thirst for voyages of discovery, but on a different level it also points to his fragmented, discontinuous and, above all, made-up identity:

> Uncle Victor... never tired of expounding on the glories hidden in my
> name. Marco Stanley Fogg. According to him, it proved that travel was in
> my blood, that life would carry me to places where no man had ever been
> before. Marco, naturally enough, was for Marco Polo, the first European to
> visit China; Stanley was for the American journalist who had tracked down
> Dr Livingstone 'in the heart of darkest Africa'; and Fogg was for Phileas,
> the man who had stormed around the globe in less than three months...
> When I was fifteen, I started signing all my papers M.S. Fogg, pretentiously
> echoing the gods of modern literature, but at the same time delighting in
> the fact that the initials stood for *manuscript*. Uncle Victor heartily
> approved of this about-face. 'Every man is the author of his own life,' he
> said. 'The book you are writing is not yet finished. Therefore, it's a manu-
> script. What could be more appropriate than that?' (*MP* 6–7)

Fogg's identity is constructed around the names of people real or imaginary who have entered our culture as the protagonists of cherished
myths. As such, Fogg is twice removed from 'reality', and heavily marked
from the beginning of the narrative. When his uncle tells him that he is
the author of his own life, his words have a layer of different meanings.
Within the fictional world, he is the author of his own life because he is
growing up and becoming responsible for his own actions. As Fogg himself knows, he is also an author because he is 'writing' his own story, the
story that makes up *Moon Palace*. At the same time, he is quite literally a
manuscript, since he is Auster's fictional creation, a paper character who
does not exist outside the pages of the novel. Finally, he is also an MS in
the sense that he is a page on which history is written, where historical
personages and events meet and converge. As an embodiment of these
things, he exemplifies the move from the universal to the personal, from
the all-encompassing unifying narrative to the partial and subjective.

The question of the distinction between subjective and objective experience lies at the heart of this book. Most of the historical facts mentioned in the narrative are in some way connected with the experience of
the protagonist. History is experienced subjectively, made to mirror
inner states and anxieties. It is non-linear, made up of arbitrary connections which only acquire meaning for the person who makes them. For
Fogg, the neon sign of the Chinese restaurant *Moon Palace*, which he sees
from his window, serves as a unifying symbol, bringing the universal into
the personal:

> the words *Moon Palace* began to haunt me with all the mystery and fasci-
> nation of an oracle. Everything was mixed up in it at once: Uncle Victor and
> China, rocket ships and music, Marco Polo and the American West... One

thought kept giving way to another, spiraling into ever larger masses of connectedness. The idea of voyaging into the unknown, for example, and the parallels between Columbus and the astronauts. The discovery of America as a failure to reach China;... the West; the war against the Indians; the war in Vietnam, once called Indochina... It went on like that, and the more I opened myself to these secret correspondences, the closer I felt to understanding some fundamental truth about the world. I was going mad, perhaps, but I nevertheless felt a tremendous power surging through me, a gnostic joy that penetrated deep into the heart of things. (*MP* 32–33)

Auster, through Fogg, is rejoicing at the random nature of things, but also at the way they can be seen to be connected. History is seen as an arbitrary web of facts which can only acquire meaning in relation to one another: 'the world is not just the sum of the things that are in it. It is the infinitely complex network of connections among them. As in the meanings of words, things take on meaning only in relationship to each other' (*IoS* 161). The fundamental truth that Fogg seeks is not a universal truth, the truth of historical fact. The only accessible truth, which is the truth of art, is to be arrived at by finding one's own place in the world and its events: 'The true purpose of art was not to create beautiful objects, he discovered. It was a method of understanding, a way of penetrating the world and finding one's place in it' (*MP* 170). In this sense, the image of the artist is linked with that of the explorer. Both the artist (the writer) and the explorer have to deal not with an ultimate, extra-linguistic reality, but with a mediated reality, as it appears in language and representation. *Moon Palace* is a quest for self-knowledge, but it is also a quest to decipher the American landscape and to understand the land's history.

Fogg begins this quest, and his artistic apprenticeship, when he accepts Effing's job offer. He is hired to be the 'eyes' of a blind man, to whom he reads every day. When the weather improves, he has to take his aged employer for a walk and describe to him everything he sees in such a way as to help Effing 'see' things for himself:

My job was not to exhaust him with lengthy catalogues, but to help him see things for himself. In the end, the words didn't matter. Their task was to enable him to apprehend the objects as quickly as possible, and in order to do that, I had to make them disappear the moment they were pronounced. It took me weeks of hard work to simplify my sentences, to learn how to separate the extraneous from the essential. (*MP* 123)

Here, Marco trains himself not only to do his job well, but also to become a writer himself. In order to do that, he must first realise the full extent of the power – and limitations – of language: 'I began to consider it as a spiritual exercise, a process of training myself how to look at the world as if I were discovering it for the first time. What do you see? And if you see, how do you put it into words? The world enters us through our eyes, but we cannot make sense of it until it descends into our mouths' (MP 122).[22] During one of their last outings, Fogg and Effing meet a man who is carrying a broken umbrella. To the amusement of the two, he pretends that it is raining, tiptoes around invisible puddles and wards off raindrops while chattering in a rapid-fire monologue of ridiculous associations and puns. 'This was imagination in its purest form: the act of bringing nonexistent things to life, of persuading others to accept a world that was not really there' (MP 209). Peter Kirkegaard compares Auster's notions on language with Roman Jakobson's definition of 'poeticity': 'Poeticity is present when the word is felt as a word and not a mere presentation of the object being named or an outburst of emotion, when words and their composition, their meaning, their external and internal form, acquire a weight and value of their own instead of referring to reality.'[23] With the recounting of his young hero's apprenticeship, Auster is returning to questions raised in City of Glass, as Fogg's task is reminiscent of Stillman's mission. Like Stillman, Fogg wanders the streets of New York and tries to create a language that will correspond to the 'true nature' of things. That both these quests take place in the streets of the city points to Auster's continuing investigation of the ability of space to convey meaning.

This space is always textual as well as geographical. Fogg may be walking the streets, or travelling across the country, but he is also moving from one page to the next, as are the readers. The narrator himself sees the connection between travelling and reading, although for him this is an imaginative experience rather than a realisation of his own ontological status. When Uncle Victor leaves to travel with his band, Fogg inherits his collection of books which amounts to 1,492 tomes arranged in boxes, and the symbolism of the number does not escape him; as his uncle remarks, 'a propitious number, I think' (MP 13). Fogg does not only read the books; first he uses them as furniture, and later he has to sell them for nourishment, thus literally living off and through books.

22. It will be recalled that Auster writes of Ponge: 'The primary act of the poet, therefore, becomes the act of seeing, as if no one had ever seen the thing before'. See 'Legacies', above.
23. Peter Kirkegaard, 'Cities, Signs, and Meaning in Walter Benjamin and Paul Auster, or: never sure of any of it', *Orbis Litterarum*, 48.2–3 (1993), p. 170.

The last ones to go are sold on the day of the first moon landing. The relation between reading, narrating and travelling is made explicit when Fogg muses:

> Each time I opened a box, I was able to enter another segment of my uncle's life, a fixed period of days or weeks or months, and it consoled me to feel that I was occupying the same mental space that Victor had once occupied – reading the same words, living in the same stories, perhaps thinking the same thoughts. It was almost like following the route of an explorer from long ago, duplicating his steps as he thrashed out into virgin territory, moving westward with the sun, pursuing the light until it was finally extinguished. Because the boxes were not numbered or labeled, I had no way of knowing in advance which period I was about to enter. The journey was therefore made up of discrete, discontinuous jaunts. Boston to Lenox, for example. Minneapolis to Sioux Falls. Kenosha to Salt Lake City. It didn't matter to me that I was forced to jump around the map. By the end, all the blanks would be filled in, all the distances would be covered. (*MP* 22)

Fogg's adventures are an attempt to fill in the blanks of his own life-story, and he has a long distance to cover. His adventures begin when he graduates from college and rents an apartment on his own, having turned down his ex-roommate's offer to share:

> It was a studio apartment on the fifth floor of a large elevator building: one medium-size room with a kitchenette in the southeast corner, a closet, a bathroom, and a pair of windows that looked out on an alley. Pigeons flapped their wings and cooed on the ledge, and six dented garbage cans stood on the ground below. The air was dim inside, tinged gray throughout, and even on the brightest days it did not exude more than a paltry radiance. (*MP* 16)

This room becomes a place of meditation and asceticism, and nearly a tomb when he runs out of money. Like the lawyer's chambers where Bartleby is reduced to complete apathy, the room is a tomb-like enclosure, but also a projection of the tenant's inner life. What Fogg does not know about his small apartment is that it also has intertextual qualities. The room is a recurring topos in Auster's fiction; the image of confinement in a room appears in all of his novels, but it does not always carry the same connotations. Indeed, it often carries its own contradictions. Quinn begins to write again in an empty room in the Stillman apartment, but he is also running away from himself. For Peter Stillman, the dark room where he was kept for nine years is a place of torture and dehumanisation. Blue and Black live in rooms of glass, mirroring each other, but the possibility of introspection afforded by solitude, or the gaze outside the window, leads to no knowledge or understanding of their situation. *The Locked Room* conceals a man who is running away, who wants to change his identity and erase the past. Anna Blume finds safety in Isabel and Ferdinand's room, but the same room is the scene of Ferdinand's attempt to rape her, which leads her to murder him. Nashe and Pozzi are prisoners in the trailer, but their imprisonment gives at least one of them the chance to assess his own life and take full control of his future. The room has positive connotations in *Leviathan*, where it is 'a sanctuary of inwardness'; in *The Invention of Solitude*, the room is the place where the writer collects his thoughts and finds happiness in creativity. Auster repeatedly quotes Pascal: 'all the unhappiness of man stems from one thing only: that he is incapable of staying quietly in his room' (*IoS* 83). The friend who saves Fogg's life in Central Park is called Zimmer, which is German for 'room'. In *The Invention of Solitude* Auster writes about Hölderlin, who spent half his life living alone in a tower built for him by a carpenter named Zimmer. The fascination with Hawthorne's voluntary confinement, Thoreau's solitude in the woods, the room where Anne Frank wrote her diary while hiding from the Nazis, are all recurring themes in Auster's writings, and the reader who is familiar with Auster's *œuvre* will recognise the importance of the description of Fogg's room. William Dow sees an interesting connection between Auster's concept of 'imaginal space' and Hawthorne's description of the writer's territory 'in some foothold between actuality and dream'. He quotes from the Custom House sketch at the beginning of *The Scarlet Letter*, where Hawthorne writes:

> Moonlight, in a familiar room, falling so white upon the carpet, and show-ing all its figures so distinctly... is a medium the most suitable for a romance-writer to get acquainted with his illusive guests... the floor of our familiar room has become a neutral territory, somewhere between the real world and fairy-land, where the Actual and the Imaginary may meet, and each imbue itself with the nature of the other.[24]

In *Moon Palace*, spatial disharmony generates plot: Fogg's eviction from his flat sets in motion an extraordinary series of events which have a strong impact on him. The bookish young man becomes homeless, and he is forced to wander aimlessly all day and sleep rough at night. His romanticised vision of a spartan existence is short-lived, but the lessons he learns signal the end of his adolescence and his initiation into adulthood.

24. William Dow, 'Never Being "This Far from Home": Paul Auster and Picturing *Moon-light* Spaces', *Q/W/E/R/T/Y*, 6 (1996), pp. 194–95.

In the process, Fogg also becomes an urban explorer mapping out a city which is already over-familiar through its myriad representations. During the day, the city which has now become his home is a friendly place: he finds some money in the street which buys him food, and he seeks shelter in a cinema where many other homeless people go to sleep during the day. However, when night falls, the city is transformed into a perilous place: 'Once I began to survey the prospects around me, I saw how dismal they really were. I was not going to stretch out on the sidewalk like some bum, I said to myself, lying there for the whole night wrapped in newspapers. I would be exposed to every madman in the city if I did that; it would be like inviting someone to slit my throat' (MP 54). Eventually, 'too exhausted to think of anything else', he ends up in Central Park where he spends the night under a bush. It is here that Marco discovers another aspect of the city, one of whose existence he had been unaware, a place which does not conform to ideas about either city or nature: 'This was New York, but it had nothing to do with the New York I had always known. It was devoid of associations' (MP 56). The New York he knows is familiar in two ways. As man-made, structured space, it can be known through maps, street numbers, landmark buildings and other way-finding devices; as a 'mythical' city that everyone can claim to know without ever having visited it, New York is known through its 'associations', its representations. In the image of Central Park, Auster explores this paradox: the existence of a man-made image of nature in the middle of a megalopolis. The park, which partakes of both nature and city, is neither. It is a place where the ordinary laws of the city are suspended, where Marco can idle the time away without anyone becoming suspicious of him, a place where people become friendlier and share their food with him, a 'sanctuary, a refuge of inwardness against the demands of the city'. As it is a place devoid of associations, it is ideal for the young explorer who is given a chance to map out 'virgin territory'. A place which does not carry a host of connotations and associations is the perfect setting for a character who is already over-determined by his fictional status, his name, and, within his own world, by the way other people see him. With his transformation in this urban wilderness, Fogg unwittingly echoes his own grandfather (at that time still unknown to him), who reinvented himself by leaving New York and losing himself in the wilderness of the untamed West.

In the park, Fogg finds momentary relief from the burden of signification: 'If the streets forced me to see myself as others saw me, the park gave me a chance to return to my inner life, to hold on to myself purely in terms of what was happening inside me. It is possible to live without a

roof over your head, I discovered, but you cannot live without establish-
ing an equilibrium between the inner and outer. The park did that for me'
(*MP* 58). However, his illusion of having learned to 'separate the extraneous from the essential' is short-lived. When autumn comes, his mood
changes with the weather: 'Outside, the weather was gloomy: a raw
sullen kind of day, all mist and hopelessness. I could feel myself gradually
running out of ideas' (*MP* 68). From that moment on, his mental and
physical condition begin to deteriorate, and he reaches the verge of
death, only to be miraculously saved by his friends.

Having retreated into a cave to protect himself from the rain, he falls
into a feverish sleep, and dreams of his city's past: 'I suddenly began to
dream of Indians. It was 350 years ago, and I saw myself following a
group of half-naked men through the forests of Manhattan. It was a
strangely vibrant dream, relentless and exact, filled with bodies darting
among the light-dappled leaves and branches' (*MP* 70). Space and time
(or history) are perceived in terms of an unusual connection here. The
city protects its inhabitants from the weather, from the perils one can be
exposed to in nature, so when Marco finds himself at the mercy of natural elements, he forgets that he lives in a modern city and thinks of
nature in terms of the past. Space contains history, and as Fogg is reduced
to lessness, his predicament is made to rhyme with the peeling away of
layers that conceal the earlier history buried in space. Fogg, however, is
not the only one to dream of Indians and the country's past in relation
to his affliction. When he finally meets his father, Solomon Barber, he
finds out that the latter had written a novel called *Kepler's Blood* when
he was seventeen. It was 'part Western and part science-fiction', and it
told the story of an artist who travels to Utah and Arizona and 'turns
native' when he stumbles across a group of Indians. Years later, his son
sets out to find him, but when he does he kills him because he is rejected.
One of the murdered man's Indian children sets out to find Kepler Jr and
avenge his father's death; he kidnaps Kepler Jr's son, and when Kepler
pursues him to take the child back, he kills his own son because he does
not recognise him. The whole story is 'a complex dance of guilt and
desire' (*MP* 263), and Barber's fascination with 'the lost colonists of
Roanoke, the accounts of white men living among Indians, the mythology of the American West' are subjects that Barber deals with in his
academic work as a historian (*MP* 263). This story-within-the-story mirrors the events of the main plot, but it is also a response to another story-
within-the-story which takes up the centre of the book, the 'real'
life-story of Thomas Effing, Barber's father.

When Fogg starts working for Effing, one of his tasks is to read to the blind man. The books, chosen by Effing himself, are mostly travel narratives:

> We began with the journeys of Saint Brendan and Sir John de Mandeville, then moved on to Columbus, Cabeza de Vaca, and Thomas Harriot. We read excerpts from Doughty's *Travels in Arabia Deserta*, plodded through the whole of John Wesley Powell's book about the mapping expedition down the Colorado River, and ended up by reading a number of eighteenth- and nineteenth-century stories, firsthand accounts written by white settlers who had been abducted by Indians. (*MP* 110)

Halfway through the reading of Powell's second expedition down the Colorado River, Effing suddenly loses interest, and decides to read *The New York Times* obituaries instead. It soon transpires that all the reading was in preparation for Effing's real intention to compose his own obituary. 'I've never heard of someone writing his own obituary. Other people are supposed to do it for you – after you're dead,' remarks Fogg, but Effing explains: 'When they have the facts, yes. But what happens when there's nothing in the file?' (*MP* 128).

The story that follows, and the questions it raises, are a mirror of the main plot and a recapitulation of Auster's themes. Effing relates how, as a young man, he was an artist, a painter of promise who inherited a lot of money from his father which enabled him to devote himself entirely to painting. At the age of thirty-three, he left his wife behind and set out on an expedition to explore and paint the West with a young aspiring topographer. After various misadventures his friend died, and Effing ended up living in a cave which had once been the retreat of a hermit whom he found murdered. The climax of the story comes when, after months of peaceful living, painting and contemplation, he confronts the hermit's killers, kills them in his turn and takes a huge sum of money they had on them. Soon after, he leaves his cave and returns to ordinary life, assuming a new name and a new identity, since he had been given up for dead. Some of the story is given in Effing's own words, and some paraphrased by Fogg. Questions of authority, authorship and authenticity are once again prominent here. The mixed point of view allows Auster to blur the lines between 'fact' and fiction, first- and third-person narration, truth and lies. Auster considers such questions to be a major concern in his writing:

> is it possible or not to speak of another person...? A large part of my work revolves around this. It is always about telling someone else's story. But if

we know nothing of them, how can we tell their story? That's why, in my books, there are often holes, blanks, endings which are not final. In *Moon Palace*, Effing wants to compose his obituary. Among the information he gives, how much is invented and how much is real?[25]

This question remains unresolved and it is no accident that, after his adventures in the wilderness, Effing has to pass through the town of Bluff before he returns to 'civilisation'. A more important issue replaces the question of whether Effing's narrative is true or false: his story is *necessary*, as Effing needs to weave this elaborate narrative in order to assume his new identity. He can only become 'Thomas Effing' if he creates a fiction around this new name. When Effing dies, no one agrees to publish his obituary, so that his life-story remains no more than a tale which is real only to the extent that it has been narrated. The teller, be it Effing or Fogg, is the only source of 'authority' or 'authenticity', so that it becomes irrelevant whether their stories are 'true' or 'false'; they are the story-tellers, and the only version of events that exists is the one they are telling. But if the emphasis lies on stories as fictional constructs, what is the place of all the historical references they contain? They are not 'details included to enhance an effect of reality; they are too esoteric to function at that level of effect. They are, rather, kernels of reality buried in [the] text... The parody is not of realism, but of irrealism. To the post-modern statement that fiction is not truth, it opposes a new paradox: fiction cannot lie.'[26]

Effing himself is aware of the power of fictional representation. His narrative takes up the theme of the explorer, and one of its functions in the book is to provide the author with an opportunity to contemplate the myth of the West, combining the theme of the artist as explorer with the question of reality and representation. Effing's Wild West is not so much a real place as one that exists in the mind, and which is available only through representation, or the qualities imposed on it. Early in his story, he tells Fogg that the West is

> where they shoot all those cowboy-and-Indian movies, the goddamned Marlboro man gallops through there on television every night. But pictures don't tell you anything about it, Fogg. It's all too massive to be painted or drawn; even photographs can't get the feel of it. Everything is so distorted,

25.   Cécile Wajsbrot, 'Paul Auster, l'Invention de l'Ecriture', *Magazine Littéraire*, 308 (1993), p. 81.
26.   William Lavender, 'The Novel of Critical Engagement: Paul Auster's *City of Glass*', *Contemporary Literature*, 34.2 (1993), p. 236.

it's like trying to reproduce the distances in outer space: the more you see, the less your pencil can do. To see it is to make it vanish. (*MP* 157)

Effing himself already had a preconceived idea of the West before he set out to explore it. The images came mostly from the work of his friend and mentor, the painter Thomas Moran, whose first name he adopted when he reinvented himself. Moran, according to Effing, was the one who showed Americans what the West looked like:

> The first painting of the Grand Canyon was by Moran...; the first painting of Yellowstone, the first painting of the Great Salt Desert, the first painting of the canyon country in southern Utah – they were all done by Moran. Manifest Destiny! They mapped it out, they made pictures of it, they digested it into the great American profit machine. Those were the last bits of the continent, the blank spaces no one had explored. Now here it was, all laid out on a pretty piece of canvas for everyone to see. (*MP* 149)

The blank spaces are filled with paintings, representations of space. The Wild West was tamed by being put on a canvas, both literally and metaphorically, and, if Moran was the one who showed Americans what the West looked like, today he is remembered as a painter who 'turned the majestic and awe-inspiring valleys and canyons of the Yellowstone and Colorado Rivers into great candy-coated, wispy confections'.[27]

Edwin Fussell explores the fascination with the West in nineteenth-century American writing, and he claims that it was writing, or representation invested with the artist's preconceived notions, that gave the West its qualities, creating a mythology around a place that had no value in and of itself:

> The simple truth is that the American West was neither more nor less interesting than any other place, except in mythology or in the swollen egos of Westerners, until by interpretation the great American writers – all of whom happened to be Eastern – made it seem so. This they did by conceiving its physical aspects (forests, rivers, lakes, clearings, settlements, prairies, plains, deserts) and its social aspects (isolation, simplicity, improvisation, criticism, chaos, restlessness, paradox, irony) as expressive emblems for the invention and development of a new national civilization, and not as things in themselves.[28]

27. Matthew Baigell, *A Concise History of American Painting and Sculpture* (New York and London: Harper & Row, 1984), p. 129.
28. Edwin Fussell, *Frontier: American Literature and the American West* (Princeton, NJ: Princeton University Press, 1965), p. 13.

Life teaches both Uncle Victor and Effing, who set out on their journeys with second-hand experience, that the myth of the West is just that: a myth. When Uncle Victor leaves Marco to travel west with his band, he envisions a mythical America where he may fulfil his dreams. The places that he has not yet visited hold the promise of an exciting future:

> Colorado, Arizona, Nevada, California. We'll be setting a westerly course, plunging into the wilderness. It should be interesting, I think, no matter what comes of it. A bunch of city slickers in the land of cowboys and Indians. But I relish the thought of those open spaces, of playing my music under the desert sky. Who knows if some new truth will not be revealed to me out there? (*MP* 12)

Alas, no truth is revealed to him. Before long, the band fall on hard times, they split up, and Uncle Victor decides to return to New York. As Marco waits for his uncle's return, he too shares in the disillusionment; the West is no longer a place of open spaces where some transcendental truth may be revealed to the traveller: 'suddenly the American continent was transformed into a vast danger zone, a perilous nightmare of traps and mazes' (*MP* 18). Throughout the novel, space is connected with the past as well as the future; depending on the individual's predicament, it either bestows liberty or conceals terror. But to give space its rightful place in the book, we need to return to the image of the moon.

As stated earlier, the moon in Blakelock's painting occupies the mathematical centre of the canvas, while the description of it occupies the centre of the novel. The narrative begins with an orphan who decides to throw his life to the winds, and in the process ends up discovering his genealogy. His grandfather tells him what his friend the topographer had taught him: 'you can't fix your exact position on the earth without referring to some point in the sky… If you think about it long enough, it will turn your brain inside-out. A here exists only in relation to a there… There's this only because there's that… Think of it, boy. We find ourselves only by looking to what we're not' (*MP* 153–54). His words recall those of Thoreau who, in *Walden*, wrote: 'Every man has to learn the points of compass again as often as he awakes, whether from sleep or any abstraction. Not till we are lost, in other words, not till we have lost the world, do we begin to find ourselves, and realize where we are and the infinite extent of our relations.'[29] It is this task that the narrator/explorer accomplishes, and only after his adventures have come to an end can he begin to write his story. On his way to the place where Effing's adven-

---

29. *The Variorum Walden*, ed. Harding, p. 149.

tures are supposed to have taken place, he loses first his newly found father, and then his inheritance. He continues to walk towards the Pacific, thinking that when he reaches the end of the continent 'some important question' will be resolved for him. When he finally reaches the ocean, his real and metaphorical journeys come to an end:

> This is where I start, I said to myself, this is where my life begins. I stood on the beach for a long time, waiting for the last bits of sunlight to vanish. Behind me, the town went about its business, making familiar late-century American noises. As I looked down the curve of the coast, I saw the lights of the houses being turned on, one by one. Then the moon came up from behind the hills. It was a full moon, as round and yellow as a burning stone. I kept my eyes on it as it rose into the night sky, not turning away until it had found its place in the darkness. (*MP* 306–307)

This is when Fogg finds his own place in the darkness, his vocation as an artist, so that he can now begin to write his narrative, the story of *Moon Palace*. The novel that followed it, *The Music of Chance*, continued with the theme of a quest for harmony, telling the story of a man who, first in travels across America and then in confinement, seeks his place among elaborate structures, fictional as well as physical. *Leviathan* makes the process even more explicit, starting with the image of a man who is blown to pieces, and charting a writer's attempt to put the fragments of this man back together.

Exploding Fictions

Leviathan is, ostensibly, Auster's most realistic novel to date. The narrative adheres to the basic principles of realist writing, and the world the characters inhabit is not predominantly the world of the text, or the realm of metaphor, but a representation of contemporary America. Narrated by Peter Aaron, *Leviathan* tells the story of Aaron's friend Benjamin Sachs. The narrative begins six days after Sachs is found dead, and it moves backwards to trace the beginning of the friendship between the two men and the extraordinary events that led up to his violent death. Sachs was a pacifist who chose to go to jail rather than fight in Vietnam. Through a series of unusual events and coincidences, Sachs killed a man; although he was never arrested, he tried to atone for his crime, and when he found out that the dead man was a terrorist he decided to carry on his work. In a symbolic gesture, he began to blow up replicas of the Statue of Liberty until one of his attacks went wrong and he was killed by one

of his own bombs. The story unfolds against a realistic background, and
the chronology is established with reference to historical events: in the
second chapter, for instance, Aaron recalls a meeting with Sachs which
took place in a restaurant: '*The New York Times* was spread out on the
Formica table in front of him, and he seemed engrossed in what he was
reading... This was early 1980, the days of the hostage crisis in Iran, the
Khmer Rouge atrocities in Cambodia, the war in Afghanistan' (*Lev* 90).
At the same time, however, this is a novel in which the categories 'fiction'
and 'reality' collapse into one another as the world and the book become
indistinguishable.

If, as Paul Auster has remarked, all his novels are really the same book,
Leviathan is another version of *The Locked Room*. Both narratives
involve a quest for a missing writer in the course of which the narrator,
a writer himself, confronts the problem of gaining access to another
person's self, and trying to turn the events of another man's life into a
coherent narrative. Aaron, like the narrator of *The Locked Room*,
becomes an investigator, and both novels attest to Auster's continuing
interest in reconciling the role of the detective with that of the artificer.
The narrator who sets out to find his missing friend has to confront his
own limitations as a seeker of truth, as a writer, but what he achieves is
not an insight into his friend's 'true self'. Instead, he is confronted with
the realisation of the unavailability of truth or objectivity. The only truth
each narrator arrives at is the truth of the story he has created in the
process of his investigation. Benjamin Sachs, the missing protagonist of
Leviathan, could be described in the words that the narrator of *The
Locked Room* uses to describe Fanshawe: 'he was there for you, and yet
at the same time he was inaccessible. You felt that there was a secret core
in him that could never be penetrated, a mysterious center of hiddenness.
To imitate him was somehow to participate in that mystery, but it was
also to understand that you could never really know him' (*LR* 210). Like
Fanshawe, Sachs 'absents himself' for a long time, and the narrator
writes about him in an attempt to understand him. In the process, Aaron
becomes another detective figure trying to piece together the fragments
of another man's life, only to be confronted by absence and gaps where
he had hoped to find answers. Sachs, like Fanshawe, becomes a symbol
of the unknowability of human nature, of the impossibility of gaining
access to another person. In *City of Glass* Quinn decided, like a latter-
day Don Quixote, to live the adventures of his own books, only to find
himself imprisoned in another kind of fictional room; in *Leviathan*, Sachs
gives up writing in order to become a terrorist and urge America to

change its ways. He steps into the real world only to find that he cannot escape his own self-mythologising.

Despite these parallels, there are obvious differences between the two texts. *The Locked Room* is more self-conscious and, towards the end, the writer shows complete disregard for realistic conventions. The book not only ends with the protagonist 'answering the question by asking another question', but it also sends the readers back to the first story in *The New York Trilogy*, thus placing all three stories primarily (though not exclusively) inside the realm of the text. If *The New York Trilogy* can be read as the image of a labyrinth, *Leviathan* becomes a garden of forking paths. The recurring imagery of explosions and fragmentation indicates dispersal which does not, as I shall be arguing, result in annihilation, be that the annihilation of self, of signification, or the possibility of being saved by fiction or representation. *Leviathan* is populated by more realistic characters than any of Auster's previous books, and it appears to be more conventional than anything he has written before it. Yet the reader acquainted with Auster's *œuvre* will recognise some familiar devices. Peter Aaron, the narrator, shares his initials, and some biographical details, with Paul Auster: he has written a novel called *Luna* (Auster's *Moon Palace*), his wife is called Iris to Auster's Siri, his first wife Delia (Auster's Lydia), and the two protagonists meet in Nashe's Tavern, whose proprietor we last saw involved in a car crash at the end of *The Music of Chance*. Brian McHale uses the phrase *retour de personnages* to refer to the authorial practice of having characters reappear in a series of novels.[30] In the case of writers such as Balzac or Trollope, the device is used to heighten the effect of realism and to reinforce the illusion that characters exist outside the text, living and growing older between novels. In postmodernist texts, on the other hand, the device is deliberately exaggerated to create confusion and impart a sense of indeterminacy; it is a defamiliarising technique aimed at drawing attention to the fictionality of the text and undermining traditional notions of delineation of character, while it is also an expression of uncertainty and indeterminacy. When a writer names a character, it does not follow that he has any insight into this person's 'real life', and the person does not have a real life anyway because he or she is a creation of the author. Auster brings together characters from 'real life' as well as from other novels, but what this achieves is not so much to underpin the narrative as to stress that the world of the novel is an alternative reality, a more self-conscious fiction. This blurring of the line that ought to separate the 'real' from the invented

30. McHale, *Postmodernist Fiction*, pp. 57–58.

also relates to the way Auster chooses to address the question of politics, how he writes about contemporary society and the writer's role in it.

As in previous novels, chance dominates the plot. Aaron and Sachs are brought together when a snowstorm prevents anyone from going to their reading. Later, Sachs ends up killing Reed Dimaggio because he receives a lift from a young man, while Aaron inadvertently helps the FBI to identify the body of Benjamin Sachs by mentioning that someone had been impersonating him and signing his books. A lost address book leads Maria Turner to her old friend Lillian Stern, who turns out to be the murdered man's ex-wife. Once again, coincidence is not used as a mechanical device to drive the plot; it gives the author the opportunity to ask questions about free will, and to explore the extent to which one can be said to have control over one's own life. This is especially apt in a novel that deals with a writer's decision to give up writing and 'step into the real world': can he ever escape the plots he weaves himself, and does he not escape into another plot made by the author and the narrator of the book?

The political aspect of the novel is stressed through a series of references to political events, but the emphasis lies more heavily on writing, as the book self-consciously refers to texts which either deal explicitly with politics or have acquired a strong political resonance. Auster explains that the title *Leviathan* is a reference to Hobbes, 'the State as a monster which devours people', but also a reference to 'the monster of consciousness', Sachs, who devours himself in the process of fulfilling his mission.[31] The novel's epigraph is taken from Emerson: 'every actual state is corrupt', he writes in 'Politics', and, in consequence, 'good men must not obey the laws too well'.[32] A similar view is expressed in 'Resistance to Civil Government', which is instrumental in shaping Sachs's attitudes and beliefs, where Thoreau proposes a model of passive resistance against unjust governments. Echoing Emerson, he writes: 'under a government which imprisons any unjustly, the true place for a just man is also in prison'.[33]

Leviathan is dedicated to Don DeLillo, whose 1991 novel *Mao II* charts similar territory, dealing as it does with a reclusive writer who reluctantly agrees to re-enter the public arena in order to save a poet

31. Wajsbrot, 'Paul Auster, l'Invention de l'Ecriture', p. 82.
32. Ralph Waldo Emerson, 'Politics' (1844), in *The Collected Works of Ralph Waldo Emerson*, ed. Joseph Slater and Douglas Emory Wilson (Cambridge, MA, and London: Belknap Press of Harvard University Press, 1983), III, p. 122.
33. Henry David Thoreau, 'Resistance to Civil Government' (1849), in *The Reform Papers*, ed. Wendell Glick (Princeton, NJ: Princeton University Press, 1973), p. 76.

taken hostage by terrorists in Beirut. The writer, Bill Gray, initially decides to come out of hiding and have his picture taken by Brita Nilsson, a photographer whose project involves taking pictures of famous writers. They have long sessions together, during which they talk about their art while she takes pictures, much as Sachs in *Leviathan* talks to the artist Maria Turner. Bill Gray tells Brita Nilsson:

> There's a curious knot that binds novelists and terrorists. In the West we become famous effigies as our books lose the power to shape and influence. Do you ask your writers how they feel about this? Years ago I used to think it was possible for a novelist to alter the inner life of the culture. Now bomb-makers and gunmen have taken that territory. They make raids on human consciousness. What writers used to do before we were all incorporated.[34]

The proximity of this view to Sachs's own beliefs about the role of the writer in society may emphasise the affinity between the two characters, but *Leviathan* is more fruitfully read as a response to, or in dialogue with, *Mao II* rather than as a recapitulation of similar thematic concerns or discursive strategies. DeLillo anchors his debate in the contemporary world, placing his characters against a background dominated by the intrusiveness of the media, and the tyranny of a visual culture in the service of consumerism. As Bill Gray notes, 'In our world we sleep and eat the image and pray to it and wear it too.' Moments of historical crisis or catastrophe are experienced as televised events in the novel, while the title reference to Andy Warhol's multiple portraits foregrounds the book's preoccupation with proliferating, self-generating images.

The Statue of Liberty replicas in *Leviathan* can be said to have a similar function, but whereas DeLillo is preoccupied with postmodern consumerist culture, Auster negotiates his writer's position in the world by invoking, as I have already indicated, the spirit and the rhetoric of nineteenth-century American writing. In doing so, he places Sachs's dilemmas and actions in a context that has few similarities with DeLillo's. Bill Gray wants to stay out of the limelight partly because he condemns the all-pervasiveness of the image as consumerist event, whereas Benjamin Sachs's withdrawal from the world is continuous with the Thoreauvian tradition of individuality and resistance. His subsequent bombing mission, and its accompanying rhetoric, are negotiated through references not only to Thoreau, but also to Hawthorne and Melville. As a result, it can be argued that Aaron (and ultimately his creator) asks that Sachs's career be read with reference to those American writers whose work

34. Don DeLillo, *Mao II* (London: Vintage, 1991), p. 41.

engaged with questions relating to prophecy, apocalypse and ultimately the sense of betrayed promise. At the same time, Auster's narrative technique involves Aaron telling another author's story, trying to do him justice, but ultimately betraying him, metaphorically because he cannot write about someone else without writing about himself, and literally because he unwittingly helps the FBI to identify Sachs's body. In this respect, the book's very process of enunciation is inextricably bound up with its historical and political project.

Even though Auster's intertextual practice places the novel in a political context, Aaron's narrative also tells a different story. The first replica of the Statue of Liberty does not explode until thirty pages before the end of the novel, and Sachs's transformation from writer to terrorist is only explained in the last twenty pages of the book, from the moment he finds out that Dimaggio was some sort of political activist and decides to carry on his work, until one of his bombings goes wrong and he ends up dead. The bulk of the narrative is taken up by the story of how Sachs killed a man and set out to atone for his crime, and the lives he touched – and was in turn transformed by – in the course of his personal odyssey.

In his much-quoted, but always relevant, 1961 essay 'Writing American Fiction', Philip Roth argued that 'the American writer in the middle of the twentieth century has his hands full in trying to understand, describe, and then make *credible* much of American reality... The actuality is continually outdoing our talents, and the culture tosses up figures almost daily that are the envy of any novelist.'[35] This was written before the Vietnam war, before the first man walked on the moon, and long before the arrest of the Unabomber. For his part, Auster has claimed that he wants to write books 'as strange as the world we live in', and that he sees this as a political act. He recently told an interviewer: 'We cannot escape politics! I belong... to the first group [of American citizens] – those who think that we live together in society and that we are all interdependent. In this sense, yes, every work of art, whether consciously or not, is a political act.'[36] As a declaration of political commitment, this statement sounds vague and detached, and it points to Auster's continuing interest in the personal rather than the political. Philip Roth concluded his essay with the remark that the 'communal predicament' is distressing, more so to the

---

35. *Commentary*, 31 (March 1961), pp. 223–33. Reprinted in *The Novel Today: Contemporary Writers on Modern Fiction*, ed. Malcolm Bradbury (London: Fontana Press, 1977), p. 29. Auster expresses a similar idea by using a quotation from Jules Verne as the epigraph to *Moon Palace*: 'Nothing can astound an American'.
36. De Cortanze, *La Solitude du labyrinthe*, p. 98.

writer than to other people. 'And it may be that when this situation produces not only feelings of disgust, rage, melancholy, but impotence too, the writer is apt to lose heart and turn finally to other matters, to the construction of wholly imaginary worlds, and to a celebration of the self, which may, in a variety of ways, become his subject, as well as the impetus that establishes the parameters of his technique.'[37] Paul Auster's fiction occupies the middle ground between writing that is primarily interested in the 'communal predicament', and writing that concerns itself with the construction of 'wholly imaginary worlds'. If he explores the political, he does so by way of the personal. Moreover, his world is not one of negation; the world of *Leviathan* may be fragmented, but there is no evidence of a total breakdown, be that the breakdown of the individual, of society, of meaning, or of narrative. As in his previous novels, Auster seeks a pattern – one that may not necessarily exist in the world around him, but one which may emerge from his narrative and, in Hawthorne's phrase, 'be shaped into a figure'. In this respect, *Leviathan* can be said to chronicle a quest for meaning; not a universal, all-encompassing pattern, but something on a smaller and more personal scale. The novel charts Peter Aaron's search for his friend, and Benjamin Sachs's quest for redemption and for his role as a writer in contemporary America. Auster deals with the political by aestheticising it, and if *Leviathan* contains many references to real historical and political events, it is equally made up of other texts, and the question of writing and representation is as important as that of politics.

There are two books within *Leviathan*: one is *The New Colossus*, Sachs's first novel, and the other is *Leviathan*, written by Peter Aaron using the title of the book Sachs never completed. *The New Colossus* functions as a mirror image of *Leviathan* (Auster's *Leviathan*), while it could also be read as a comment on Auster's own earlier fiction. 'As every reader knows, *The New Colossus* is a historical novel, a meticulously researched book set in America between 1876 and 1890 and based on documented, verifiable facts. Most of the characters are people who actually lived at the time, and even when the characters are imaginary, they are not inventions so much as borrowings, figures stolen from the pages of other novels' (*Lev* 37). The cast of characters in the novel includes Emerson, Whitman, Hawthorne's daughter Rose, and fictional characters such as Raskolnikov, Huck Finn, and Ishmael. It is curious, then, that in a novel of such overt literariness the 'dominant emotion was anger, a full-blown, lacerating anger that surged up on nearly every page: anger

37. In *The Novel Today*, ed. Bradbury, p. 42.

against America, anger against political hypocrisy, anger as a weapon to destroy national myths' (*Lev* 40). Like the Auster of *Leviathan*, Sachs addresses questions pertaining to historical fact in terms of other books, fictional characters and writers; from Sachs's formative reading of Thoreau to the writing of his own historical novel, his attitude stems from reading. Time, however, renders Sachs's novel almost obsolete:

> The era of Ronald Reagan had began. Sachs went on doing what he had always done, but in the new American order of the 1980s, his position became increasingly marginalized... Almost imperceptibly, Sachs came to be seen as a throwback, as someone out of step with the spirit of the time. The world had changed around him, and in the present climate of selfishness and intolerance, of moronic, chest-pounding Americanism, his opinions sounded curiously harsh and moralistic. It was bad enough that the Right was everywhere in the ascendant, but even more disturbing to him was the collapse of any effective opposition to it. The Democratic Party had caved in; the Left had all but disappeared; the press was mute. All the arguments had suddenly been appropriated by the other side, and to raise one's voice against it was considered bad manners. (*Lev* 104)

If Sachs and his work can be read as an image of Auster and his novel, two things are happening in this passage. It can be read as an 'apology' on the author's part, a way of signalling an awareness of the political climate, and thus seeking to pre-empt criticisms of the novel for its perceived lack of involvement. At the same time, as Sachs and his work are framed by Aaron's narrative, the marginalised author and his writings are saved, recovered: the fiction they become part of becomes a justification, and also a vindication, of Sachs's perceived failings.

The image that dominates *Leviathan* is that of the Statue of Liberty, a conceit which works on various levels. Sachs's first visit to the statue at the age of six is recounted early on in the narrative. Aaron points out that Sachs was prone to self-mythologising, and this incident is a good example of how Sachs linked personal experience with the world around him. Two things happened during that visit, and Sachs ascribes to them what may seem a disproportionate significance. First, he recalls how his mother made him wear a pair of 'terrible short pants with the white knee socks', whereas he wanted to wear jeans and sneakers, especially since he was going to meet two boys his own age. This trivial episode is now remembered as a formative experience in Sachs's career: 'Even then, the irony of the situation didn't escape me. There we were, about to pay homage to the concept of freedom, and I myself was in chains. I lived in an absolute dictatorship, and for as long as I could remember my rights had been trampled underfoot' (*Lev* 33). After that visit, Sachs became 'master of his own wardrobe': 'I felt as if I'd struck a blow for democracy, as if I'd risen up in the name of oppressed peoples all over the world' (*Lev* 33). During the ascent inside the Statue, his mother and her friend suffered from vertigo, and as a result they had to go down the stairs sitting down. '"It was my first lesson on political theory," Sachs said, turning his eyes away from his mother to look at Fanny and me. "I learned that freedom can be dangerous. If you don't watch out, it can kill you"' (*Lev* 35). Aaron recognises the fact that the statue must have held some secret attraction for Sachs, and he also points out that Sachs's novel contained numerous references to the Statue of Liberty: 'If not for Sachs's novel... I might have forgotten all about it. But since that book is filled with references to the Statue of Liberty, it's hard to ignore the possibility of a connection' (*Lev* 35). The same, of course, is true of Aaron's own narrative and Auster's novel, in which the statue becomes the scene of conflict and is, in a sense, the key to Sachs's development: the statue is associated with the formative childhood experience, the crisis he suffers, and the answer he finds to his predicament. It is therefore significant that, as soon as the statue makes its first appearance in the narrative, Sachs is seen to weave plots around it, using it as a landmark for his own development.

Sachs's second encounter with the Statue of Liberty is equally important, as it marks the beginning of a phase that transforms him forever. On 4 July 1986 Sachs attended a party to celebrate the one hundredth anniversary of the Statue of Liberty. The circumstances led Aaron and Sachs's wife, Fanny, to recall Sachs's childhood incident, but no sooner had that descent been recalled than Sachs fell from the fire escape. Both the cause and the effects of this accident remain a mystery to Aaron, and they become an emblem of his own ignorance: 'This is the thing I'm still struggling to come to terms with, the mystery I'm still trying to solve. His body mended, but he was never the same after that. In those few seconds before he hit the ground, it was as if Sachs lost everything. His entire life flew apart in midair, and from that moment until his death four years later, he never put it back together again' (*Lev* 107). The circumstances of his death confirm this, as he is blown to bits, his body burst into dozens of small pieces, and it is left up to Aaron to put the pieces back together, even when he knows that Sachs can never be whole again.

The theme of the Fall is a recurrent one in Auster's fiction. The Fall of Man is the shaping force of Stillman's argument in *City of Glass*, and it concerns not only humankind's fall from grace but also the fall of language. Theological and linguistic connotations give way to personal tragedy when Stillman ends his life by jumping off a bridge. In *In the Country of Last Things*, Anna Blume jumps out of a window to escape her persecutor; the fall becomes a means of struggle for survival in a brutal world where the protagonist can only rely on her own resources to preserve her humanity. Nashe's story in *The Music of Chance* is introduced with these words: 'Without the slightest tremor of fear, Nashe closed his eyes and jumped' (*MC* 1). What he jumped into was an adventure that would change his life for ever. In *Moon Palace*, Solomon Barber falls into a freshly dug grave, and Fogg loses his father the moment he has found him. The fall therefore represents loss, but at the same time it is seen as a necessary stage in each character's development, an unburdening that can lead to recovery.

With his accident, Sachs falls out of his social milieu; by refusing to talk to his friends as he is lying on a hospital bed, he becomes a stubborn recluse who wants to sever his ties with the outside world. Like a latter-day Transcendentalist, he withdraws from the outside world in order to contemplate in isolation:

> Something extraordinary had taken place, and before it lost its force within him, he needed to devote his unstinting attention to it. Hence his silence. It was not a refusal so much as a method, a way of holding on to the horror of that night long enough to make sense of it. To be silent was to enclose himself in contemplation, to relive the moments of his fall again and again, as if he could suspend himself in midair for the rest of time – forever just two inches off the ground, forever waiting for the apocalypse of the last moment. (*Lev* 119–20)

Yet it is not only the Transcendentalist practice of withdrawal from society that is ironically echoed here. Auster is also returning to the story of Jonah in the belly of the fish, which had excited his imagination in *The Invention of Solitude*. In 'The Book of Memory', he imagines Jonah inside the great leviathan, and he writes:

> In the depth of that solitude, which is equally the depth of silence, as if in the refusal to speak there were an equal refusal to turn one's face to the other... – which is to say: who seeks solitude seeks silence; who does not speak is alone; is alone, even unto death – Jonah encounters the darkness of death... And when the fish vomits Jonah onto dry land, Jonah is given back to life, as if the death he had found in the belly of the fish were a preparation for new life, a life that has passed through death, and therefore a life that can at last speak. For death has frightened him into opening his mouth... In the darkness of the solitude that is death, the tongue is finally loosened, and at the moment it begins to speak, there is

an answer. And even if there is no answer, the man has begun to speak.
(*IoS* 125–26)

Like Jonah, Sachs experiences death in his self-imposed linguistic prison.
When Sachs recovers from this spell of intense introspection, he decides
to trade words for action: 'The idea of writing disgusts me. It doesn't
mean a goddamned thing to me anymore... I don't want to spend the rest
of my life rolling pieces of blank paper into a typewriter. I want to stand
up from my desk and do something... I've got to step into the real world
now and do something' (*Lev* 122). 'And even if there is no answer, the
man has begun to speak': despite his decision, Sachs has no specific plans
for accomplishing his mission. He gives up writing for a while, and he
turns down a number of commissions from editors, but later he starts
working on a new novel, which he calls *Leviathan*. He is only a third into
it when fate intervenes and forces him to 'step into the real world'.

Taking a break from the composition of his new novel, Sachs goes for
a walk and gets lost in the woods. He is offered a lift by a young man,
and they meet another car that blocks their way. In a twisted re-enactment of the murder of Laius, Sachs kills the aggressor, after the latter has
killed the young man. This sets in motion a whole series of events that
will determine Sachs's passage from guilt to redemption, and lead to the
discovery of what he sees as his vocation. Going through the dead man's
possessions, he finds out that his name was Reed Dimaggio, and that he
carried in the car large quantities of explosives and a big sum of money.
The first person that he confides in, Maria Turner, turns out to be
acquainted with the victim, and Sachs sets out to atone for his crime by
giving the money to the man's ex-wife, an old friend of Maria's. A large
part of the narrative is then devoted to the relationship that develops
between the two, but this is not the happy conclusion to the story. During
his stay with Lillian, Sachs does not learn much about his victim until he
decides to look into his room. There, he finds Dimaggio's dissertation, a
reappraisal of the life and works of anarchist activist Alexander Berkman.
One thing Sachs learns from it is that terrorism 'had its place in the struggle, so to speak. If used correctly, it could be an effective tool for drama-
tizing the issues at stake, for enlightening the public about the nature of
institutional power' (*Lev* 224). This, in turn, leads him to a comparison
between himself and his victim, and he comes to the conclusion that 'I'd
sat around grumbling and complaining for the past fifteen years, but for
all my self-righteous opinions and embattled stances, I'd never put myself
on the line. I was a hypocrite and Dimaggio wasn't, and when I thought

about myself in comparison to him, I began to feel ashamed' (*Lev* 225). Although he does not realise it, Sachs cannot escape from the world of books, and it is ironic that, despite the fact that he felt 'a lot of anger towards America', it is a dissertation that forces him to reappraise his own position as a writer. Even at this late stage in his awareness of his role in society, his first impulse is to write something about Dimaggio, 'something similar to what he had written about Berkman'. However, for reasons he cannot comprehend, he cannot perform the task and his inability to do so is the only indication that this is not his true vocation, not the way to step into the real world and do something. Once again, the answer to his problem comes from a book. Taking refuge in a book-shop to avoid an old acquaintance in the street, he buys a copy of his own book; he spends a lot of time just gazing at the cover, and it is then that he experiences an epiphany:

> The Statue of Liberty, remember? That strange, distorted drawing of the Statue of Liberty. That was where it started, and once I realised where I was going, the rest followed, the whole cockeyed plan fell into place... I would be using it [Dimaggio's money] to express my own convictions, to take a stand for what I believed in, to make the kind of difference I had never been able to make before. All of a sudden, my life seemed to make sense to me. Not just the past few months, but my whole life, all the way back to the beginning. It was a miraculous confluence, a startling conjunction of motives and ambitions. I had found the unifying principle, and this one idea would bring all the broken pieces of myself together. For the first time in my life, I would be whole. (*Lev* 227–28)[38]

This is how Sachs justifies his decision to blow up replicas of the Statue of Liberty. In his newly found zeal, he is 'less like a political revolutionary than some anguished, soft-spoken prophet' (*Lev* 217), accompanying his explosions with messages that read 'Wake up, America', or 'Democracy is not given. It must be fought for every day.' However, the unifying principle that Sachs thinks he has discovered is just a fiction he has created, a synthesis of his various encounters with the Statue of Liberty, whose value, in turn, is symbolic rather than intrinsic. Like Rousseau, who thought that hitting a tree with a stone could determine the course of his life, Sachs seizes on this arbitrary connection in an attempt to find an answer to his dilemmas. However, as in previous novels, arbitrary connections do not amount to a post-modernist loss of faith. Instead, they lead to a sense of personal recovery.

---

38. The cover of *Moon Palace* depicts the Statue of Liberty seen from many different angles.

Leviathan opens with the image of a man who has been blown to pieces, and the subsequent narrative chronicles the attempt of the dead man's best friend to put the pieces back together by telling the story of how this man came to blow himself up by the side of a road in northern Wisconsin. This in effect reverses Hobbes's procedure in his *Leviathan* (1651), where he begins with the image of an artificial body in its entirety and then goes on to analyse its parts. In his introduction, he writes: 'For by Art is created that great LEVIATHAN called a COMMON-WEALTH, or STATE, (in latine CIVITAS) which is but an Artificiall Man.'[39] Auster borrows Hobbes's main conceit, the image of the artificial man, a construct which has parts corresponding to nature but which is 'of greater stature and strength', but he uses it not so much for its political implications as for the way in which it can be seen as a metaphor for the act of writing, and what that writing reflects of people's lives. Writing thus becomes an attempt to find a pattern, to put together the fragments. The novel is an artificial body whose parts correspond metaphorically to real life, just as Hobbes's body has 'soveraignty' for a soul, magistrates for joints, reward and punishment for nerves. This move from Hobbes's analysis to Aaron's (and Auster's) attempted, but not quite accomplished, synthesis is indicative of a more general trend in contemporary writing which rejects the grand, totalising narratives of the past in favour of internalisation and subjectivity. Paul Auster as the author of the novel puts together the fragments of his limited knowledge while, within the text, Peter Aaron does so too, by putting together the parts of his friend's shattered life; the fiction he creates he calls *Leviathan* in homage to his friend's unfinished novel of the same name. Sachs's work in progress is curiously absent from the text. Whereas *The New Colossus* is described in detail, Aaron says little of *Leviathan*. Tantalisingly, he does remark that this was the book he had always imagined Sachs could write, but he goes on to add that 'as it stands now, the book is no more than the promise of a book, a potential book buried in a box of messy manuscript pages and a smattering of notes' (*Lev* 142). Aaron's own novel, though coherently narrated and complete, is equally fragmented to the extent that the writer confesses the limitations of his own perception and acknowledges the impossibility of turning another man's life into a story that could correspond to that man's 'real' life.

Leviathan tells the story of Benjamin Sachs and his transformation from writer to terrorist, but it is also the story of Peter Aaron. At the

39. Thomas Hobbes, *Leviathan*, ed. A.D. Lindsay (London: J.M. Dent, 1962), p. 1.

beginning of his narrative, Aaron promises to confine himself to verifiable facts, but his promise is as questionable as that of the narrator in *City of Glass* who claims to have refrained from any interpretation. Peter Aaron is aware of his limitations as observer and writer: 'I can only speak of the things I know, the things I have seen with my own eyes and heard with my own ears... I have nothing to rely on but my own memories... I don't want to present this book as something it's not. There is nothing definitive about it. It's not a biography or an exhaustive psychological portrait' (*Lev* 22). However, he often presents his own theories concerning his friend, and he also records 'facts' he has not been able to verify. Above all, what emerges from his narrative is the realisation that writing about someone else's life is a process of fiction-making. Lives do not unfold in a linear sequence and effects cannot always be traced to a single cause. Inevitably, then, the novel is the portrait of two artists, Sachs and Aaron, whom Auster himself thinks of as two sides of the same coin.[40] At the same time, both characters are given biographical details which belong to the real, extratextual Paul Auster. In this complicated relationship, the boundaries between self and other are constantly blurred, and it is no accident that impersonation and representation play a big part in the novel.

The recurring Austerian theme of imagining the self as other is reflected here in the character of Maria Turner, who is herself based on a real artist, Sophie Calle, whom Auster thanks for 'permission to mingle fact with fiction'.[41] Maria Turner is an artist whose work defies traditional categorisation. 'Her subject was the eye,' writes Aaron, 'the drama of watching and being watched, and her pieces exhibited the same qualities one found in Maria herself: meticulous attention to detail, a reliance on arbitrary structures, patience bordering on the unendurable' (*Lev* 63). Among other projects, Maria hires a detective to watch her and write reports of her movements. When she studies these reports, she feels 'as if she had become a stranger, as if she had been turned into an imaginary being' (*Lev* 63). Later, she takes a job as a stripper and invites a friend to take pictures of her to 'satisfy her own curiosity about what she looked like' (*Lev* 65). Conversely, she herself takes pictures of strangers and composes imaginary biographies. Although Peter Aaron has a limited understanding of what happened the night Sachs fell from the fire escape,

40. De Cortanze, *La Solitude du labyrinthe*, p. 67.
41. Fact and fiction were further mingled when Sophie Calle mounted an exhibition in which she recreated the art described by Auster in the novel. Sophie Calle, *Double Game* (London: Violette Editions, 1999).

he knows that Maria Turner was somehow involved in it. Sachs's version of the story is that he was tempted by her, and chose to fall rather than give in to that temptation. But if she was the cause of his accident, she was also the agent of his partial recovery. Although at the time it was assumed that the two were no longer in touch, Aaron later found out that they met regularly, spending every Thursday together as part of a loosely defined project of Maria's. During those meetings they would sometimes talk, and Maria would tape their conversations, while at other times she would take pictures of him, occasionally dressing him up in costume, or she would follow him in the streets. Aaron thinks that these projects saved Sachs from himself:

> When Sachs came to visit her in October, he had withdrawn so far into his pain that he was no longer able to see himself. I mean that in a phenomenological sense, in the same way that one talks about self-awareness or the way one forms an image of oneself. Sachs had lost the power to step out from his thoughts and take stock of where he was, to measure the precise dimensions of the space around him. What Maria achieved over the course of those months was to lure him out of his own skin... They say that a camera can rob a person of his soul. In this case, I believe it was just the opposite. With this camera, I believe that Sachs's soul was gradually given back to him. (*Lev* 129–30)

Maria enables Sachs to exit his solipsistic world by allowing him to see himself in representation, to re-establish a sense of identity in relation to others. With his narrative, Aaron saves his friend in a similar way.

It is chance that brings the two men together. An author who is due to give a reading alongside Sachs cancels at the last minute, and Aaron is invited to take his place. However, a snowstorm forces the cancellation of the event, and when Aaron arrives at Nashe's Tavern, the only people there are the bartender and Sachs. The two writers spend the evening drinking in the bar, talking about their lives and their work. By the end, Aaron has had so much to drink that he begins to see double: 'Whenever I looked at Sachs, there were two of him. Blinking my eyes didn't help, and shaking my head only made me dizzy. Sachs had turned into a man with two heads and two mouths' (*Lev* 22). With the recounting of this episode, the effect is twofold: Aaron introduces the theme of the double, while he is also giving a warning. Not only during this initial meeting but throughout their friendship, and when he finally sits down to write the story of his friend, Aaron will be unable to focus clearly. All he can hope to achieve with his story is to give his partial, fragmented perception of a man whose personality is multiple, and whose actions and ideas are

contradictory. There are numerous disclaimers in Aaron's narrative, especially when he writes of events related to the time prior to his own meeting with Sachs. No sooner does he give some information about Sachs's
family than he adds that 'I doubt that I'm trying to make a specific point
about this. These kinds of partial observations are subject to any number
of errors and misreadings' (*Lev* 29–30). When, following his accident,
Sachs withdraws from his friends, Aaron writes: 'Knowing what I know
now, I can see how little I really understood. I was drawing conclusions
from what amounted to partial evidence, basing my responses on a clus-
ter of random, observable facts that told only a small piece of the story'
(*Lev* 126). The same holds true for Aaron's narrative 'now'; the evidence
remains partial, and the process of representing his friend forces Aaron to
look at himself as well. The final irony of the novel is that Aaron, who is
racing against time to give his side of the story before the FBI can identify his friend's body, actually helps them to solve the case by mentioning
that someone has been impersonating him: that person turns out to have
been Sachs himself.

   In conclusion, despite the ostensible realism of the text, *Leviathan* asks
the same questions that Auster's previous novels had raised. The lines
that ought to separate the text from the world are constantly blurred:
Sachs's appreciation of books leads him to the decision to give up writing and involve himself actively in the world. His story survives because
another author writes it down from his own limited perspective, thus
putting Sachs back into a book. That book, Aaron's narrative, helps the
FBI to identify Sachs, thus putting the writer back into the extratextual
world. And just before Sachs dies, another writer who had been imprisoned steps into the real world: Vaclav Havel becomes president of
Czechoslovakia (*Lev* 237). The activities of writing and reading, far from
producing a clear distinction between the 'real' and the textual, emphasise their interconnectedness. As Valéry Hugotte observes, 'if Auster's
novels are at heart literary because of their erudition and their implicit
allusions to certain literary traditions, they do not cease equally to affirm
their relation to life'.[42] If Blue were to get out of the room that is the
book, he would find himself in another book, the world which is known
through its representations.

---

42. 'Paul Auster ou l'art de la fugue', p. 57.

Epilogue

'*Mr Vertigo* is different from my other books,' says Paul Auster. Asked how it fits into the cycle of complex novels followed by simpler ones, he says that that circle has closed: '*Mr Vertigo* constitutes a leap towards another place. After *Leviathan*, which was a very difficult book to write, very tough, an altogether strenuous effort, I wanted to engage in a much lighter project. Deep down, this desire to talk of levitation seems to me like a resistance to heaviness, to a certain weightiness of the previous novel.'[1] This desire to escape the 'weightiness' of previous novels may one day be read as the beginning of a second phase in Auster's novelistic career, a suggestion which his latest novel, *Timbuktu*, seems to confirm. Although both books contain certain motifs that can be traced back to Auster's earlier work, they are more notable for their difference from their predecessors. They therefore fall outside the scope of this book, since a detailed study of them would necessitate an entirely different set of theoretical parameters and critical perspectives.

Narrated in the first person, *Mr Vertigo* tells the story of Walter Claireborne Rawley, a nine-year-old orphaned urchin who is picked up by the mysterious Master Yehudi in the streets of St Louis in 1924. Master Yehudi promises to teach Walt to fly, and, after a gruelling three-year apprenticeship, Walt lifts himself off the ground. Reinvented as Walt the Wonder Boy, he tours the country with his master and becomes famous but, as puberty sets in, he loses the ability to levitate. Having lost his mentor, he drifts aimlessly through life until, at the age of seventy-seven, he begins to write his memoirs, which he instructs his nephew to publish after his death. Although the novel is written in such a way that the opportunity arises, Auster deliberately avoids the questions he had asked in all his previous novels. Questions of authorship and authority are

1.   De Cortanze, *La Solitude du labyrinthe*, p. 75.

mostly absent from the text. Although towards the end of the narrative
Walt says that he was 'rescued by the idea of writing this book' (MV 275),
which he entrusts to Daniel Quinn, the question of Walt's (inter)textual
identity is not a central concern of the novel. Similarly, questions of identity, the nature of the self as defined in language and representation, the
elaboration of patterns and systems of signification are all absent from
this text, as are references to other writers and books.

Mr Vertigo has a fairy-tale opening: 'I was twelve years old the first time
I walked on water' (MV 3). What follows, however, is a largely realistic
narrative; as Auster explains, 'I think that Mr Vertigo is a realist book. The
only element which is improbable, but which we must obviously accept,
is the question of levitation. Once we accept that, everything else is true:
the characters' psychology, the historical references, everything. This
story, which unfolds against a realist background, emerges literally from
the ground and from truth.'[2] This realistic effect is achieved partly
through the use of earlier themes and techniques which receive a different treatment. The retrospective first-person narrative is reminiscent of
Moon Palace, as is the hero's implication in the historical events of his
time, but the two novels also display marked differences. Marco Stanley
Fogg's story concentrates on his early adulthood, and it is narrated in a
cultured, literary voice. Walt's narrative focuses mainly on his childhood,
and the narrating voice is a mixture of the illiterate small boy's and the
old man's recollection of his childhood. In terms of the time-span it
covers, Mr Vertigo may again be compared to Moon Palace. However,
whereas the previous novel told three related stories in which 'each generation repeats the mistakes of the previous generation' (AH 318), in Mr
Vertigo the bulk of the narrative focuses on events that took place in the
1920s, and it concerns the life of one character.

The father–son relationship once again concerns a surrogate, rather than
a biological, father. Walt's mischievous appearance at the beginning of the
novel has echoes of Pinocchio, and the theme continues with the rigorous
training with which the master effects the little boy's transformation.
Unlike Pinocchio, though, Walt cannot save his adoptive father. When the
villainous Uncle Slim attacks Walt and Master Yehudi, the latter is seriously
wounded; he asks Walt to shoot him, Walt refuses to do so, and Master
Yehudi shoots himself. From that moment on, both Walt's life and the narrative take a turn for the worse. Walt turns 'back into the beggar [he] was
born to be' (MV 215), and travels for three years plotting his revenge. Walt

2.   De Cortanze, La Solitude du labyrinthe, p. 81.

is not the first of Auster's characters to turn into a beggar, nor the first to undertake a long journey, but what sets his adventures apart is the fact that these events are not invested with the significance they carried in previous novels. Walt, once the Wonder Boy, travels on foot, hitchhikes, sleeps in doorways, sweeps floors and steals, but his condition is neither beyond his control, as was Anna Blume's, nor an aesthetic gesture or a desire to find meaning in randomness, as in the adventures of Jim Nashe or MS Fogg. Once he has attained his goal and killed his uncle, Walt continues to drift aimlessly through life until he decides to write his memoirs.

As previous novels did, *Mr Vertigo* promises, and simultaneously eludes, an allegorical reading. The protagonist's literal rise and fall, and his passage from innocence to experience, are related to the changes that his country also undergoes. When Walt tours America at the height of his fame, the entire country is transformed into a stage, the backdrop of his incredible feats. However, geographical space does not convey meaning in the same way that it did in previous novels, and this is due to the fact that this is mainly a comic novel. The theme of levitation may be read as an inversion of the earlier fall motif, and it is this inversion that produces a comic effect. Auster thinks of *Moon Palace* as an essentially comic coming-of-age story which has some sad moments,[3] but the protagonist's artistic dilemmas and aspirations, and the broader issues the novel deals with, do not quite allow the comical elements of the tale to take centre-stage. As for Walt, he may seem like an entirely new creation, but the author thinks that he has created similar characters before him; he thinks of Walt as someone like Pozzi in *The Music of Chance*, or Boris Stepanovich in *In the Country of Last Things*: 'Walt doesn't come out of nowhere. My books are after all full of Walts who act in the shadow of the main character.'[4]

In order to understand just how this novel differs from Auster's previous work, we need to look at the ending of the narrative, and read that as a metaphor for the author's transformation. Walt begins to suspect that his gruelling training was not, after all, responsible for his later success: 'Master Yehudi had been trained in the old school... But what if his way wasn't the only way? What if there was a simpler, more direct method... What then?' (MV 278). It is this question that *Mr Vertigo* attempts to answer. Whereas previous novels were self-consciously placed within a specific context, deliberately asking to be read in the

3.   Del Rey, 'Paul Auster: Al compas de un ritmo pendular', p. 26. ('*Moon Palace* is a comic novel. It is not a tragedy, although it has its sad moments.')

4.   De Cortanze, *La Solitude du labyrinthe*, p. 76.

network of their acknowledged connections, the desired effect here is one of transparency. Walt's narrative ends with these words:

> Deep down, I don't believe it takes any special talent for a person to lift himself off the ground and hover in the air. We all have it in us – every man, woman, and child – and with enough hard work and concentration, every human being is capable of duplicating the feats I accomplished as Walt the Wonder Boy. You must learn to stop being yourself. That's where it begins, and everything else follows from that. You must let yourself evaporate. Let your muscles go limp, breathe until you feel your soul pouring out of you, and then shut your eyes. That's how it's done. The emptiness inside your body grows lighter than the air around you. Little by little, you begin to weigh less than nothing. You shut your eyes; you spread your arms; you let yourself evaporate. And then, little by little, you lift yourself off the ground. Like so. (*MV* 278)

With this novel perhaps Walt's creator, too, is learning to stop being himself. Two years after the publication of *Mr Vertigo*, Auster told an interviewer: 'I think all my father figures are dead. Everyone has died now. Edmond Jabès is dead. He was more like a grandfather than a father... I think I looked up to Beckett in a way, even though he was not someone I was close to personally. We met a couple of times, corresponded a little bit, but he was certainly a paternal figure for me.'[5] Seen in this light, *Mr Vertigo* may be read as Auster's attempt to lay the ghosts of his progenitors to rest, and move to an entirely different place.

The novel that followed *Mr Vertigo*, *Timbuktu*, may further support this view. It is a book that is largely free of the literary and textual ghosts that had haunted previous novels, and despite its unrealistic elements, it seems to be aspiring to transparency. *Timbuktu* is narrated from the point of view of a dog, Mr Bones, and it tells of the dog's relationship with his master, Willy G. Christmas, his adventures following Willy's death, and the dog's subsequent adoption by a happy, all-American suburban family. Once again, familiar motifs underlie the narrative. The relationship between Willy and Mr Bones is recognisable in terms of Auster's earlier preoccupations: part father–son, part Don Quixote and Sancho Panza. Willy seems to have been loosely based, at least in part, on H.L. Humes, whose acquaintance Auster recalls in *Hand to Mouth*, and elements of whose personality have found their way, as I have shown, into *Moon Palace*, and more covertly into *Leviathan*. Willy is a vagabond, a familiar

5.   Michel Contat and Paul Auster, 'The Manuscript in the Book: A Conversation', trans. Alyson Waters, *Yale French Studies*, 89 (1996), pp. 186–87.

figure in Auster's fiction, and the novel's opening ('Mr Bones knew that Willy wasn't long for this world') once again announces endings instead of beginnings.

Like its predecessor, *Timbuktu* is a comic novel with allegorical overtones. The lightness of this simple story is often interrupted by more sombre passages, but the overall tone remains light and unapologetically sentimental (Auster has explained how using a dog as the centre of consciousness allowed him to 'express very pure, intense emotions that we all feel').[6] The comic and the allegorical do not, of course, have to be incompatible, but Auster's method of delivery creates hermeneutic problems. For instance, the early parts of the narrative offer a brief sketch of Willy's life; phrases such as 'His father had always been a riddle to him, a man prone to weeklong silences and sudden outbursts of rage' (*Tm* 15), by evoking Auster's autobiographical writing as well as being reminiscent of previous novels, promise the availability of a reading that subsequently the novel does not sustain. Similarly, the issue of Willy's ethnic identity is raised early in the book, but the prominence given to it does not appear to be supported by the rest of the narrative. Willy was born William Gurevitch, the son of Polish Jews who fled their country, were pursued across Europe, and finally arrived in America in 1946 while the rest of the family perished in the Holocaust. Willy grew up 'American, a Brooklyn boy who played stickball in the streets, read *Mad Magazine* under the covers at night, and listened to Buddy Holly and the Big Bopper' (*Tm* 14). He changed his name from Gurevitch to Christmas after the 'real' Santa Claus appeared on television and addressed him directly, asking him to spread the message of 'goodness, generosity, and self-sacrifice' (*Tm* 21). The novel confounds the expectations raised by this conversion, and indeed the details of Willy's background do not, on the whole, relate to the rest of the story, which centres on Mr Bones's life without his master. When they do, they risk appearing offensive and unacceptable. For instance, following Willy's death Mr Bones becomes a stray dog and suffers tiredness, hunger, and cruelty at the hands of men. Willy then appears in a dream and tells his dog how his own mother had also suffered hardship and persecution at the hands of the Nazis: 'They hunted her down like a dog, and she had to run for her life. People get treated like dogs, too, my friend' (*Tm* 123).

Willy dies in front of Poe's house in Baltimore, having first explained to Mr Bones that Poe was 'the great forebear and daddy of all us Yankee

6. Mackenzie, 'The Searcher', p. 23.

scribes' (*Tm* 46), while earlier in his career he had thought of himself as 'the second coming of François Villon' (*Tm* 16). The references to mad visionaries, tormented or marginalised writers, would in previous Auster novels have established the kind of intertextual link that would encourage a recognition of affinity; here, they seem to suggest very little apart from Willy's illusions and delusions. 'We've wound up in Poe-land,' Willy announces, 'and if you say it quick enough, that's the same country my own dead ma was born in' (*Tm* 46). This is the kind of association that may not stand up to closer scrutiny, but it points to one of the book's saving graces, which is its engagement with notional and nominal space. The Timbuktu of the novel's title is not the real, geographical place in Africa; it is the Timbuktu of the phrase 'from here to Timbuktu', an imaginary place with a real name. When Willy knows that he is going to die, he tells Mr Bones that he will go to Timbuktu. The philosophical dog imagines Timbuktu by turns as a place of fear and hope, despair and happiness: 'in Timbuktu dogs would be able to speak man's language and converse with him as an equal'; but then, 'What if Timbuktu turned out to be one of those places with fancy carpets and expensive antiques? What if no pets were allowed?' (*Tm* 50). Mr Bones eventually decides to take his chances and join his master by playing 'dodge the car' on a busy six-lane super-highway. In doing so, he resolves several dilemmas that have informed Auster's *œuvre*: his sacrifice stems from a desire to be reunited with Willy, and it thus restores the father–son relationship as well as realising the dream of connectedness that haunts earlier novels. His literal leap of faith seeks to reconcile the discrepancies between ideas and words, between real and imagined spaces, between randomness and order. However, the novel ends before Mr Bones gets to Timbuktu; in fact, it ends before he is even killed on the highway, so that once again everything remains unfinished. The book as *text* therefore posits the impossibility of attainment that its discourse dreams of. If Auster, like his character Fanshawe, has answered the question by asking another question, subsequent novels may confirm whether it is the terms or merely the mode of the enquiry that has changed.

A Parable for all Seasons

On 25 December 1990, 'Auggie Wren's Christmas Story' was published in *The New York Times*.[7] This was eventually turned into *Smoke*, and the

7.   Paul Auster, 'Auggie Wren's Christmas Story'; repr. in *Smoke and Blue in the Face: Two Films* (London: Faber, 1995). Further references are to this edition.

success of the film may have overshadowed the literary merit of this short tale. In the context of my approach to Auster's fiction, 'Auggie Wren's Christmas Story' may be read as a parable for the author's novelistic practices. The story is narrated in the first person by a character who is a writer, identified only by his first name, Paul. Paul has been commissioned to write a Christmas story for *The New York Times*, but finds it hard to do so. When he confides in his tobacconist friend, Auggie Wren, the latter promises to tell him the best Christmas story he has ever heard, and which he may use for the newspaper. What comes to the reader is not only Auggie's tale, but also an account of how it came to be told. Paul's narrative begins by charting the beginning of the friendship between the two men. It all began when Auggie realised that his customer was a famous writer, and asked him to look at his collection of photographs. It transpired that Auggie took a picture of the same street corner, at the same time in the morning, every day over twelve years. At first, the four thousand photographs look identical to Paul, who turns the pages of Auggie's albums with growing impatience and bewilderment. 'You're going too fast,' Auggie tells him. 'You'll never get it if you don't slow down.'

> He was right, of course. If you don't take the time to look, you'll never manage to see anything. I picked up another album and forced myself to go more deliberately... Eventually, I was able to detect subtle differences in the traffic flow, to anticipate the rhythm of the different days... And then, little by little, I began to recognize the faces of the people in the background... Once I got to know them... I could imagine stories for them, as if I could penetrate the invisible dramas locked inside their bodies... Auggie was photographing time, I realized,... and he was doing it by planting himself in one tiny corner of the world and willing it to be his own, by standing guard in the space he had chosen for himself. (152)

Auster has also planted himself in one tiny corner of the world. The implication here is that life is random and amorphous and, if it is turned into a work of art, it is not because the artist penetrates the invisible dramas played around him, but because he reads – and writes – the world *as if* he were doing so. By standing guard in his small space, observing the everyday world and the world of literature, the author creates an alternative world, one which is small, seen from a partial point of view, but no less significant for that. Writing, Auster's work suggests, does not reflect a perceived pattern which is embedded in the real; it creates this pattern in the process of its own enunciation.

The second half of 'Auggie Wren's Christmas Story' is narrated in the first person by Auggie himself, who tells Paul how he acquired his first camera and started taking those photographs. One day, Auggie chased a shoplifter out of his shop and during the pursuit the shoplifter dropped his wallet. Auggie, who felt pity for him, decided to return it in the spirit of Christmas goodwill, and an address inside the wallet led him to the young man's grandmother, an old, blind woman who mistook him for her grandson. After having a festive Christmas dinner with her, Auggie found a box of cameras stacked in the bathroom. Arguing to himself that they were stolen anyway, and the blind woman clearly had no use for them, he helped himself to one and left the house. Paul tells him that what he did was a kind gesture, to which Auggie replies: 'I lied to her, and then I stole from her. I don't see how you can call that a good deed.' Paul replies that he gave her joy, and did not steal the camera from its rightful owner anyway. 'Anything for the sake of art, right Paul?' is Auggie's reply. Reading this episode in the light of Auster's actively intertextual practice, the question I asked in the introduction needs to be asked again: who does literature belong to? With his reply to Auggie, Paul is suggesting that it has no rightful owner, and can only exist as long as it is put to new use by different people, producers and receivers alike. The same implication is woven into the very structure of the story: the title suggests that the Christmas story is Auggie's, but Auggie gives it to Paul in exchange for nothing more than a lunch. The story that Paul narrates tells his own story as well as Auggie's, and both tellers speak in their own voice. This question of authorship is related to questions of authenticity, truth and lies, the real and the fictive. Like his character Paul, Auster was commissioned to write a story for the Christmas edition of *The New York Times*. As it was going to appear in the Op-Ed section in the guise of an article, Auster wanted to produce a story that would deliberately blur the lines between fact and fiction: 'It was an interesting proposal, I thought – putting a piece of make-believe in a newspaper, the paper of record, no less.' 'Everything gets turned upside down in "Auggie Wren"', continues Auster; 'What's stealing? What's giving? What's lying? What's telling the truth?'[8] Perhaps his character Paul has the answer to these questions. When he has heard Auggie's story, he pauses for a moment, studying his friend's face:

> I couldn't be sure, but the look in his eyes at that moment was so mysterious, so fraught with the glow of some inner delight, that it suddenly occurred to me that he had made the whole thing up. I was about to ask him if he he'd been putting me on, but then I realized he would never tell. I had been tricked into believing him, and that was the only thing that

8.   Annette Insdorf, 'The Making of Smoke', in *Smoke and Blue in the Face*, p. 3.

mattered. As long as there's one person to believe it, there's no story that can't be true. (156)

Auster, who like his character Fanshawe answers each question by asking another question, gives at least one answer, which is a vindication – and a celebration – of his art, the art of creating fictions and telling stories.

And this, after all, may be the only answer available. The study of a living author, more so than any other, is provisional, open-ended. Therefore, everything remains 'open, unfinished, to be started again'. 'Portrait of an Invisible Man' ends with the words 'To end with this'.

Michel Contat: It's kind of mysterious to me. 'To end with this.' It can be matter of fact: 'let's end with this'...

Paul Auster: No, 'to end with this', meaning on this image, on this thought. This is the place where the story comes to an end. 'To end with *this*.' Not this [shows something large], but this [shows something tiny]. Very small.[9]

To end with this.

---

9.   Contat and Auster, 'The Manuscript in the Book', p. 187.

Bibliography

Works by Paul Auster

Fiction

Auster, Paul. *City of Glass*. Los Angeles: Sun and Moon Press, 1985.
    Ghosts. Los Angeles: Sun and Moon Press, 1986.
    The Locked Room. Los Angeles: Sun and Moon Press, 1986.
    These three novels published in Britain as *The New York Trilogy*. London: Faber, 1987.
    In the Country of Last Things. London: Faber, 1987.
    Moon Palace. London: Faber, 1989.
    The Music of Chance. London: Faber, 1990.
    Leviathan. London: Faber, 1992.
    Mr Vertigo. London: Faber, 1994.
    Timbuktu. London: Faber, 1999.
    Smoke and Blue in the Face: Two Films. London: Faber, 1995. [Includes 'Auggie Wren's Christmas Story'.]
    Lulu on the Bridge. London: Faber, 1998.
Benjamin, Paul. *Squeeze Play*. London: Faber, 1992.

Non-Fiction

Auster, Paul. 'Moonlight in the Brooklyn Museum'. *Art News*, 86.7 (1987), 104–105.
    The Invention of Solitude. Los Angeles: Sun and Moon Press, 1982; repr. London: Faber, 1988.
    Ground Work: Selected Poems and Essays 1970–1979. London: Faber, 1990.
    The Art of Hunger: Essays, Prefaces, Interviews. New York: Penguin, 1993.
    The Red Notebook and Other Writings. London: Faber, 1995.
    Hand to Mouth: A Chronicle of Early Failure. London: Faber, 1997.

Edited by Paul Auster
The Random House Book of Twentieth Century French Poetry. New York: Random House, 1982.

Filmography
The Music of Chance. Philip Haas, Columbia Tristar, 1992.
Smoke. Wayne Wang and Paul Auster, Miramax, 1995.
Blue in the Face. Wayne Wang and Paul Auster, Miramax, 1995.
Lulu on the Bridge. Paul Auster, Trimark, 1999.

Other Primary Sources

Beckett, Samuel. *The Beckett Trilogy: Molloy, Malone Dies, The Unnamable*. London: Picador, 1976.
Calle, Sophie. *Double Game*. London: Violette Editions, 1999.
DeLillo, Don. *Mao II*. London: Vintage, 1991.
Emerson, Ralph Waldo. *Selected Essays*. Ed. Larzer Ziff. Harmondsworth: Penguin, 1982.
— *The Collected Works of Ralph Waldo Emerson*, 5 vols. Ed. Joseph Slater and Douglas Emory Wilson. Cambridge, MA and London: Belknap Press of Harvard University Press, 1983.
Hamsun, Knut. *Hunger*. Trans. Robert Bly. New York: Farrar, Straus, 1967.
Hawthorne, Nathaniel. *Nathaniel Hawthorne's Tales: Authoritative Texts, Backgrounds, Criticism*. Ed. James McIntosh. New York and London: W.W. Norton, 1987.
— *The House of the Seven Gables*. Ed. Allan Lloyd-Smith. London: Everyman, 1995.
— *The Marble Faun*. Ed. Malcolm Bradbury. London: Everyman, 1995.
— *Selected Tales and Sketches*. Ed. Michael Colacurcio. Harmondsworth: Penguin, 1987.
Hobbes, Thomas. *Leviathan*. Ed. A.D. Lindsay. London: J.M. Dent, 1962.
Jabès, Edmond. *The Book of Questions*. Trans. Rosemarie Waldrop. Middletown: Wesleyan University Press, 1983.
Kafka, Franz. *The Great Wall of China and Other Pieces*. Trans. Edwin Muir. London: Martin Secker, 1933.
— *The Penal Colony: Stories and Short Pieces*. Trans. Willa and Edwin Muir. New York: Schocken, 1961.
Karasik, Paul and David Mazzucchelli. *Paul Auster's City of Glass: A Graphic Mystery*. New York: Avon Books, 1994.
Melville, Herman. *Selected Tales and Poems*. Ed. Richard Chase. New York: Holt, Rinehart and Winston, 1966.
— *The Confidence Man*. Ed. Tony Tanner. Oxford and New York: Oxford University Press, 1989.

Poe, Edgar Allan. *The Complete Works of Edgar Allan Poe*, 17 vols. Ed. James A. Harrison. New York: AMS, 1965.

— *The Narrative of Arthur Gordon Pym of Nantucket*. Ed. Harold Beaver. Harmondsworth: Penguin, 1975.

Rimbaud, Arthur. *Œuvres Complètes*. Ed. Rolland de Renéville and Jules Mouquet. Paris: Pléiade, 1963.

— *Complete Works*. Trans. Paul Schmidt. New York and London: Harper & Row, 1975.

Robbe-Grillet, Alain. *Les Gommes*. Paris: Editions de Minuit, 1953.

Thoreau, Henry David. *The Variorum Walden*. Ed. Walter Harding. New York: Twayne, 1962.

— *Reform Papers*. Ed. Wendell Glick. Princeton, NJ: Princeton University Press, 1973.

Secondary Sources

Abrams, M.H. *The Mirror and the Lamp: Romantic Theory and the Critical Tradition*. London, Oxford and New York: Oxford University Press, 1953.

Addy, Andrew. 'Narrating the Self: Story-Telling as Personal Myth-Making in Paul Auster's *Moon Palace*'. *Q/W/E/R/T/Y*, 6 (1996), 153–61.

Alexander, Marguerite. *Flights from Realism: Themes and Strategies in Postmodernist British and American Fiction*. London: Edward Arnold, 1990.

Alford, Steven E. 'Mirrors of Madness: Paul Auster's *The New York Trilogy*'. *Critique: Studies in Contemporary Fiction*, 37.1 (Fall 1995), 17–33.

— 'Spaced-Out: Signification and Space in Paul Auster's *The New York Trilogy*'. *Contemporary Literature*, 36.4 (1995), 613–32.

Auerbach, Jonathan. *The Romance of Failure: First Person Fictions of Poe, Hawthorne, and James*. New York and Oxford: Oxford University Press, 1989.

Baigell, Matthew. *A Concise History of American Painting and Sculpture*. New York and London: Harper & Row, 1984.

Bakhtin, Mikhail. *Problems of Dostoevsky's Poetics*. Trans. and ed. Caryl Emerson. 1963; repr. Manchester: Manchester University Press, 1984.

— *Rabelais and His World*. Trans. Helene Iswolsky. 1965; repr. Bloomington: Indiana University Press, 1984.

— *The Dialogic Imagination*. Trans. Caryl Emerson and Michael Holquist. Ed. Michael Holquist. 1975; repr. Austin: University of Texas Press, 1981.

Barbour, James and Thomas Quirk, eds. *Romanticism: Critical Essays in American Literature*. New York and London: Garland, 1986.

Barone, Dennis, ed. *Beyond the Red Notebook: Essays on Paul Auster*. Philadelphia: University of Pennsylvania Press, 1995.

Barth, John. 'The Literature of Exhaustion'. *Atlantic Monthly*, 220 (August 1967), 23–34.

— 'The Literature of Replenishment'. *Atlantic Monthly*, 245 (January 1980), 65–71.

— *The Friday Book: Essays and Other Nonfiction*. New York: G.P. Putnam's Sons, 1984.

Barthes, Roland. *The Pleasure of the Text*. Trans. Richard Miller. Oxford: Basil Blackwell, 1990.

— *Image–Music–Text*. Trans. Stephen Heath. London: Fontana, 1977.

Bate, Walter Jackson. *The Burden of the Past and the English Poet*. Cambridge, MA: Harvard University Press, 1970.

Baudrillard, Jean. *America*. Trans. Chris Turner. New York and London: Verso, 1988.

Bawer, Bruce. 'Doubles and More Doubles'. *New Criterion*, 7.8 (April 1989), 67–74.

Beckett, Samuel. *Proust and Three Dialogues*. London: Calder and Boyars, 1965.

Begley, Adam. 'The Public Eye'. The *Guardian Weekend Supplement*, October 17, 1992, 18–21.

Benjamin, Walter. *Illuminations*. Trans. Harry Zohn. Ed. Hannah Arendt. London: Fontana, 1973.

Birkerts, Sven. *American Energies: Essays on Fiction*. New York: William Morrow, 1992.

— 'Reality, Fiction, and *In the Country of Last Things*'. *The Review of Contemporary Fiction*, 14.1 (Spring 1994).

Bloom, Harold. *The Anxiety of Influence: A Theory of Poetry*. New York: Oxford University Press, 1973.

— *A Map of Misreading*. New York: Oxford University Press, 1975.

— *The Western Canon: The Books and School of the Ages*. London: Macmillan, 1994.

Bloom, Harold, ed. *Edgar Allan Poe*. New York: Chelsea House Publishers, 1985.

Booth, Wayne C. *The Rhetoric of Fiction*. Chicago and London: University of Chicago Press, 1961.

Bradbury, Malcolm. *The Modern American Novel*. Oxford and New York: Oxford University Press, 1992.

Bradbury, Malcolm, ed. *The Novel Today: Contemporary Writers on Modern Fiction*. London: Fontana, 1977.

Bradbury, Malcolm and James McFarlane, eds. *Modernism: A Guide to European Literature 1890–1930*. 1976; repr. Harmondsworth: Penguin, 1991.

Bradbury, Malcolm and Richard Ruland. *From Puritanism to Postmodernism: A History of American Literature*. New York: Viking Penguin, 1991.

Bradbury, Malcolm and Sigmund Ro, eds. *Contemporary American Fiction*. London: Edward Arnold, 1987.

Bray, Paul. 'The Currents of Fate and *The Music of Chance*'. *The Review of Contemporary Fiction*, 14.1 (Spring 1994).

Brooker, Peter. *New York Fictions: Modernity, Postmodernism, The New Modern*. London and New York: Longman, 1996.

Brooke-Rose, Christine. *A Rhetoric of the Unreal: Studies in Narrative and Structure, Especially of the Fantastic*. Cambridge: Cambridge University Press, 1981.

Butler, Lance St John and Robin J. Davis, eds. *Rethinking Beckett: A Collection of Critical Essays*. London: Macmillan, 1990.

Calvino, Italo. *Six Memos for the Next Millennium*. Trans. Patrick Creagh. 1988; repr. London: Jonathan Cape, 1992.

— *The Literature Machine*. Trans. Patrick Creagh. 1982; repr. London: Picador, 1989.

Canty, Daniel. 'L'œil d'Emerson et la sphère de Pascal: *City of Glass* de Paul Auster'. *Révue Française d'Etudes Américaines*, 64 (May 1995), 375–83.

Carton, Evan. *The Rhetoric of American Romance: Dialectic and Identity in Emerson, Dickinson, Poe, and Hawthorne*. Baltimore and London: Johns Hopkins University Press, 1985.

Chai, Leon. *The Romantic Foundations of the American Renaissance*. Ithaca and London: Cornell University Press, 1987.

Chénetier, Marc. *Beyond Suspicion: New American Fiction since 1960*. Trans. Elizabeth A. Houlding. Liverpool: Liverpool University Press, 1996.

— *Paul Auster as the Wizard of Odds: Moon Palace*. Paris: Didier Erudition/CNED, 1996.

Chénetier, Marc, ed. *Critical Angles: European Views of Contemporary American Literature*. Carbondale and Edwardsville: Southern Illinois University Press, 1986.

Clayton, Jay and Eric Rothstein, eds. *Influence and Intertextuality in Literary History*. Wisconsin: University of Wisconsin Press, 1991.

Coale, Samuel Chase. *In Hawthorne's Shadow: American Romance from Melville to Mailer*. Kentucky: University Press of Kentucky, 1985.

Cohen, Ralph, ed. *The Future of Literary Theory*. New York and London: Routledge, 1989.

Cohn, Ruby. *Samuel Beckett: The Comic Gamut*. New Brunswick, NJ: Rutgers University Press, 1962.

Connor, Steven. *The English Novel in History 1950–1995*. London and New York: Routledge, 1996.

Contat, Michel and Paul Auster. 'The Manuscript in the Book: A Conversation'. Trans. Alyson Waters. *Yale French Studies*, 89 (1996), 160–87.

Cortanze, Gérard de. 'Les Romans en dix mots-clés. *Magazine Littéraire*, 338 (December 1995), 43–48.

— *La Solitude du labyrinthe: essai et entretiens.* Paris: Actes Sud, 1997.

Coulomb-Buffa, Chantal. 'Réconciliation dans *Moon Palace* de Paul Auster'. *Révue Française d'Etudes Américaines*, 62 (November 1994), 404–15.

Culler, Jonathan. *The Pursuit of Signs: Semiotics, Literature, Deconstruction.* London and Henley: Routledge and Kegan Paul, 1981.

— *On Deconstruction: Theory and Criticism after Structuralism.* London: Routledge, 1983.

— *Framing the Sign: Criticism and its Institutions.* Oxford: Basil Blackwell, 1988.

Cunliffe, Marcus, ed. *The Penguin History of Literature.* 8. *American Literature to 1900.* Harmondsworth: Penguin, 1993.

Davies, Philip John, ed. *Representing and Imagining America.* Keele: Keele University Press, 1995

Debevec Henning, Sylvie. *Beckett's Critical Complicity: Carnival, Contestation, and Tradition.* Lexington: University of Kentucky Press, 1988.

Derrida, Jacques. 'The Purveyor of Truth'. *Yale French Studies*, 52 (1975), 31–113.

— *Acts of Literature.* Ed. Derek Attridge. New York and London: Routledge, 1992.

Dillard, Annie. *Living by Fiction.* New York: Harper & Row, 1982.

Doctorow, E.L. *Poets and Presidents: Selected Essays 1977–1992.* London: Macmillan, 1993.

Dow, William. 'Never Being "This Far from Home": Paul Auster and Picturing *Moonlight* Spaces'. *Q/W/E/R/T/Y*, 6 (1996), 193–98.

Drenttel, William, ed. *Paul Auster: A Comprehensive Bibliographic Checklist of Published Works 1968–1994.* New York: Delos Press, 1994.

Duperray, Annick, ed. *L'Œuvre de Paul Auster: Approches et lectures plurielles.* Paris: Actes Sud/Université de Provence, 1995.

Eagleton, Terry. *Literary Theory: An Introduction.* Oxford: Basil Blackwell, 1983.

Eco, Umberto. *Reflections on The Name of the Rose.* Trans. William Weaver. London: Secker and Warburg, 1985.

Eco, Umberto with Richard Rorty, Jonathan Culler, Christine Brooke-Rose. Ed. Stefan Collini. *Interpretation and Overinterpretation.* Cambridge and New York: Cambridge University Press, 1992.

Eliot, T.S. *Selected Essays.* London: Faber, 1961.

Ellmann, Maud. *The Hunger Artists: Starving, Writing and Imprisonment.* London: Virago Press, 1993.

Ellmann, Richard and Charles Feidelson, eds. *The Modern Tradition: Backgrounds of Modern Literature.* New York: Oxford University Press, 1965.

Ertel, Jean-Marc. 'Paul Auster et ses doubles'. *Critique*, 50 (1994), 378–89.

Esslin, Martin, ed. *Samuel Beckett: A Collection of Critical Essays.* Englewood Cliffs, NJ: Prentice-Hall, 1965.

Fallix, François, ed. *Lectures d'une œuvre: Moon palace de Paul Auster*. Paris: Editions du Temps, 1996.

Federman, Raymond. *Critfictions: Postmodern Essays*. New York: State University of New York Press, 1993.

Feidelson, Charles, Jr. *Symbolism and American Literature*. Chicago and London: University of Chicago Press, 1953.

Fiedler, Leslie. *Love and Death in the American Novel*. 1960; repr. London: Jonathan Cape, 1967.

Fletcher, John. *The Novels of Samuel Beckett*. New York: Barnes and Noble, 1970.

Floc'h, Sylvain. 'Ascétisme et Austérité dans *Moon Palace*'. *Q/W/E/R/T/Y*, 6 (1996), 199–207.

Ford, Mark. 'Inventions of Solitude: Thoreau and Auster'. *Journal of American Studies*, 33.2 (1999), 201–19.

Fredman, Stephen. '"How to Get Out of the Room that is the Book?" Paul Auster and the Consequences of Confinement'. *Postmodern Culture*, 6.3 (May 1996), http://muse.jhn.edu/journals/punc

Freitag, Michael. 'The Novelist out of Control: An Interview with Paul Auster'. *New York Times Book Review*, March 19, 1989, 9.

Friedman, Melvin, ed. *Samuel Beckett Now: Critical Approaches to his Novels, Poetry and Plays*. Chicago and London: University of Chicago Press, 1970.

Frye, Northrop. *The Secular Scripture: A Study of the Structure of Romance*. Cambridge, MA, and London: Harvard University Press, 1976.

Fussell, Edwin. *Frontier: American Literature and the American West*. Princeton, NJ: Princeton University Press, 1965.

Gado, Frank, ed. *First Person: Conversations on Writers and Writing*. New York: Union College Press, 1973.

Granjeat, Yves-Charles, ed. *Moon Palace, collectif*. Paris: Ellipses, 1996.

Grimal, Claude. 'Paul Auster au coeur des labyrinthes'. *Europe: Revue Littéraire Mensuelle*, 68.733 (May 1990), 64–66.

Grossvogel, David. *Mystery and its Fictions: From Oedipus to Agatha Christie*. Baltimore and London: Johns Hopkins University Press, 1979.

Gutman, Yisrael. *The Jews of Warsaw 1939–1943: Ghetto, Underground, Revolt*. Trans. Ina Friedman. Brighton: Harvester, 1982.

Hassan, Ihab. *The Literature of Silence: Henry Miller and Samuel Beckett*. New York: Alfred Knopf, 1967.

Herzogenrath, Bernd. *An Art of Desire: Reading Paul Auster*. Amsterdam and Atlanta, GA: Rodopi, 1999.

Hilfer, Tony. *American Fiction Since 1940*. London and New York: Longman, 1992.

Hoffman, Frederick J. *Samuel Beckett: The Language of Self*. Carbondale: South Illinois University Press, 1962.

Horne, Philip. 'It's Just a Book'. *London Review of Books*, 14.24 (December 17, 1992), 20–2.

Howe, Irving. *The American Newness: Culture and Politics in the Age of Emerson*. Cambridge, MA, and London: Harvard University Press, 1986.

Hugotte, Valéry. 'Paul Auster ou l'art de la fugue'. *Esprit*, 10 (1994), 39–64.

Hühn, Peter. 'The Detective as Reader: Narrativity and Reading Concepts in Detective Fiction'. *Modern Fiction Studies*, 33.3 (Autumn 1987), 451–56.

Hutcheon, Linda. *A Theory of Parody: The Teachings of Twentieth-Century Art Forms*. New York and London: Methuen, 1985.

— *A Poetics of Postmodernism: History, Theory, Fiction*. New York and London: Routledge, 1988.

— *The Politics of Postmodernism*. London: Routledge, 1989.

Irwin, John. *American Hieroglyphics: The Symbol of the Egyptian Hieroglyphics in the American Renaissance*. Baltimore and London: Johns Hopkins University Press, 1980.

Iser, Wolfgang. *The Implied Reader: Patterns of Communication in Prose Fiction from Bunyan to Beckett*. Baltimore and London: Johns Hopkins University Press, 1974.

— *The Act of Reading: A Theory of Aesthetic Response*. London: Routledge, 1978.

Jackson, Rosemary. *Fantasy: The Literature of Subversion*. London and New York: Methuen, 1981.

Jarvis, Brian. *Postmodern Cartographies: The Geographical Imagination in Contemporary American Culture*. London: Pluto Press, 1998.

Jauss, Hans Robert. *Towards an Aesthetic of Reception*. Trans. Timothy Bahti. Minneapolis: University of Minnesota Press, 1982.

Johnson, Barbara. *The Critical Difference*. Baltimore and London: Johns Hopkins University Press, 1980.

Kennedy, Andrew K. *Samuel Beckett*. Cambridge and New York: Cambridge University Press, 1989.

Kenner, Hugh. *Samuel Beckett: A Critical Study*. Berkeley: University of California Press, 1973.

Kermode, Frank. *The Sense of an Ending*. London, Oxford and New York: Oxford University Press, 1966.

— *Modern Essays*. London: Fontana, 1971.

Kiely, Robert. *Reverse Tradition: Postmodern Fictions and the Nineteenth Century Novel*. Cambridge, MA, and London: Harvard University Press, 1993.

Kirkegaard, Peter. 'Cities, Signs and Meaning in Walter Benjamin and Paul Auster; or, never sure of any of it'. *Orbis Litterarum*, 48.2–3 (1993), 161–79.

Klinkowitz, Jerome. *Literary Disruptions: The Making of a Post-Contempo-*

rary American Fiction. Urbana and London: University of Illinois Press, 1975.

Knowlson, James. *Damned to Fame: The Life of Samuel Beckett.* London: Bloomsbury, 1996.

Kopcewicz, Andrej. 'Paul Auster's Masquerades in *City of Glass*', in *American Cultures: Assimilation and Multiculturalism*, ed. Elzbieta Olesky. San Francisco and London: International Scholars Publications, 1995, 63–73.

— 'The Dark Rooms and Bartleby: An Intertextual Study', in *Canons, Revisions, Supplements in American Literature and Culture*, ed. Marek Wilczynski. Poznan: Bene Nati, 1997, 109–24.

Kristeva, Julia. *Desire in Language: A Semiotic Approach to Literature and Art.* Trans. Thomas Gora, Alice Jardine, and Leon S. Roudiez. Ed. Leon S. Roudiez. New York: Columbia University Press, 1980.

Lacan, Jacques. 'Seminar on "The Purloined Letter"'. *Yale French Studies*, 48 (1956), 339–72.

Lavender, William. 'The Novel of Critical Engagement: Paul Auster's *City of Glass*'. *Contemporary Literature*, 34.2 (1993), 219–39.

LeClair, Tom and Larry McCaffery, eds. *Anything Can Happen: Interviews with Contemporary American Novelists.* Urbana, Chicago and London: University of Illinois Press, 1983.

Levin, David, ed. *Emerson: Prophecy, Metamorphosis, and Influence.* New York and London: Columbia University Press, 1975.

Levin, Harry. *The Power of Blackness.* New York: Alfred Knopf, 1958.

Levine, Robert S. *Conspiracy and Romance: Studies in Brockden Brown, Cooper, Hawthorne, and Melville.* Cambridge: Cambridge University Press, 1989.

Lewin, Abraham. *A Cup of Tears: A Diary of the Warsaw Ghetto.* Trans. Christopher Hutton. Ed. Antony Polonsky. Oxford: Blackwell, 1988.

Lodge, David, ed. *Modern Criticism and Theory: A Reader.* London and New York: Longman, 1988.

Lüthi, Max. *The European Folktale: Form and Nature.* Trans. John D. Niles. Philadelphia: Institute for the Study of Human Issues, 1982.

Macherey, Pierre. *A Theory of Literary Production.* Trans. Geoffrey Wall. London and Boston: Routledge, 1978.

Mackenzie, Suzie. 'The Searcher'. *The Guardian Weekend*, May 29, 1999, 18–23.

Massa, Ann and Alistair Stead, eds. *Forked Tongues? Comparing Twentieth-Century British and American Literature.* London and New York: Longman, 1994.

Matthiessen, F.O. *American Renaissance: Art and Expression in the Age of Emerson and Whitman.* New York: Oxford University Press, 1941.

McCaffery, Larry and Sinda Gregory, eds. *Alive and Writing: Interviews with*

American Authors of the Eighties. Chicago: University of Illinois Press, 1987.

McCaffery, Larry and Sinda Gregory. 'An Interview with Paul Auster'. *Contemporary Literature*, 33.1 (1992), 1–23.

McCaffery, Larry. 'An Interview with Paul Auster'. *Mississippi Review*, 20.1–2 (1991), 49–62.

McHale, Brian. *Postmodernist Fiction*. London and New York: Routledge, 1989.

— *Constructing Postmodernism*. London: Routledge, 1992.

McPheron, William. 'Remaking Narrative'. *Poetics Journal*, 7 (1987), 140–49.

Messent, Peter. *New Readings of the American Novel: Narrative Theory and its Application*. London: Macmillan, 1990.

Michlin, Monica. 'Bitter-Sweet Gravity: *Moon Palace*'. *Q/W/E/R/T/Y*, 6 (1996), 217–24.

Miller, Nancy. *Subject to Change: Reading Feminist Writing*. New York: Columbia University Press, 1988.

Morse, David. *American Romanticism. 1. From Cooper to Hawthorne*. London: Macmillan, 1987.

Most, Glenn and William Stowe, eds. *The Poetics of Murder*. San Diego, New York and London: Harcourt Brace Jovanovich, 1983.

Newman, Charles. *The Post-Modern Aura: The Act of Fiction in an Age of Inflation*. Evanston: Northwestern University Press, 1985.

Nicholls, Peter. *Modernisms: A Literary Guide*. London: Macmillan, 1995.

Nores, Dominique, ed. *Les critiques de notre temps et Beckett*. Paris: Garnier Frères, 1971.

O'Donnell, Patrick and Robert Con Davis, eds. *Intertextuality and Contemporary American Fiction*. Baltimore and London: Johns Hopkins University Press, 1989.

O'Faolain, Julia. 'The Phantom of Liberty'. *The Times Literary Supplement*, 4673 (October 23, 1992), 20.

Osteen, Mark. 'Phantoms of Liberty: The Secret Lives of *Leviathan*'. *Review of Contemporary Fiction*, 14.1 (Spring 1994).

Pesso-Miquel, Catherine, ed. *Toiles Trouées et déserts lunaires dans Moon palace de Paul Auster*. Paris: Presses de la Sorbonne Nouvelle, 1996.

Poirier, Richard, ed. *Ralph Waldo Emerson*. Oxford: Oxford University Press, 1990.

Porte, Joel. *The Romance in America: Studies in Cooper, Poe, Hawthorne, Melville, James*. Middletown, CT: Wesleyan University Press, 1969.

Propp, Vladimir. *Morphology of the Folktale*. Trans. Laurence Scott. Ed. Louis A. Wagner. Austin and London: University of Texas Press, 1968.

Quinn, Patrick F. *The French Face of Edgar Poe*. Carbondale and Edwardsville: Illinois University Press, 1954.

Reising, Russell. *The Unusable Past: Theory and the Study of American Literature*. New York and London: Methuen, 1986.

Rey, Santiago del. 'Paul Auster: Metamorfosis del misterio'. *Quimera: Revista de Literatura*, 90–91, n.d., 28–33.

— 'Paul Auster: Al compas de un ritmo pendular'. *Quimera: Revista de Literatura*, 109 (May 1992), 22–27.

Reynolds, David S. *Beneath the American Renaissance: The Subversive Imagination in the Age of Emerson and Melville*. Cambridge, MA, and London: Harvard University Press, 1989.

Richardson, Robert. *Myth and Literature in the American Renaissance*. Bloomington and London: Indiana University Press, 1978.

Robbe-Grillet, Alain. *Towards a New Novel*. Trans. Barbara Wright. London: Calder and Boyars, 1965.

Robinson, Douglas. *American Apocalypses: The Image of the End of the World in American Literature*. Baltimore and London: Johns Hopkins University Press, 1985.

Rose, Margaret. *Parody: Ancient, Modern and Postmodern*. Cambridge: Cambridge University Press, 1993.

Rowen, Norma. 'The Detective in Search of the Lost Tongue of Adam: Paul Auster's *City of Glass*'. *Critique: Studies in Modern Fiction*, 32.4 (Summer 1991), 224–34.

Rushdie, Salman. *Imaginary Homelands: Essays and Criticism 1981–1991*. London: Granta, 1991.

Russell, Alison. 'Deconstructing *The New York Trilogy*: Paul Auster's Anti-Detective Fiction'. *Critique: Studies in Contemporary Fiction*, 31.2 (Winter 1990), 71–83.

Saltzman, Arthur. *Designs of Darkness in Contemporary American Fiction*. Philadelphia: University of Pennsylvania Press, 1990.

— *The Novel in the Balance*. Columbia: University of South Carolina Press, 1993.

Santos, Maria Irene Ramalho de Sousa. 'Plagiarism in Praise: Paul Auster and Melville'. *Revista Portuguesa de Literatura Comparada*, 1 (December 1991), 105–14.

Scholes, Robert. *The Fabulators*. New York: Oxford University Press, 1967.

Silverman, Kenneth, ed. *New Essays on Poe's Major Tales*. Cambridge: Cambridge University Press, 1993.

Simha, Rotem. *Memoirs of a Warsaw Ghetto Fighter: The Past within Me*. Trans. and ed. Barbara Harshav. New Haven and London: Yale University Press, 1994.

Smyth, Edmund J., ed. *Postmodernism and Contemporary Fiction*. London: B.T. Batsford Ltd, 1991.

Soja, Edward. *Postmodern Geographies: The Reassertion of Space in Critical Social Theory*. London: Verso, 1989.

Spanos, William. *Repetitions: The Postmodern Occasion in Literature and Culture*. Baton Rouge and London: Louisiana State University Press, 1987.

Spilka, Mark and Caroline McCracken-Flesher, eds. *Why the Novel Matters: A Postmodern Perplex*. Bloomington and Indianapolis: Indiana University Press, 1990.

Steiner, George. *Language and Silence: Essays 1958–1966*. London and Boston: Faber, 1967.

Swann, Charles. *Nathaniel Hawthorne: Tradition and Revolution*. Cambridge: Cambridge University Press, 1991.

Tani, Stefano. *The Doomed Detective: The Contribution of the Detective Novel to Postmodern American and Italian Fiction*. Carbondale and Edwardsville: Southern Illinois University Press, 1984.

Tanner, Tony. *The Reign of Wonder: Naivety and Reality in American Literature*. Cambridge: Cambridge University Press, 1965.

— *City of Words: American Fiction 1950–1970*. New York: Harper & Row, 1971.

— *Scenes of Nature, Signs of Men*. Cambridge: Cambridge University Press, 1987.

Todorov, Tzvetan. *The Poetics of Prose*. Trans. Richard Howard. Oxford: Blackwell, 1977.

Towers, Robert. 'Enigma Variations'. *The New York Review of Books*, 38.1–2 (January 17, 1991), 31–3.

Vallas, Sophie. '*Moonpalace*: Marco Autobiographe, ou les errances du Bildungsroman'. *Q/W/E/R/T/Y*, 6 (1996), 225–33.

Wasjbrot, Cécile. 'Paul Auster, L'Invention de l'Ecriture'. *Magazine Littéraire*, 308 (1993), 79–82.

Waugh, Patricia. *Metafiction: The Theory and Practice of Self-Conscious Fiction*. London and New York: Methuen, 1984.

Weisenburger, Steven. 'Inside *Moon Palace*'. *The Review of Contemporary Fiction*, 14.1 (Spring 1994).

Wesseling, Elizabeth. '*In the Country of Last Things*: Paul Auster's Parable of the Apocalypse'. *Neophilologus*, 75.4 (1991), 496–504.

White, Hayden. *Metahistory: The Historical Imagination in Nineteenth-Century Europe*. Baltimore: Johns Hopkins University Press, 1973.

— *Tropics of Discourse: Essays in Cultural Criticism*. Baltimore: Johns Hopkins University Press, 1978.

Wilde, Alan. *Horizons of Assent: Modernism, Postmodernism and the Ironic Imagination*. Baltimore and London: Johns Hopkins University Press, 1981.

— *Middle Grounds: Studies in Contemporary American Fiction*. Philadelphia: University of Pennsylvania Press, 1987.

Williams, Michael J.S. *A World of Words: Language and Displacement in the*

Fiction of Edgar Allan Poe. Durham and London: Duke University Press, 1988.

Winks, Robin, ed. *Detective Fiction: A Collection of Critical Essays*. Englewood Cliffs, NJ: Prentice-Hall, 1980.

Worton, Michael and Judith Still, eds. *Intertextuality: Theories and Practices*. Manchester: Manchester University Press, 1990.

Ziegler, Heide, ed. *Facing Texts: Encounters Between Contemporary Writers and Critics*. Durham and London: Duke University Press, 1988.

Ziff, Larzer. *Literary Democracy: The Declaration of Cultural Independence in America*. New York: Viking Press, 1981.

Periodicals with special Paul Auster issues

Critique. 39.3 (Spring 1998).

Magazine Littéraire. Paul Auster: de la Trilogie new-yorkaise à Smoke. 338 (December 1995).

Review of Contemporary Fiction. Paul Auster and Danilo Kis. 14.1 (Spring 1994).

Index